THE TRUTH ABOUT MARY:

THE TRUTH ABOUT MARY:
A SCRIPTURAL INTRODUCTION
TO THE MOTHER OF JESUS
FOR BIBLE-BELIEVING CHRISTIANS

VOLUME ONE:
From Human Invention to the
Truths Taught by Scripture

by Robert Payesko

Queenship
PUBLISHING COMPANY
P.O Box 42028 Santa Barbara, CA 93140-2028
(800) 647-9882 • (805) 957-4893 • Fax: (805) 957-1631

All Scripture citations in this book are taken from the King James Version of the Bible since this is the version most commonly used by Protestant Fundamentalists. It must be said, however, that both Protestant and Catholic scholars have shown that this version of the Bible has grave errors of translation but we use it here because it is the Version on which most of our expected readers rely.

Front Cover Painting:
  Martha G. Storm
  Mesquite, Texas

©1996 Queenship Publishing

Library of Congress Number # 96-70137

Published by:
  Queenship Publishing
  P.O. Box 42028
  Santa Barbara, CA 93140-2028
  (800) 647-9882 • (805) 957-4893 • Fax: (805) 957-1631

Printed in the United States of America

ISBN: 1-882972-82-1

THE TRUTH ABOUT MARY
VOLUME ONE
From Human Inventions to the Truths Taught by Scripture

TABLE OF CONTENTS OF THE TWO OTHER VOLUMES IN THE TRILOGY:

VOLUME TWO
Mary in Scripture and the Historic Christian Faith

VOLUME THREE
A Response to Fundamentalist Misconceptions and a Return to Historic Christianity

MARY IN SCRIPTURE BY CHAPTER AND VERSE: ARK OF THE COVENANT, DAUGHTER OF ZION, WOMAN CLOTHED WITH THE SUN

A. THE WOMAN AND HER SEED: THE NEW EVE AND THE NEW ADAM

"And the Lord God said unto the serpent, ... *I will put enmity between thee and the woman, and between thy seed and her seed." Genesis* 3:14-15:

"Therefore the Lord himself shall give you a sign; Behold, a virgin shall conceive, and bear a son, and shall call his name Immanuel." *Isaiah* 7:14:

"But when the fulness of the time was come, God sent forth his Son, made of a woman, made under the law." *Galatians* 4:4:

"We see a crucial statement in Genesis 3:15: 'I will put enmity between you [Satan] and the woman, between your seed and her seed; he will crush your head, and you will strike at his heel.' This passage is especially significant in that it refers to the 'seed of the woman,' a singular usage. The Bible, following normal biology, otherwise only refers to the man, the seed of the father, but never to the seed of the woman. Who is the woman mentioned here? The only possibility is Mary, the only woman to give birth to a child without the aid of a human father, a fact prophesied in Isaiah 7:14. If Mary were not completely sinless this prophecy becomes untenable. Why is that? The passage points to Mary's Immaculate Conception because it mentions a complete enmity between the woman and Satan. Such an enmity would have been impossible if Mary were tainted by sin, original or actual (see 2 Corinthians 6:14). This line of thinking rules out Eve as the woman, since she clearly was under the influence of Satan in Genesis 3." *Patrick Madrid, "Ark of the New Covenant."*

"Jesus said unto her, Woman, what have I to do with thee? mine hour is not yet come." *John* 2:4.

"Now there stood by the cross of Jesus his mother ... When Jesus therefore saw his mother, and the disciple standing by, whom he loved, he saith unto his mother, Woman, behold thy son! Then saith he to the disciple, Behold thy mother." *John* 19:25-27:

"In the scene at the Cross the making of Eve from Adam's side is repeated symbolically, when the new Adam, in the sleep of death, breathes the life-giving breath of the Spirit upon the figure of Mary standing below his opened side." **L.S. Thornton, Anglican theologian.**

"Ye are of your father the devil, and the lusts of your father ye will do." *John* 8:44

"He that committeth sin is of the devil ... Whosoever is born of God doth not commit sin; for his seed remaineth in him: and he cannot sin, because he is born of God. In this the children of God are manifest, and the children of the devil: whosoever doeth not righteousness is not of God." 1 *John* 3:8-10

"I will put enmity between thee and the woman, and between thy seed and her seed." *Genesis* 3:15:

"And the dragon was wroth with the woman, and went to make war with the remnant of her seed, which keep the commandments of God, and have the testimony of Jesus Christ." *Revelation* 12:17:

Martin Luther (1523):

"Mary is the Mother of Jesus and the mother of us all. If Christ is ours, we must be where he is; and all that he has must be ours, and his mother is therefore also ours."

Martin Luther (1529):

"We are the children of Mary."

"And the serpent said unto the woman, Ye shall not surely die: For God doth know that in the day ye eat thereof, then your eyes shall be opened, and ye shall be as gods, knowing good and evil. And when the woman saw that the tree was good for food, ... she took of the fruit thereof, and did eat." *Genesis* 3:4-6.

"And the Lord God said unto the woman, What is this that thou hast done? ... I will greatly multiply thy sorrow." *Genesis* 3:13,16

"And the angel said unto her, Fear not, Mary: for thou hast found favour with God. And behold thou shalt conceive in thy womb, and bring forth a son, and shalt call his name JESUS." *Luke* 1:30

"And Mary said, Behold the handmaid of the Lord; be it unto me according to thy word." *Luke* 1:38

"Elisabeth was filled with the Holy Ghost ... and said, blessed art thou among women ... *blessed is she that believed.*" *Luke* 2:41,45.

"The knot of Eve's disobedience was loosed by the obedience of Mary. What the virgin Eve had bound in unbelief, the Virgin Mary loosed through faith." **Irenaeus (189 A.D.), Against Heresies, 3:22:24.**

"Through man came death, and through man salvation. The first man fell into sin; the second raised up the fallen. Woman has spoken in behalf of woman. The first woman gave entrance to sin; this woman helped justice enter in. The former followed the serpent's counsel; the latter presented the serpent's destroyer and brought forth the author of light. The former introduced sin through the wood; through the wood the latter introduced blessing instead. By the wood I mean the cross; and the fruit of this wood becomes life ever green and imperishable for those who taste of it." **Gregory of Nyssa (394 A.D.), In diem natalem Christi; PG, 46, 1148.**

"It shall bruise thy head, and thou shalt bruise his heel." *Genesis* 3:15

"For this purpose the Son of God was manifested, that he might destroy the works of the devil." 1 *John* 3:8

From Genesis *to* Revelation, *from Bethlehem to Cana to Calvary, the most powerful procession of images in Scripture is the* dazzling vision of the Woman and her Seed, the Virgin and her Son, the Queen-Mother and the King, the Daughter of Zion and the messianic Son of Man, the New Adam and the New Eve. This striking sequence of scriptural icons locked itself into the minds and hearts of the Christian faithful starting with the Apostolic Community of the first century, the first Fathers and the earliest Councils and resulted in a vast treasury of doctrinal and devotional masterpieces. The union of Mother and Son in the Son's mission of salvation and in the war against the Serpent/Dragon is a persistent theme of Scripture mirrored in Christian doctrine and devotion through the centuries. This union of the New Adam and the New Eve has been portrayed from a wide variety of perspectives, the most recent such expression being the union of the Sacred Heart of Jesus and the Immaculate Heart of Mary. To see the Son without the Virgin Mother, the Seed without the Woman, the King without the Queen-Mother, the New Adam without the New Eve is to do violence both to Scripture and to all of Christian history. For the Christian who enters the mind of the New Testament Church, the idea of "Jesus alone" without Mary is as unthinkable as the idea of the New Testament alone without the Old or the divinity of Jesus without the Humanity.

B. NEW ARK OF THE COVENANT

"The cloud covered the Tent of meeting and the glory of Yahweh filled the tabernacle." *Exodus* 40:34.

"The power of the Most High will cover you with its shadow. And so the child will be holy and will be called Son of God." *Luke* 1:35.

"And the Word was made flesh and pitched his tent among us." *John* 1:14

"'The power of the Holy Ghost shall come upon thee, and the power of the Most High shall overshadow thee: Wherefore also that which is to be born shall be called holy, the Son of God.' (*Luke* 1:35). These two sentences constitute the first part of the angelic reply to a question. Mary had asked: 'How shall this be?' The answer given in the above quotation contains two distinct echoes from the book of Exodus to which we must now give our attention.

In the second clause of the quotation the word rendered 'overshadow' is significant. Its literary associations suggest the cloud of the divine presence which rested upon the tabernacle. This appears from Exodus xl. 35, where the cloud 'abode' upon the tent of meeting. From *shakan* ('abode') is formed *shekinah*, a word coined to represent the divine presence over the ark in the Holy of Holies. In the Greek bible, moreover, *shakan* is rendered by a word of similar sound meaning 'overshadowed.' It is this word (*episkiazein*) which St. Luke employs in the phrase: 'the power of the highest shall overshadow thee.' That the word is here used designedly by the evangelist is evident from the story of Our Lord's Transfiguration, where all three gospels have it. There St. Peter's talk of three tents or tabernacles is answered by the divine voice from the overshadowing cloud indicating the true tabernacle in the flesh of 'Jesus only.' So here, in the earlier scene at Nazareth, the origination of that same tabernacle of flesh is announced in the angelic words. The tabernacle of the divine indwelling is the flesh of Mary which Jesus took." *L.S. Thornton, Anglican theologian.*

> "Not born of blood or of the desire of the flesh or of the desire of God." *John* 1:13.
>
> *"I do not know man." Luke* 1:34.
>
> "But of God." *John* 1:13.
>
> "The power of the Most High will cover you ..." *Luke* 1:35:

The parallelism of Mary and the Ark is continued in the visitation narrative.

> "However can the Ark of Yahweh (= My Lord) come to me?" *2 Samuel* 6:9.
>
> *"Why should I be honored with a visit from the mother of My Lord?" Luke* 1:43.
>
> "And David danced before the Lord with all his might ... So David and all the house of Israel brought up the ark of the Lord with shouting, and with the sound of the trumpet." *2 Samuel* 6:14-15.

"As soon as the voice of thy salutation sounded in mine ears, the babe leaped in my womb for joy." Luke 1:44.

"And the Ark of the Lord continued in the house of Obededom the Gittite three months." 2 *Samuel* 6:11.

"And Mary abode with her about three months." Luke 1:56.

"And the Lord blessed Obededom and all his household." 2 *Samuel* 6:11. [In Old Testament times, fertility was associated with God's blessing.]

"Now Elisabeth's full time came that she should be deliverd; and she brought forth a son." Luke 1:57

When Mary brings Jesus to the Temple, Simeon greets Him as *"the glory of thy people Israel,"* a divine title. The "glory" had departed from the Temple when the Ark had been taken away but now Mary the Daughter of Zion who is the new Ark brings the "glory of thy people Israel" back to the Temple and Simeon can die "in peace" because he has seen "the glory".

The Ark symbolism and its relationship to Mary continues in the Book of *Revelation*.

"I saw the holy city, the new Jerusalem, coming down from God out of heaven, as beautiful as a bride all dressed for her husband, and then I heard a loud voice call out from the throne, 'Behold the tent of God with men' ..." *Revelation* 21:2-3.

"Then the sanctuary of God in heaven opened, and the Ark of the Covenant could be seen inside it ... Now a great sign appeared in heaven: a woman, adorned with the sun ... She was pregnant." *Revelation* 11:19-12:1.

C. DAUGHTER OF ZION

"Rejoice, Daugher of Zion, the King of Israel, Yahweh, is IN you. Do not be afraid Zion, Yahweh your God is in your womb as a strong Savior." *Zephaniah* 3:14-17.

"Sing and rejoice, O daughter Zion! See, I am coming to dwell among you, says the Lord." *Zechariah* 2:14.

"Rejoice heartily, O daughter Zion, shout for joy, O daughter Jerusalem! See, your king shall come to you." *Zechariah* 9:9.

"Rejoice so highly favored. The Lord is WITH you. Do not be afraid, Mary ... Listen, you are to conceive in your womb and bear a son and you must name him "Yahweh Savior." *Luke* 1:28-33.

"My soul proclaims the greatness of the Lord, my spirit rejoices in God my savior." *Luke* 1:46.

D. ABRAHAM

"[Abraham] said, My Lord, if now I have found favour in thy sight, pass not away, I pray thee, from thy servant." *Genesis* 18:3.

"And the angel said unto her, Fear not, Mary: for thou hast found favour with God." *Luke* 1:30.

"I will bless them that bless thee, and curse him that curseth thee: and in thee shall all families of the earth be blessed." *Genesis* 12:3.

"All the nations of the earth shall be blessed in him." *Genesis* 18:18.

"And in thy seed shall all the nations of earth be blessed; because thou hast obeyed my voice." *Genesis* 22:18.

"Blessed art thou among women, and blessed is the fruit of thy womb." *Luke* 1:42.

"Behold, from henceforth all generations shall call me blessed." *Luke* 1:46.

"And he believed in the Lord; and he counted it to him for righteousness." *Genesis* 15:6.

"And blessed is she that believed: for there shall be a performance of those things which were told her from the Lord." *Luke* 1:45.

"And he said, Take now thy son, thine only son Isaac, whom thou lovest, and get thee into the land of Moriah; and offer him there for a burnt offering upon one of the mountains which I will tell thee of... And Isaac spake unto Abraham his father, and said, ... where is the lamb for a burnt offering? And Abraham said, My son, God will provide himself a lamb for a burnt offering... [And the angel of the Lord] said, By myself have I sworn, saith the Lord, for because thou has done this thing, and hast not withheld thy son, thine only son: That in blessing I will bless thee, and in multiplying I will multiply thy seed as the stars of the heaven ... and thy seed shall possess the gate of his enemies." *Genesis* 22:2,7-8, 16-17.

"He is brought as a lamb to the slaughter." *Isaiah* 53:7.

"But when the fulness of the time was come, God sent forth his Son, made of a woman, made under the law, To redeem them that were under the law, that we might receive the adoption of sons." *Galatians* 4:4-5.

"And when the days of her purification according to the law of Moses were accomplished, they brought him to Jerusalem, **to present him** to the Lord ...And Simeon blessed them, and said **unto Mary his mother**, Behold this child is set for the fall and rising again of many in Israel; and for a sign which shall be spoken against (Yea, A sword shall pierce through thy own soul also.)" *Luke* 2:22,34-35.

———

"Behold the Lamb of God, which taketh away the sin of the world." *John* 1:29.

"The lamb slain from the foundation of the world." *Revelation* 13:8.

"Ye were not redeemed with corruptible things ... but with the precious blood of Christ, as a lamb without blemish and without spot who verily was foreordained before the foundation of the world." 1 *Peter* 1:18-19.

"Now there stood by the cross of Jesus his mother." *John* 19:25.

"The tabernacle of the divine indwelling is the flesh of Mary which Jesus took. We now turn back from the scene where the tabernacle was set up to the earlier story of the great deliverance. When the firstborn of Egypt were slain, Israel, God's own firstborn son (Exodus iv.22), went free. In grateful acknowledgement of this fact it is laid down that all the firstborn males of Israel and of their live-stock shall be set apart or 'sanctified to the Lord.' To that expression Westcott and Hort refer us, in their edition of the Greek Testament, when they come to St. Luke's phrase: 'that which is to be born shall be called holy,' in the crucial verse which we are considering... The tabernacle was not simply and solely the abode of the divine presence, the place where God meets man. As such, it was also the center of the cultus, the place in which sacrifice was offered. If Mary is here the sanctuary, Jesus her promised Son is already the victim. All the firstborn of Israel's sons were redeemed under the Law by substitution of animal sacrifices. Mary's Son, however, is the true sacrifice by which alone all are redeemed." *L.S. Thornton, Anglican theologian.*

E. MOSES

"And Moses went up unto God, and the Lord called unto him ... tell the children of Israel ... if ye will obey my voice indeed, and keep my covenant, then ye shall be a peculiar treasure unto me above all people ... And **Moses** came and called for the elders of the people, and laid before their faces all these words which the Lord commanded him. And all the people answered together, and said, **All that the Lord hath spoken we will do**. And Moses returned the words of the people unto the Lord... And it came to pass on **the third day** in the morning, that there were thunders and lightnings, and a thick cloud upon the mount, and the voice of the trumpet exceeding loud; so that all the people that was in the camp trembled ... And Moses said unto the people, Fear not: for God is come to prove you, and that his fear may be before your faces, that you sin not." *Exodus* 19:3,5,7-8.,16; 20:20.

___

"And **the third day** there was a marriage in Cana of Galilee; and the mother of Jesus was there ... **His mother** saith unto the servants, **Whatseover he saith unto you, do it**... This beginning of miracles did Jesus in Cana of Galilee, and manifested forth his glory; and his disciples believed on him. *John* 2:1,5,11.

___

"My servant Moses is not so, who is faithful in all mine house ... Wherefore then were ye not afraid to speak against my servant Moses? And the anger of the Lord was kindled against them." *Numbers* 12:7-9.

———

"And the angel said unto her, Fear not, Mary: for thou hast found favour with God... Elisabeth was filled with the Holy Ghost ... and said, blessed art thou among women ... blessed is she that believed." *Luke* 2:30, 41,45.

F. PROTOTYPES OF MARY IN THE OLD TESTAMENT

[Derived from **All Generations Shall Call Me Blessed** by Stefano Manelli]

SARAH

"Free" wife of Abraham unlike Hagar the slave wife. Although sterile she bears Isaac in her old age through a miracle of God. Isaac is the father of a great nation [*Genesis* 11].

MARY

Mary is the "free" wife who is free of any subjection to sin - "whoever commits sin is the slave of sin" [*John* 8:34]. She is a voluntary virgin who nevertheless conceives and bears her Son through a miracle. Her Son Jesus is the Head of the Mystical Body, the "firstborn among many brethren." [*Romans* 8:29].

"Is anything too hard for the Lord?" *Genesis* 18:14.

"With God nothing shall be impossible." *Luke* 2:37.

———

REBECCA

Wife of Isaac who played a key role in the history of salvation. Abraham asked his servant Eliezer to request Rebecca to be the wife of Isaac. Her brothers tell Rebecca: "May you increase to thousands of thousands and may your seed possess the gates of their enemies." [*Genesis* 24:60]. Rebecca dresses Jacob in the clothes of his older brother Esau to secure the blessing of Isaac.

MARY

God the Father asks the angel Gabriel to request Mary to be the Mother of God the Son. Mary's seed are the multitudes "which keep the commandments of God, and have the testimony of Jesus Christ." Mary clothes Jesus in human flesh and offers Him to the Father to secure His blessing on the human race.

RACHEL

Jacob is entranced by Rachel's beauty. Rachel is the mother of Joseph who was sold for 20 pieces of silver. Rachel's sorrow at the loss of Joseph is recalled in Jeremiah 31:15. Joseph comes to power in Egypt and is the savior of his family.

MARY

Mary has "found favor with God." Her Son Jesus is sold for thirty pieces of silver. Mary's sorrow at the Cross is prefigured by the sorrow of Rachel at the loss of her son. By His death He becomes the savior of the human race.

MIRIAM

Miriam the sister of Moses, the liberator of the People of God, and the sister of Aaron, the first priest of the Old Covenant. Miriam is present with Moses and Aaron at the "Tent of Meeting" in which the Lord descended and spoke to them. "For I brought thee out of the land of Egypt, and redeemed thee out of the house of servants; and I sent before thee Moses, Aaron and Miriam." *Micah* 6:4.

MARY

Just as Miriam was associated with the lawgiver of the People of God, Mary is associated with the Supreme Lawgiver Who Moses pre-figured. Similarly Mary is associated with the High Priest of the New Covenant who again is prefigured by Aaron. Whereas Miriam flees from Egypt, Mary flees to Egypt.

DEBORAH

Deborah saves her people from the Canaanites by helping Barak victoriously lead a small army against the much larger army of Sisera. Deborah is a prophetess and renowned for her mercy. Judges 5 is a song of praise from Deborah to the Almighty thanking Him for the victory over Sisera.

MARY

Mary assists Christ in His redemptive mission - a mission He performs against all odds. Mary is the Queen of Prophets and Merciful Mother. Deborah's song is a foreshadowing of the Magnificat.

RUTH

Ruth, a Moabite, is the wife of Boaz and the mother of Obed the grandfather of David. She leaves her people behind and declares herself the servant of Boaz.

MARY

Mary will bear a Son in the line of David. She offers herself as a handmaiden of the Lord.

"And Ruth said ... whither thou goest I will go." *Ruth* 1:16.

"And Mary said, Behold the handmaid of the Lord; be it unto me according to thy word." *Luke* 1:38.

HANNAH

"And Hannah prayed, and said, My heart rejoiceth in the Lord, mine horn is exalted in the Lord ... I rejoice in thy salvation. There is none holy as the Lord ... Talk no more so exceeding proudly ... The bows of the mighty men are broken, and they that stumbled are girded with strength ... He raiseth up the poor out of the dust ... The adversaries of the Lord shall be broken to pieces." 1 *Samuel* 2:1-4,8,10.

MARY

"And Mary said, My soul doth magnify the Lord, And my spirit hath rejoiced in God my Saviour. For he hath regarded the low estate of his handmaiden ... and holy is his name ... He hath shewed strength with his arm; he hath scattered the proud in the imagination of their hearts. He hath put down the mighty from their seats, and exalted them of low degree." *Luke* 1:46-9,51-2.

———

ABIGAIL

Abigail means "exaltation of the Father." Because of her great virtue David marries her and makes her queen of the house of David. In 1 *Samuel* 25:41, she tells David, "Behold your servant ..."

MARY

Mary's exaltation of the Father is seen especially in the Magnificat. Because she has won favor with Him, God the Father makes her the Spouse of the Holy Spirit and the Mother of the Son. At the Annunciation, *Luke* 1:38, she says, "Behold the handmaid of the Lord."

———

ESTHER

Esther is chosen to be queen by King Ahasuerus for her beauty. All of Esther's people have been condemned to death through the schemes of an enemy. She alone is excepted from this condemnation. Esther manages to foil the schemes of the enemy and saves her people from death.

"For the king loved Esther above all the women, and she obtained grace and favor in his sight more than all the virgins; so that he set the royal crown upon her head." *Esther* 2:17.

"And Esther spake yet again before the king, and fell down at his feet, and besought him with tears to put away the mischief of Haman the Agagite, and his device that he had devised against the Jews ... For how can I endure to see the evil that shall come unto my people? or how can I endure to see the destruction of my kindred?" *Esther* 8:5-6.

MARY

Alone of her race, Mary was not subject to Original Sin, the condemnation to spiritual death. She assists her Son in His mission of defeating the enemy and rescuing her people from the decree of damnation. She continues to intercede for her people as they continue in their journey from death.

G. QUEEN MOTHER

> "And the king rose to meet her, and bowed down to her; then he sat on his throne, and had a seat brought for the king's mother; and she sat on his right. Then she said, 'I have one small request to make of you; do not refuse me.' And the king said to her, 'Make your request, my mother; for I will not refuse you.' 1 *Kings* 2: 19-20.

> "And whence is this to me, that the mother of my Lord should come to me?" *Luke* 2:43.

> "And he went down with them, and came to Nazareth, and was subject unto them." *Luke* 2:51.

> "Jesus said unto her,... Mine hour is not yet come." *John* 2:4.

> "And there appeared a great wonder in heaven; a woman clothed with the sun, and the moon under her feet, and upon her head a crown of twelve stars ... And she brought forth a man child, who was to rule all nations with a rod of iron." *Revelation* 12:1,5.

The position of the Queen-Mother was its highest in the reign of the Davidic Kings. Concerning Jesus, we are told in the Gospels that "the Lord God shall give unto him the throne of his father David." [*Luke* 1:32]. How entirely fitting then that His Mother too is a Queen-Mother with the same dignity and stature as the other Davidic Queen-Mothers - but with the one difference that of her Son's kingdom "there shall be no end." [*Luke* 1:33]

"Elizabeth makes a substantial contribution to the scriptural theology of Mary. When she greets her as "Mother of my Lord," she speaks in familiar terms founded upon the Old Testament. These words indicate that Mary is Queen-Mother, the Great Lady of Judah's court. Because of the polygamy practiced by the Near Eastern monarchs, it was the mother of the royal son, the woman who had given the king to his nation, who enjoyed a position of pre-eminence surpassed only by her son. Mary was Mother of "the Lord," a word whose meaning at the opening of our era contained overtones of royalty and divinity. The Old Testament gives us pictures of Solomon's and Belshazzar's mothers dominating an incident in the court... [David Stanley:] 'With these two instances in mind, we are in a position to appreciate the deeply theological significance of Luke's application to our Lady of the title, 'Mother of my Lord.' ... We may say that the Mother of Jesus was admittedly next in importance to her divine Son in the veneration offered by the apostolic Church. Moreover, as the incident between Solomon and Bathsheba would appear to indicate, this solemn title expressed Mary's intercessory or mediatorial power with her glorified Son.'"

Thomas F. O'Meara, Mary in Protestant and Catholic Theology.

H. INTERCESSOR, MEDIATRIX

"Abraham stood yet before the Lord. And Abraham drew near, and said, Wilt thou also destroy the righteous with the wicked? Peradventure there be fifty righteous within the city: wilt thou also destroy and not spare the place for the fifty righteous that are therein? ... And the Lord said, If I find in Sodom fifty righteous within the city, then I will spare all the place for their sakes." *Genesis* 18:22-24, 26.

"Moses said unto the people, Ye have sinned a great sin: and now I will go up unto the Lord; peradventure I shall make an atonement for your sin. And Moses returned unto the Lord, and said, Oh, this people have sinned a great sin, and have made them gods of gold. Yet now, if thou wilt forgive their sin -; and if not, blot me, I pray thee, out of thy book which thou has written." *Exodus* 32:30-32.

"And the Lord spake unto Moses, saying, Phinehas, the son of Eleazar, the son of Aaron the priest, hath turned my wrath away from the children of Israel, while he was zealous for my sake among them, that I consumed not the children of Israel in my jealousy. Wherefore say, Behold, I give unto him my covenant of peace: And he shall have it, and his seed after him, even the covenant of an everlasting priesthood; because he was zealous for his God, and made an atonement for the children of Israel." *Numbers* 25: 10-13.

"They forgat God their saviour, which had done great things in Egypt; wondrous works in the land of Ham, and terrible things by the Red Sea. Therefore he said that he would destroy them, had not Moses his chosen stood before him in the breach, to turn away his wrath, lest he should destroy them." *Psalm* 106:21-3.

"They joined themselves also unto Baalpeor, and ate the sacrifices of the dead. Thus they provoked him to anger with their inventions: and the plague brake in upon them. Then stood up Phinehas, and executed judgment: and so the plague was stayed. And that was counted unto him for righteousness unto all generations for evermore." *Psalm* 106:28-31.

"Then she said, 'I have one small request to make of you; do not refuse me.' And the king said to her, 'Make your request, my mother; for I will not refuse you.'" 1 *Kings* 2: 19-20.

"Which of you shall have a friend, and shall go unto him at midnight, and say unto him, Friend, lend me three loaves; **For a friend of mine in his journey is come to me, and I have nothing to set before him**? ... I say unto you, Though he will not rise and give him, because he is his friend, yet because of his importunity he will rise and give him as many as he needeth." *Luke* 11:5-6,8.

"Let him know, that he which converteth the sinner from the error of his way **shall save a soul from death**, and shall hide a multitude of sins." *James* 5:20

"Take heed unto thyself, and unto the doctrine; continue in them: for in doing this **thou shalt both save thyself, and them that hear thee**." 1 *Timothy* 4:16

"Wherefore seeing we also are compassed about with so great a cloud of witnesses, let us lay aside every weight." *Hebrews* 12:1.

"I saw under the altar the souls of them that were slain for the word of God, and for the testimony which they held: And they cried with a loud voice, saying, How long, O Lord, holy and true, dost thou not judge and avenge our blood on them that dwell on the earth?" *Revelation* 6:9-10.

"And another angel came and stood at the altar, having a golden censer; and there was given unto him much incense, that he should offer it **with the prayers of all saints upon the golden altar** which was before the throne. And the smoke of the incense, which came **with the prayers of the saints, ascended up before God** out of the angel's hand." *Revelation* 8:3-4.

"And when they wanted wine, the mother of Jesus saith unto him, They have no wine. Jesus said unto her, Woman, what have I to do with thee? **mine hour is not yet come.** His mother saith unto the servants, **Whatsoever he saith** unto you, do it." *John* 2:3-5.

"Now there stood by the cross of Jesus his mother ... When Jesus therefore saw his mother, and the disciple standing by, whom he loved, he saith unto his mother, **Woman, behold thy son!** Then saith he to the disciple, **Behold thy mother.**" *John* 19:25-27.

"These all continued with one accord in prayer and supplication. with the women, and Mary the mother of Jesus ... And there appeared unto them cloven tongues like as of fire, and it sat upon each of them. And they were all filled with the Holy Ghost." *Acts* 1:14, 2:3-4.

"And the dragon was wroth with the woman, and went to make war with the remnant of **her seed**." *Revelation* 12.

"She [Mary] stands at the beginning of the life of each Christian as she stood once at the beginning of Christ's life Himself." [Christ was] "the first-born of Mary as she was in Him and after Him to give life to many others." [Irenaeus].

Modern exegetes like F.M. Braun have shown that all Jesus's words on the Cross concerned His divine mission and so it is not unthinkable that His words to His Mother, "Woman, behold thy son," were an exception. Moreover, since all the incidents from verses 17 to 42 of *John* 19 concern the fulfillment of prophecy it has to be concluded that this statement is also prophetically significant. Jesus crushes the head of the serpent (*Genesis* 3:15 and *Revelation* 12:9) and "casts him down" forever (*John* 12:31) on the cross. The reference to the Devil and his seed (*Genesis* 3) is followed through in *John* 8:41-4 and 1 *John* 3:8-10. Since the *Genesis* prophecy is consciously recalled in *John* (with the victory over the Devil and his seed), we see then that the last figure in the great prophecy, the Woman who shares in the Victory of her seed, belongs to this picture. In *Genesis* the first woman is the mother of the human race; in *John* and *Revelation* (as prophesied in *Genesis*), Mary would appropriately be appointed mother of all who follow her Son. Finally, it is critical to note that the beloved disciple is first entrusted to Mary and not vice versa. Most modern exegetes agree that the disciple here represents all who follow and love Jesus (Jesus has said that those who love Him are those who follow His commandments). When Jesus speaks He does not simply declare but He causes what He says to happen (*John* 1:3; 2:7-8; 4:15) - thus Mary now actually becomes the spiritual mother of all the beloved disciples of her Son (as confirmed in *Revelation* 12). Her role is to bring her Son's followers to Him.

When we talk about going "to Jesus through Mary" we are not suggesting that Mary's function is to "introduce" us to Jesus. We are talking about growing deeper in our life in Jesus with and through Mary's assistance. With Mary as our model, teacher and guide we become the kind of Christian God wants us to be. With and through Mary we become more and more like Jesus. Thus "through Mary" does not mean that she functions as a door-opening "go-between." In actuality, it means that she is acting as our Mother trying to make us more like her divine Son. We are simply doing what Jesus commanded in *John* 19 and what the book of *Revelation* teaches when it says that those who "keep the commandments of God, and have the testimony of Jesus Christ" are "**her seed**." *Revelation* 12:17.

Once we recognize Mary to be our spiritual Mother given to us by our Savior to guide and draw us in our growth in His Life we will see why "Marian mediation" in no sense competes with our faith in Christ. All of Christian life is designed to draw us closer to Christ, to make us more like Him. Like the Bible, Mary is one more instrument in this life-long process of conforming ourselves to Christ. She is our Mother who helps us become like her Son - that is the basis and object of Marian devotion.

"We fly to thy patronage, O holy Mother of God, despise not our petitions in our necessities, but deliver us from all danger, O ever glorious and blessed Virgin." [Third century document containing the ancient prayer of the early Christians.]

I. IMMACULATELY CONCEIVED

"Then the word of the Lord came unto me, saying, Before I formed thee in the belly I knew thee; and **before thou camest forth out of the womb I sanctified thee**, and I ordained thee a prophet unto the nations." *Jeremiah* 1:4-5.

"When Elisabeth heard the salutation of Mary, **the babe leaped in her womb**; and Elisabeth was **filled with the Holy Ghost**." Luke 1:41.

———

"The lamb slain from the foundation of the world." *Revelation* 13:8.

"Ye were not redeemed with corruptible things ... but with the precious blood of Christ, as a lamb without blemish and without spot who verily was foreordained before the foundation of the world." 1 *Peter* 1:18-19.

———

"And the angel came in unto her, and said, Hail, **thou that art highly favoured**, the Lord is with thee: blessed art thou among women. And when she saw him, she was troubled at his saying, and cast in her mind what manner of salutation this should be. And the angel said unto her, Fear not, Mary: for **thou hast found favour with God**. And behold thou shalt conceive in thy womb, and bring forth a son, and shalt call his name JESUS." *Luke* 1:28-31.

"The glory of **his grace, wherein he hath made us accepted in the beloved**. In whom we have redemption through his blood, the forgiveness of sins, according to the richness of his grace." *Ephesians* 1:6-7.

The Angel Gabriel's greeting to Mary, variously rendered as "thou that art highly favored" and "full of grace" is a translation of the Greek word *kecharitomene* which refers to one who has been transformed by God's grace. This word is used only one other time in the New Testament and that is in the epistle to the Ephesians where Paul is addressing those who by becoming Christians are transformed by grace and receive the remission of sins. In Ephesians the reference is to those who have been transformed with the grace of God by accepting Christ. In the description of Mary, we are told she was transformed by grace even before the birth of Christ.

"In what then would this transformation of grace consist? According to the parallel text of the Letter to the *Ephesians* 1:6 the Christians have been 'transformed by grace' in the sense that 'according to the richness of his grace, they find redemption by his blood, the *remission of sins*.' (Ephesians 1:7). This grace, in reality, takes away sin. This is elucidating for our particular case. Mary is 'transformed by grace,' because she has been *sanctified* by the grace of God... Sophronius of Jerusalem, for example, interprets the term 'full of grace' in this manner: 'No one has been fully sanctified as you ...; no one has been *purified in advance* as you.' In addition, he takes from the total context that Mary had been 'transformed by the grace' of God in view of the task which she awaits, that of becoming the Mother of the Son of God, and to do so while remaining a virgin." ***Ignace de la Potterie.***

Martin Luther:

"But the other conception, namely the infusion of the soul, it is piously and suitably believed, was without any sin, so that while the soul was being infused, she would at the same time be cleansed from original sin and adorned with the gifts of God to receive the holy soul thus infused. And thus, in the very moment in which she began to live, she was without all sin..."

"God has formed the soul and body of the Virgin Mary full of the Holy Spirit, so that she is without all sins, for she has conceived and borne the Lord Jesus."

Ulrich Zwingli:

"Christ ... was born of a most undefiled Virgin."

"It was fitting that such a holy Son should have a holy Mother."

J. MARY AND THE HOLY SPIRIT

"The **Holy Ghost** shall come upon **thee**, and the power of the Highest shall overshadow thee: therefore also that holy thing which shall be born of thee shall be called the Son of God... And Mary said, Behold the handmaid of the Lord; be it unto me according to thy word." *Luke* 1:35.

———

"When as his mother Mary was espoused to Joseph, before they came together, **she** was found with child of the **Holy Ghost**." *Matthew* 1:18.

———

"Elisabeth was filled with the **Holy Ghost**: and she spake out with a loud voice, and said, blessed art **thou** among women, and blessed is the fruit of thy womb." *Luke* 2:41-42.

———

"The **Holy Ghost** was upon him ... and he came by the Spirit into the temple ... And Simeon blessed them, and said unto **Mary** his mother ... A sword shall pierce through thy own soul also." *Luke* 2:25,27,34-5.

———

"These all continued with one accord in prayer and supplication. with the women, and **Mary** the mother of Jesus ... And when the day of Pentecost was fully come, they were all with one accord in one place... And there appeared unto them cloven tongues like as of fire, and it sat upon each of them. And they were all filled with the **Holy Ghost**." *Acts* 1:14, 2:3-4.

In ancient Christianity the name given to Mary, "Panagia", ("all holy" in Greek) was the same as the name given to the Holy Spirit, "Panagion".

"As the Son is the natural image of the Father, and consequently an image entirely similar, and the Paraclete is in the same way the image of the Son, so also the Mother of the Son is the image of the Paraclete, not really a natural one, but by participation and grace, in such wise that incomparably above all created nature, she represents the prototype, and in her alone most eminently shine and are beheld all the graces and splendours of the Spirit related to her Son." ***Theophanes of Nicaea.***

K. EVER-VIRGIN MOTHER OF IMMANUEL

"Therefore the Lord himself shall give you a sign; Behold, a **virgin** shall conceive, and bear a son, and shall call his name **Immanuel**." *Isaiah* 7:14.

___

"Therefore will he give them up, until the time that **she** which travaileth hath brought forth ... And he shall ... be great unto the ends of the earth. And this man shall be the peace." *Micah* 5:3-5.

___

"And behold **thou** shalt conceive in thy womb, and bring forth a son, and shalt call his name JESUS. He shall be great, and shall be called the Son of the Highest." *Luke* 1:31-2.

___

"And whence is this to me, that **the mother of my Lord** should come to me?" *Luke* 1:43.

Martin Luther:

"The council [Ephesus] has not offered anything new to faith but has strengthened the old faith against the new arrogance of Nestorius. This article of faith - that Mary is the Mother of God - is present in the Church from the beginning and is not a new creation of the Council but the presentation of the Gospel and Scriptures."

"In this work whereby she was made the Mother of God, so many and such great good things were given her that no one can grasp them."

John Calvin:

"Elizabeth called Mary Mother of the Lord, because the unity of the person in the two natures of Christ was such that she could have said that the mortal man engendered in the womb of Mary was at the same time the eternal God."

"It cannot be denied that God in choosing and destining Mary to be the Mother of his Son, granted her the highest honor."

Ulrich Zwingli:

"It was given to her what belongs to no creature, that in the flesh she should bring forth the Son of God."

"Then said the Lord unto me: This gate shall be shut, it shall not be opened, and no man shall enter in by it; because the Lord, the God of Israel, hath entered in by it, therefore it shall be shut. It is for the prince ... he shall enter by the way of the porch of that gate, and shall go out by the way of the same." *Ezekiel* 44:2-3.

———

Luke 1:34 "How shall this be, seeing I know not a man?"

Luke 1:34 has historically been understood as a reference by Mary to a vow of life-long virginity. Rene Laurentin notes that here we must "recognize the present tense 'I do not know' as having to do with a condition rather than an instant of time. To give an example, if someone to whom a cigarette is offered replies, 'I don't smoke,' he is understood to mean 'I never smoke' and not 'I am not smoking right now.'"

Martin Luther:

"It is an article of faith that Mary is Mother of the Lord and still a Virgin."

John Calvin:

"Helvidius has shown himself too ignorant, in saying that Mary had several sons, because mention is made in some passages of the brothers of Christ." Calvin translated "brothers" in this context to mean cousins or relatives.

Ulrich Zwingli:

"I firmly believe that Mary, according to the words of the gospel as a pure Virgin brought forth for us the Son of God and in childbirth and after childbirth forever remained a pure, intact Virgin."

L. MERCIFUL MOTHER

"Behold thy father and I have sought thee sorrowing." *Luke* 2:48.

———

"There came then his brethren and his mother, and standing without, sent unto him, calling him. And the multitude sat about him, and they said unto him, Behold thy mother and thy brethren without seek for thee." *Mark* 3:31-2.

———

"And when they wanted wine, the mother of Jesus saith unto him, They have no wine." *John* 2:3.

_____

"A sword shall pass through thy own soul, also." *Luke* 2:35.

_____

"In the midst of the elders, stood a Lamb as it had been slain." *Revelation* 5:5.

_____

"And she being with child cried." *Revelation* 12:2.

_____

"Now there stood by the cross of Jesus his mother." *John* 19:25.

M. EXALTATION

"And the angel came in unto her, and said, Hail, thou that art highly favoured, the Lord is with thee: blessed art thou among women. And when she saw him, she was troubled at his saying, and cast in her mind what manner of salutation this should be. And the angel said unto her, Fear not, Mary: for thou hast found favour with God." *Luke* 1:28, 30.

_____

"And it came to pass, that, when Elisabeth heard the salutation of Mary, the babe leaped in her womb; and Elisabeth was filled with the Holy Ghost: and she spake out with a loud voice, and said, blessed art thou among women, and blessed is the fruit of thy womb. And whence is this to me, that the mother of my Lord should come to me? For, lo, as soon as the voice of thy salutation sounded in mine ears, the babe leaped in my womb for joy." *Luke* 2:41-44.

_____

"From henceforth all generations shall call me blessed." *Luke* 2:48.

Rene Laurentin:

"No other biblical personage has been given such strong praise, and without anything said to the contrary.

In Luke 1:35 the angel tells Mary, 'The Holy Spirit will come upon *you* and the power of the Most High will cover *you* with its shadow.' In the light of Isaiah 11:2 would it not have been more normal to say that the Holy Spirit was coming on the Emmanuel rather than on his Mother? In Luke 1:42 Elizabeth proclaims Mary's blessing before that of her Son and adds, 'Why should I be honoured with a visit from the *Mother of my Lord*?' even though the honour that falls to her is actually the visit of the *Lord* rather than of the Mother. She adds, 'For the moment *your greeting* reached my ears, the child in my womb leapt for joy,' even though in reality the benefit of the visitation is to be attributed to the action of Mary's child rather than to Mary's voice. That Mary should thus be placed in the forefront is most astonishing and gives food for reflection to those who fear that they do Christ some offense in exalting his Mother."

John McHugh:

"There is nothing improbable in the suggestion that the early Christians sang hymns of praise in honour of Mary... That her special rank was acknowledged by the Church is implied by the text of the Magnificat, where Luke says that 'from this present time' (1:48b) all generations will call her blessed. Could Luke have written that phrase if, at the time when he was writing (A.D. 70-80), his own generation had not begun to call her blessed? The text of Lk 1:42 would seem conclusive proof that the early Church expressed its reverence for the mother of its Lord by singing hymns in her honour."

Martin Luther:

"Is Christ only to be adored? Or is the holy Mother of God rather not to be honoured? This is the woman who crushed the Serpent's head. Hear us. For your Son denies you nothing."
"The veneration of Mary is inscribed in the very depths of the human heart."

John Calvin:

"To this day we cannot enjoy the blessing brought to us in Christ without thinking at the same time of that which God gave as adornment and honour to Mary, in willing her to be the mother of his only-begotten Son."

Ulrich Zwingli:

"The more the honor and love of Christ increases among men, so much the esteem and honor given to Mary should grow."

Heinrich Bullinger:
"She can hardly be compared with any of the other saints, but should by rights be elevated above all of them."

N. ASSUMPTION

"And Enoch walked with God: and he was not; for God took him." *Genesis* 5:24.

"And it came to pass, as they still went on, and talked, that, behold, there appeared a chariot of fire, and horses of fire, and parted them both asunder; and Elijah went up by a whirl-wind into heaven." 2 *Kings* 2:11.

"[Jesus] was transfigured before them: and his face did shine as the sun, and his raiment was white as the light. And, behold, there appeared unto them Moses and Elias talking with him." *Matthew* 17:2-3.

"From henceforth all generations shall call me **blessed**." *Luke* 2:48.

"And there appeared a great wonder **in heaven; a woman clothed with the sun**, and the moon under her feet, and upon her head a crown of twelve stars." *Revelation* 12:1.

Martin Luther:
"There can be no doubt that the Virgin Mary is in heaven. How it happened we do not know."

Heinrich Bullinger [Cranmer's brother-in-law and successor of Zwingli]:
Mary's "sacrosanct body was borne by angels into heaven."

O. THE WEDDING FEAST

"Thy Maker is thine husband; the Lord of hosts is his name." *Isaiah* 54:5.

"And the third day there was a marriage in Cana of Galilee; and the mother of Jesus was there: and ... Jesus." *John* 2:1-2.

———

"The marriage of the Lamb is come, and his wife hath made herself ready ... Blessed are they which are called unto the marriage supper of the Lamb." *Revelation* 19:7,19.

———

"I saw the holy city, the new Jerusalem, coming down from God out of heaven, as beautiful as a bride all dressed for her husband, and then I heard a loud voice call out from the throne, 'Behold the tent of God with men.'" *Revelation* 21:2-3.

———

"The Word is joined to flesh; the Word is married to flesh, and your womb is the bridal chamber of that great marriage." [Augustine, *Sermon* 291,6.]

———

"Thy Mother she is, she alone, and thy sister along with all; she became thy Mother, she became thy sister. She is also thy Bride." [Ephrem of Syria, 373 A.D.]

Rene Laurentin:

John saw in the feast and marriage of Cana a symbol not only of the Eucharistic feast but of the eschatological marriage of God and humanity signified and prepared by the Eucharist. It will be recalled that in Jesus' parables the banquet is symbolically presented as the type of the eschatological banquet (Mt 22:1-14; 25:1-13; Lk. 12:37; 22:2,9). Marriage, such as at Cana when Jesus began his mission, is presented as the figure and pledge of the heavenly nuptials which will be consummation of this ministry.

Stefano Manelli:

As regards the entire episode of Cana, a literal interpretation of the miracle and a spiritual interpretation of the marriage are to be preferred as more faithful to the text and exegetical tradition. The miracle anticipated by Jesus solely because of Mary's motherly care for two young spouses is to be understood literally. The marriage, however, is to be interpreted spiritually, as symbolizing the espousals between the Word and humanity in

Mary and through Mary, espousals shown as approved by God via the sign of water changed into wine through the mediative action of Mary, who motivates the creative action of Christ.

The fundamental fact of "transposition" in the meaning of "spouses," who no longer are the two young persons of Cana, but Jesus and Mary, the unique workers of the transformation of the water into new wine, that is, of the passage from the Old to the New Testament, from the Old to the New Covenant must be noted with special care... If Jesus, in fact, is the divine "Spouse" of the new people of God, represented in the small group of early disciples, how is Mary's role and position to be interpreted? It is certainly a role of mediation, as has already been said. But there is something more and different. Here Mary is both Spouse and Mother. She is Spouse of the Word Incarnate, Mother of the Church.

Ignace de la Potterie:

From the outset, the evangelist underlines this theme [of the wedding feast] with insistence: "On the third day, there was a *wedding feast* at Cana in Galilee. The mother of Jesus was there. Jesus also was invited to the *wedding feast*, and also his disciples. Now they had no wine, for the wine of the *wedding feast* was used up. The mother of Jesus said to him: 'They have no wine'" (Jn 2:1-3). In the first three verses, the word "wedding feast" occurs three times. What is astonishing - we have already pointed this out - is that nothing is said about the married couple. John is not interested in them but rather in the fact that *Jesus* and *Mary* were there, at this *wedding feast*. Besides, let us recall a detail of the literary structure: the theme of the *wedding feast* is supported in the first narrative part (vv.1-3: A), and returns in an equivalent form in the third (vv.9-12: A') where the theme of the *bridegroom* as applied to Jesus prevails. At the narrative level, one has the impression that it is Jesus who "functions" here as the bridegroom of the wedding feast; and, as we shall state later, there are indications which permit us to say that the mother of Jesus "functions" here as the bride...

This is also what results from the study of the Protestant exegete, P. Geoltrain, a specialist in structuralism, who published a structural analysis of the Cana account... Jesus and

Mary truly act as if they were the principal personages of the narrative. Saint Augustine had already seen this quite well, at least for Christ, and he knew how to express this in a very fine text ..."The bridegroom of these nuptials represented the person of the Lord, of him to whom it had been said: 'You have kept the choice wine until now.' The choice wine, Christ had kept till now: this is his Gospel." Jesus took upon himself the role of the bridegroom of Cana, and becomes at the spiritual level, the true Bridegroom of the whole episode.

This interpretation is confirmed by the word of John the Baptist a little later when he designates Jesus as the Bridegroom. He himself, "the friend of the Bridegroom" (Jn 3:29), had "come to baptize in water in order that he might be revealed to Israel" (Jn 1:31); now, he is "filled with joy" because he has heard the voice of the Bridegroom ...

We also need to remember what was said formerly concerning the theme of the messianic covenant, which was announced by the prophets under the espousals between Yahweh and his people (Ho 2:16-25; Jr 2:1-2; 3:1,6-12; Ezk 16; Is 50:1; 54:4-8; 62:4-5)...

J.P. Charlier in his fine book on the sign of Cana, sums up all of his exegesis in this key sentence which says all that is essential: "In their gestures and their dialogue, the Virgin Mary and Christ surpass by far the human and material part of the local festivities, supplanting the young couple of Cana in order to become the spiritual Bridegroom and Bride of the messianic banquet." ... From a purely functional point of view ... Jesus and Mary take the place here of the bridegegroom and bride of Cana.

As far as Mary is concerned, the substitution clearly appears in the text from the fact that Jesus calls his mother in this place, "Woman." "The word could not have been better chosen," says J.P. Charlier, "to make it understood that the role of Bride is taken by Mary." Mary, likewise, conducts herself as a close "collaborator" fo Jesus in the preparation of the "choice wine," the sign of the messianic wedding feast. "As Bride she is the first collaborator with Christ ... As the Bride of Christ she becomes a veritable helpmate similar to him (Gn 2:19). At Cana, she helps him prepare the wine, to set the table of the

banquet, and she dispatches those in the house (Pr 9:1-5) ...
Already at the hour of the sign, John shows us the Virgin-Bride
integrated at the deepest level in the plan of redemption." Mary
in reality says to the servants: "Do whatever he tells you." This
means, at the symbolic level, that she incites them to keep the
true attitude of the Covenant, by obedience to God in Christ.
And the fact that they are called "servants," "*diakonoi*," is an
explicit reference to the true "disciples" of Jesus. "*Diakonos*,"
let us recall, is a term that John employs for designating those
who are "disciples" of Jesus.

M. J. Scheeben:

The factor that really forms the *personal character* in the divine motherhood and ... represents *the grace of the divine motherhood* is a *supernatural, spiritual union of the person of Mary
with the divine Person of her Son, which is effected by the will
and power of God* ... The simplest, most precise and most natural description of this union with the divine Person is the term
matrimonium divinum or *conubium Verbi* in the strictest sense
of the word ... and which therefore is just as much the most
perfect image of the Hypostatic Union of a created nature with
God as human marriage is the image of the union of the body
with the spiritual soul. Seen in this way, this union, according
to the nature of marriage, involves a togetherness of both persons in one organic whole, in which they are grown together,
and a mutual belonging, in which Mary is joined to the Logos
and completely possessed by him, whilst the Logos, as being
infused into her ... gives himself to her and receives her as his
companion and help into the most intimate, complete and perfect communion. That Mary's divine motherhood really includes such a *matrimonium divinum* follows from the nature
of the case as necessarily as every properly established human
motherhood ... presupposes a *matrimonium humanum*.

INTRODUCTION TO THE TRILOGY: THE TRUTH ABOUT MARY AND THE HISTORIC CHRISTIAN FAITH

This is a series of three books about Mary - the truth about Mary. From the very beginning, the Christian doctrines about Mary have been an indivisible part of the historic Christian faith and of the Christian interpretation of Scripture. These Marian doctrines were proclaimed by the New Testament Church long before the very books that constitute the New Testament were assembled and defined as canonical at the end of the fourth century. The foundational doctrine that Mary is the Mother of God was defined right at the Church's third major Council - even before the final consolidation of Christology at Chalcedon. Mary's divinely-ordained role as the New Eve, the theme that underlies all Marian doctrines, was recognized by the earliest Church Fathers in the second century and documents evidencing the New Testament Church's belief in the intercession of Mary have been traced back to the second and third centuries. The Marian doctrines were defined in parallel with the Christological doctrines and were accepted by all Christians from the beginning, by the Founding Fathers of the Protestant Reformation (with the exception of the doctrine of Marian mediation because the Reformers would not allow any role for the human response to God's offer of salvation) and by almost all major Christian denominations even into the nineteenth century. The Marian doctrines are in reality Christological doctrines because every doctrine about Mary derives entirely from her relationship to her Son and tells us something more about Him.

The historic Christian consensus on Mary was shattered only under the influence of the so-called Enlightenment Era [the age of atheism and anti-supernaturalism that began in the eighteenth century] and the dominance of the doctrines of private interpretation [which began as *sola scriptura* or Scripture Alone] and of God's predetermination of salvation and damnation for all men [which began as *sola fidei* or Faith Alone]. Although Catholic, Eastern Orthodox and many Episcopalian/Anglican, Lutheran, Methodist and Presbyterian Christians continue to affirm the Marian doctrines of the New Testament Church, Protestant Fundamentalists allege that these doctrines are unscriptural and therefore heretical [overlooking the fact that these very doctrines were affirmed by Luther, Calvin and Zwingli]. This book is intended to reopen the scriptural case for Mary and to bring Protestants and Catholics back to the truth about Mary affirmed by historic Christianity.

The Modern Return to Mary

Happily for us all, there is today a return to the Mary of biblical historic Christianity that is the fruit of four separate developments.

First, modern scriptural exegesis has enabled Scripture scholars to bring to light new insights about Mary in Scripture that illuminate the historic understanding of Mary's significance in the Christian revelation. For instance, there is a new awareness today among biblical scholars of Mary's role in "the mystery of the Covenant" as the embodiment of both Old Testament Israel and the New Testament Church.

Second, Mary's role in Scripture and doctrine is the focus of serious and fruitful dialogue among Christians from all the major denominations. Polemics and emotions have been set aside as Protestants, Catholics and Eastern Orthodox Christians come to Scripture and historic Christianity with an open mind in trying to understand better the mission of the Mother of Jesus. The Ecumenical Society for the Blessed Virgin Mary is the best-known organization devoted primarily to this purpose. Pioneering books that have furthered inter-denominational understanding of Mary in Scripture and the New Testament Church include the following: *Mary in the New Testament* produced by a group of New Testament scholars from various denominations; *The One Mediator, The Saints and Mary* produced by eminent Lutheran and Catholic scholars; *The Mother of God* produced by a group of Eastern Orthodox and Anglican theologians; *The Blessed Virgin Mary*, a collection of essays by Anglicans on Marian doctrine; *Down to Earth: The New Protestant Vision of the Virgin Mary* by the Evangelical scholar John de Satge; and *Mary for All Christians* by the Anglican theologian John Macquarrie. Major essays on Marian doctrine have been produced not just by Catholic, Anglican and Eastern Orthodox scholars but by Lutherans, Methodists, Presbyterians and Baptists [some of whom are extensively cited in this Trilogy].

Donald Dawe, a Presbyterian who is Professor of Systematic Theology at Union Theological Seminary, writes:

> Evangelical conservatives within Protesantism have come to realise that polemics against Marian devotion must be rethought. Evangelicals, Anglicans and Protestants have come to see with increasing clarity the biblical witness to Mary and to the virgin birth...
>
> One can trace the work of the Holy Spirit in the formation of groups such as the Ecumenical Society for the Blessed Virgin Mary and of church councils reflecting on the place of Mary in the life of the Christian. One can point to the consultations and dialogues such as the recently concluded one in the United States between Lutherans and Roman Catholics on Mary and the Saints. There is a vast and scholarly literature that has recaptured the vital place of Mary in the sermons, prayers, poems and hymns of Luther, Calvin, Wesley and a host of our spiritual forebears. We are finding in new ways the truth about Mary. For Protestants - particularly for American Protestants - it is the discovery that Mary is just there all about us. Speaking personally, it is the realisation that long before I learned of Mary's place in the plan of salvation from great theologians, I heard of it in Bible stories simply told and sang it in gospel songs and Christmas hymns.
>
> Protestant Christians are increasingly aware as they look about them of the sheer presence of Mary. Christian art would disappear without the Blessed Virgin, as would much poetry and hymnody. If you are going to have anything to do with most of the rest of the Christians in the world, you have to deal with Mary as not only the one who once bore Christ, but the one who is still bearing Christ to the people. This was a fact, however, that took a long time for me to comprehend.[1]

---

1 Donald Dawe, *Mary, Pilgrimages and Protestants: Do They Belong Together?* (Wallington, Surrey: Ecumenical Society for the Blessed Virgin Mary, 1993), 6.

The third factor in the modern return to Mary is the steady pilgrimage of Protestant Evangelicals and Fundamentalists to churches and communities that remain committed to the central tenets of historic Christianity rejected by Fundamentalism. Many of these pilgrims are joining the Anglican/Episcopalian, Eastern Orthodox and Catholic churches and regaining the Marian heritage of the historic Faith.

Finally, there has been a worldwide resurgence of Marian devotion and interest in Marian doctrine that cuts across denominations and churches. This resurgence was even documented in a cover story in *Time* magazine titled "The Search for Mary":

> When her womb was touched by eternity 2,000 years ago, the Virgin Mary of Nazareth uttered a prediction: 'All generations will call me blessed.' Among all the women who have ever lived, the mother of Jesus Christ is the most celebrated, the most venerated, the most portrayed, the most honored in the naming of girl babies and churches....
>
> Yet even though the Madonna's presence has permeated the West for hundreds of years, there is still room for wonder - now perhaps more than ever... A grass-roots revival of faith in the Virgin is taking place worldwide. Millions of worshippers are flocking to her shrines, many of them young people. Even more remarkable are the number of claimed sightings of the Virgin, from Yugoslavia to Colorado, in the past few years...
>
> Some Protestants are softening aspects of their hostility. Church of England theologian John Macquarrie has proposed revisions of such dogmas as the Assumption of Mary into heaven, which could then be seen as a symbol of the redemption that awaits all believers. Theologian Donald Bloesch of the University of Dubuque says fellow conservative Protestants 'need to see Mary as the pre-eminent saint' and 'the mother of the church.' ...
>
> No one can take more satisfaction in the growth of faith in the Virgin ... than John Paul II ... He firmly believes that her personal intercession spared his life when he was shot at St.Peter's Square in Rome in 1981; the assassination attempt occurred on May 13, the exact anniversary of the first Fatima apparition.
>
> Moreover, John Paul is firmly convinced, as are many others, that Mary brought an end to communism throughout Europe. His faith is rooted in the famed prophecies of

Mary at Fatima in 1917. According to Sister Lucia, one of the children who claimed to see her, the Virgin predicted the rise of Soviet totalitarianism before it happened. In a subsequent vision, she directed the Pope and his bishops to consecrate Russia to her Immaculate Heart in order to bring communism to an end...

[Mary] remains one of the most compelling and evocative icons of Western civilization. Renewed expressions of her vitality and relevance are signs that millions of people are still moved by her mystery and comforted by the notion of her caring. Whatever aspect of Mary they choose to emphasize and embrace, those who seek her out surely find something only a holy mother can provide.[2]

Mary in Scripture

The book is deliberately sub-titled "A Scriptural Introduction to the Mother of Jesus" because the Mary of theology is first and foremost the Mary we find in Scripture. The richest and most powerful source of Marian doctrine and devotion is Scripture. This may seem shocking to both Catholics and Protestants because the conventional wisdom of our day tells us that scriptural texts "refute" Marian doctrines and prohibit Marian devotion. This conventional wisdom is the product of numerous Fundamentalist books and pamphlets parading verses from the Bible that allegedly demolish the basis of Marian doctrine and devotion. It is here, above all, that those who seek the truth about Mary, whether Protestant, Catholic or Eastern Orthodox, must resolve to make a decision on the basis of the full range of evidence.

We must first state the obvious. There is no battle beween Scripture and Marian doctrine. The battle is between competing interpretations of Scripture as it relates to Mary. On the one side we have the 20th century Fundamentalists who have dispensed with many essential elements of the historic Christian Faith and who have themselves split into hundreds and thousands of sects that differ on fundamental interpretations of Scripture on various issues. On the other side we have the consistent interpretation of Scripture held for 20 centuries from the time of the New Testament Church. This interpretation, the early Church Fathers taught,

---

2   "The Search for Mary", *Time* magazine, December 30, 1991.

was the interpretation of the divinely inspired New Testament writers themselves and this was the interpretation that was ratified by Church Councils and Creeds and accepted even by the Protestant Reformers. This is the Faith of the Fathers that has been held from the beginning and that continues to be affirmed today by Christians of many different denominations. The one century-old Fundamentalist interpretations of Scripture deny Marian doctrine and devotion - and in many cases even Christological and Trinitarian doctrine. Twenty centuries of the historic Christian Faith, however, affirm the fundamental Marian doctrines as essential and true. If a Fundamentalist were to read the writings of the ancient Church Fathers, both East and West, he will be shocked to see that every one of them writes of Mary with the highest reverence, showering her with affectionate praise. These are the men who helped establish the canon of Scripture and gave us the great doctrines of Christendom. We should at least pay them the courtesy of attending to their testimony.

Scripture as Christians have historically read it shows Mary from seven different perspectives: her salvific mission with her Son the Redeemer of humanity in *Genesis* [the salvific splendor]; the prophecy of her virginal conception of the Messiah in *Isaiah* and *Micah* [the prophetic splendor]; her spousal union with the Holy Spirit and motherhood of the God-man in *Matthew* and *Luke* [the maternal splendor]; her merciful seeking after the needs of her Son during His public ministry and her merciful intervention at Cana in *Matthew*, *Mark*, *Luke* and *John* [the merciful splendor]; her sorrow at the sacrifice of her dying Son, prefigured in *Luke* and portrayed in *John* and *Revelation* [the sorrowful splendor]; her prayerful participation during the outpouring of the Holy Spirit on the Church in *Acts* [the holy splendor]; and her glorious participation in the ongoing battle between her Son and the serpent in *Revelation* and the consummation at the Wedding Feast of the Lamb [the heavenly splendor]. Two other themes have been prominent in the Apostolic Community's meditation on Scripture. Mary in Scripture is seen within the overall pattern of God's salvific plan for humanity as the New Eve cooperating with the New Adam. Secondly, Mary has been understood as the bridge between the Old and New Testaments: the references to her in Scripture show that she represents both the Chosen People of the Old Testament and the Church of the New Testament.

From *Genesis* to *Revelation* we are told that a new Adam and a new Eve, the Woman and her Seed, will overcome the Evil One and bring salvation to the human race. Just as the first Eve brought damnation to the human race through her disobedience to God, the second Eve brings salvation through her obedience [Eve's disobedience led to Adam's damning sin and Mary's obedience led to Christ's salvific sacrifice]. In *Genesis* after the damnation brought by Eve we see the prophecy of enmity between Satan and the Woman and her Seed and the culmination of this enmity in the defeat of Satan. The prophecy in *Genesis* is followed by the prophecies in *Isaiah* and *Micah*: "a virgin shall conceive, and bear a son, and shall call his name Immanuel" [*Isaiah* 7:14] and "Therefore will he give them up, until the time that she which travaileth hath brought forth: then the remnant of his brethren shall return unto the children of Israel" [*Micah* 5:3]. These prophecies come to fulfillment in the Gospel narratives where Mary's obedience results in the miraculous conception and birth of Jesus followed by Simeon's prophecy to Mary that "a sword shall pierce through thine own soul, too," a prophecy fulfilled in Mary's sorrow at the foot of the cross. Mary's continuing cooperation with her Son in the scheme of salvation is prophesied in the Book of *Revelation* where we read, "And there appeared a great wonder in heaven; a woman clothed with the sun, and the moon under her feet, and upon her head a crown of twelve stars: And she being with child cried ... and the dragon stood before the woman which was ready to be delivered, for to devour her child as soon as it was born. And she brought forth a man child, who was to rule all nations with a rod of iron ... And the dragon was wroth with the woman, and went to make war with the remnant of her seed, which keep the commandments of God, and have the testimony of Jesus Christ." [*Revelation* 12].

The poverty of Fundamentalist exegesis is evident from the critics' silence about the rich scriptural witness to Mary. Take the first chapter of *Luke*. Exegete Rene Laurentin says about it, "This exaltation of Mary by God's gratuitous choice is one of the salient themes of the first chapter of Luke's Gospel. The angel Gabriel greets her with the name *kecharitomene* (1:28). The word defies translation in most languages. Recourse must be had to a circumlocution such as 'one who has won God's favor,' or 'object of God's favor.' ... This name is given her from on high; it is Mary's true name in the eyes of God, her name of grace. Indeed, the name *kecharitomene* is formed from the word *charis*, meaning 'grace,' as its root. Mary is the 'object of favor' in a pre-eminent way. She is 'the-one-who-has-found-grace' (*charin*), in the words of the Angel Gabriel in Luke 1:30. This initial greeting of praise is prolonged throughout the accounts of the annunciation and the visitation. The Lord is with her (1:28), the Holy Spirit comes down upon her (1:35), great things are accomplished in her (1:49) thanks to her faith (1:45), and 'that is why' (as she herself recognizes) 'all generations will call [her] blessed' (1:48). *No other biblical personage has been given such strong praise, and without anything said to the contrary.* Were it not the inspired text, one would be tempted almost to wonder whether the Christocentrism of the gospels were here in default. In Luke 1:35 the angel tells Mary, 'The Holy Spirit will come upon *you* and the power of the Most High will cover *you* with its shadow.' In the light of Isaiah 11:2 would it not have been more normal to say that the Holy Spirit was coming on the Emmanuel rather than on his Mother? In Luke 1:42 Elizabeth proclaims Mary's blessings before that of her Son and adds, 'Why should I be honoured with a visit from the *Mother of my Lord*?' even though the honour that falls to her is actually the visit of the *Lord* rather than of the Mother. She adds, 'For the moment *your greeting* reached my ears, the child in my womb leapt for joy,' even though in reality the benefit of the visitation is to be attributed to the action of Mary's Child rather than to Mary's voice. That Mary should thus be placed in the forefront is most astonishing and gives food for reflection to those who fear that they do Christ some offense in exalting his Mother."[3]

Curiously, Fundamentalists who read these passages ignore, downplay or deny the significance so obviously attributed to Mary in *Luke* 1 - a habit that repeats itself in their reading of other Marian passages. In one way or another the Fundamentalist mind has been innoculated against a good many of the truths so plainly and powerfully presented in Scripture. In opening their eyes to the Scriptural portrait of Mary we might also help Fundamentalists see Scripture as a whole in all its depth and majesty. A true understanding of Scripture comes not just from a knowledge of Greek and Hebrew and the principles of Fundamentalist or Liberal exegesis. It comes

---

3   Rene Laurentin, *A Short Treatise on the Virgin Mary* (Washington, New Jersey: AMI Press, 1991), pp.20-1.

primarily from an understanding of the truths that God intended to teach through Scripture. These truths are presented in outline on the surface of Scripture and fleshed out as doctrines in the Spirit-inspired interpretations of the historic Christian Faith.

The stunning testimony of Scripture to an Adam-Christ/Eve-Mary plan of salvation is obvious to anyone who reads the Word of God with the mind of the Apostolic Community and without the ideological baggage of post-Reformation polemics. It was certainly obvious to the New Testament Church and to the Fathers and Councils of the Apostolic Community who gave us the doctrines of the Trinity and the Incarnation. And, most interestingly, it was obvious to the fathers of the Protestant Reformation who accepted and affirmed most of the major Marian titles.

The Reformers and Mary

Fundamentalists who consider themselves heirs of the Protestant Reformation should not assume that the Reformation as such was a denial of Marian doctrine. The three primary Reformers, Martin Luther, John Calvin and Ulrich Zwingli, all accepted the doctrinal definition of Mary as the Mother of God and her Perpetual Virginity. Luther and Zwingli, in fact, accepted the consequences of Mary's role as the new Eve and affirmed her freedom from sin and Assumption into Heaven. Said Luther, "In this work whereby she was made the Mother of God, so many and such great good things were given her that no one can grasp them."[4] John Calvin wrote, "Elizabeth called Mary Mother of the Lord, because the unity of the person in the two natures of Christ was such that she could have said that the mortal man engendered in the womb of Mary was at the same time the eternal God."[5] Zwingli said, "I esteem immensely the Mother of God, the ever chaste, immaculate Virgin Mary."[6] If Marian devotees are victims of diabolic deception, then so are the fathers of the Protestant Reformation. If the Fundamentalists charge that the Reformers were deceived in their Marian theology, then they will have to admit that the Reformers could have been deceived on their other theological pronounce-

---

4   Martin Luther, Weimar edition of *Martin Luther's Works*, English translation edited by J. Pelikan [Concordia: St. Louis], volume 7, 572.
5   John Calvin, *Calvini Opera* [Braunshweig-Berlin, 1863-1900], Volume 45, 35.
6   E. Stakemeier, *De Mariologia et Oecumenismo*, K. Balic, ed., (Rome, 1962), 456.

ments - and these are the very same pronouncements that the Fundamentalists embrace whole-heartedly.

The Fundamentalist and Liberal Rejection of Marian Doctrine

Christians and historic Christianity have understood Mary against the seven Scriptural backdrops, the "splendors," given us in *Genesis, Isaiah, Micah,* the Gospels, the *Acts of the Apostles, Galatians* and *Revelation.* Marian theology cannot be comprehended if we do not first comprehend these backdrops and the related themes of Mary as the bridge between the Old and the New Testaments who is the new Ark of the Covenant, the New Eve who has been "transformed by grace" [*Luke* 1:28]. The various Marian doctrines are faint echoes of this great Scriptural vision of Mary and the exaltation of Mary in *Luke* and *John.* In the light of the New Adam-New Eve theme of salvation history revealed in Scripture we understand more fully the place and message of each of the seven splendors of Mary. Without this fuller understanding, unfortunately, it is impossible to grasp the Scriptural Mary of the historic Christian faith.

The heart-rending tragedy of the last 200 years is the fury with which both Fundamentalist and Liberal Christians have torn to shreds the great scriptural tapestry of the seven splendors of Mary [although the term "Fundamentalist" is fairly modern it applies in this book to the theory of private interpretation deriving from the sola scriptura viewpoint popularized at the Reformation]. The "biblical Mary" of most Fundamentalists bears little resemblance to the Mary of Scripture. In their minds Mary's role is reduced to their negative interpretations of certain references to her in the public ministry of Jesus. Following in the wake of the Fundamentalists, the Liberals not only ridiculed all seven of the splendors of Mary but rejected even the divine splendors of her Son. Whereas the Fundamentalists read Scripture in isolation from the historic Christian Faith the Liberals read it in isolation from any kind of faith at all.

And just as Liberal New Testament scholars have pursued their so-called quest for the "historical Jesus," Fundamentalists have embarked on their own search for the "biblical Mary." Discarding the witness of Scripture, the historic teachings of the New Testament Church and the faith of the Apostolic Community, the Liberals have concocted a Jesus who is dramatically different from the Savior worshipped by Christians. Similarly Fundamentalists have discarded the seven-splendored story of Scripture and the historic faith of Christians and have created a "Mary" who is dramatically different from the Mary to whom Elizabeth said, "Whence is this to me, that the mother of my Lord should come to me?" Fundamentalists introduced a way of approaching Scripture that is different from the approach taken by the Christianity of the first 19 centuries. It is this new - and alien - approach that led to the loss of the truth about Mary (and often the truth about Jesus).

The Doctrine of Private Interpretation

Protestant Fundamentalists are totally committed to the principles of *sola scriptura* [Scripture alone], *sola fidei* [Faith alone] and *sola Christus* [Christ alone]. In practical application these principles are entirely different from what they mean by definition. *Sola scriptura* has become a doctrine of private interpretation whereby every reader's interpretation of Scripture is equally acceptable. *Sola fidei* has become a doctrine of divine pre-determination whereby God pre-programs the salvation and damnation of every man (this leaves no room for freedom or responsibility). *Sola Christus* has become a form of pantheism whereby God is the only Actor on the stage of salvation and even life itself. The consequences of the doctrine of private interpretation are particularly troubling because the need for authoritative interpretation of Scripture is unaddressed. The authoritative interpretation of Scripture made by the Fathers and Councils of the New Testament Church is what we call the historic Christian Faith. Fundamentalists, however, reject the authoritative nature of the historic Faith and this leaves them with an insoluble problem: if no interpretation is authoritative then no interpretation can be known to be true and this means that we cannot know what Scripture teaches. There is no point in affirming "Scripture Alone" if we also affirm that we cannot know what Scripture authoritatively teaches.

Since they reject the idea of a *true* interpretation, neither Liberal New Testament scholars nor Fundamentalists can offer any help to the Bible-believing Christian who seeks to know the truths shown in Scripture. Although the Liberal scholars can speculate on the sources and dates and the various possible meanings and senses of the New Testament texts they cannot tell us what truths *God* intended to teach through these texts. Only the Apostolic Community inspired by the Holy Spirit could determine the true divinely-intended meaning and interpretation of these texts. The Fundamentalists are in the same bind as the Liberals because they have cut themselves off from 20 centuries of Spirit-inspired Christian interpretation. As a result, Fundamentalist writers can only offer us their own speculations on the meanings and senses of the various passages in Scripture. And these speculations are just as uncertain and arbitrary as the speculations of the Liberal scholars and, of course, contradict each other. *The real issue for the Christian believer is not whether he should rely on Scripture alone but whether or not he can have an authoritative interpretation of Scripture.* From the time of the New Testament Church, the Apostolic Community has affirmed and taught what they hold to be an authoritative, consistent and binding interpretation of Scripture. It is this possibility of an authoritative interpretation that is denied by the Fundamentalists - with disastrous consequences.

Fundamentalists themselves by the hundreds of thousands have migrated to cults and Liberal churches. *Christianity Today*[7] reported that only two out of five Evangelicals (i.e., 43%) affirm that Jesus Christ is fully God and fully man!

In Liberal attacks on the historic interpretation of Scripture, the bandleader is Robert Funk, a former Fundamentalist who leads the circus act of modern Liberalism, the so-called Jesus Seminar. Funk brings his zeal as a Fundamentalist to his new project of totally denying the historical reliability of the teachings of Jesus. "Even now," said a story in *U.S. News and World Report*, "when Robert Funk addresses an audience, there are hints of the precocious young preacher who once led revival meetings in rural Texas... But the Jesus who Funk commends to his audiences bears little resemblance to the Savior of his gospel-preaching youth." Funk's methods and end-results are the inevitable fruit of the Fundamentalist doctrine of private interpretation and the Fundamentalist rejection of Councils and Creeds: "Stripped of what he now considers to be the artificial accretions of centuries of church tradition, the historical Jesus of Nazareth, in Funk's view, was probably more akin to a Jewish Socrates ... than the divine Son of God. The goal

---

7   *Christianity Today*, April 18 & May 2, 1980.

of his seminar, Funk recently told a California audience, is *to 'set Jesus free' from the 'scriptural and creedal prisons in which we have entombed him.'*[8] [emphasis added]. Funk and the other participants in the "Jesus Seminar" claim to be able to discern which words in the Gospels were uttered by Christ and which were not, which events actually took place and which were fabricated. It should seem obvious to most onlookers (not just Christians) that such confidence in jumping to judgments on a 2000 year-old document is at best naive if not plainly senseless. But this presumptuous program is simply the heir to the throne of Fundamentalism - what the Fundamentalists began by interpreting the Gospels and Epistles in near-total isolation from the historic understanding, the Liberals end by giving a final shove to the historic understanding. Once you remove the fish of Scripture from the ocean of historic Christianity using the hook of private interpretation, it will thrash around for a few moments and then be still.

If Fundamentalism and Evangelicalism want to remain true to the historic Faith, they should beware of overthrowing historic interpretations of Scripture in favor of their own recent and novel interpretations. Fundamentalists and Evangelicals would do well to heed the warnings in "Is Evangelicalism Christian?," a recent article in *The Evangelical Journal*:

> Evangelicalism at its best has marched off at a tangent from the trajectory of the historic church. It has followed interests it has perceived as important in the confidence that it, more than others, has a true understanding of the Christian faith. It has rarely stopped to ask whether the movement itself was a capitulation to philosophical voices from outside the church. In reality, evangelicalism is a variant form of Christianity and one that, due to the dangerously loose lines that connected it to the heritage of the wider historic faith, could now be in danger of losing its grasp of the faith it seemingly holds dear...
>
> Evangelicalism as known in the modern world (individualistic, pietistic, missionary) is a child of the enlightenment and thus is disintegrating and dying with the passing of the world of the enlightenment.[9]

---

8   "In Search of Jesus," *U.S. News and World Report*, April 8, 1996, 48.
9   Robert Letham, "Is Evangelicalism Christian?," *The Evangelical Quarterly*, 67:1, 1993, 3ff.

The Basis of Marian Doctrine

Historically the Marian doctrines were discerned hand in hand with the development of the Christological doctrines. In fact the definition of Mary as the Mother of God came even before the final consolidation of Christology. Thus the Marian doctrines come to us from the witness of Scripture, from the Councils and from the writings of Church Fathers and other holy men and women of God as well as from the experience of the faithful through the centuries. In a sense, every Marian doctrine is simply a consequence of the fundamental Christological affirmations. It was John Damascene who said of Mary, "This name - Theotokos (the Mother of God) - contains the whole mystery of the Incarnation." The deeper we delve into Mary the more we learn about Christ. By the same token, the more we learn about Christ the more we discover the truth about Mary. Hence we say that the Marian doctrines can rightly be called Christological doctrines.

The Marian doctrines that are part of the historic Christian Faith are not "Roman Catholic" or "papist" and were actually most powerfully articulated by Eastern Orthodox Fathers and theologians. Some of the best expositions of Marian doctrine in this century have come from scholars writing from within the mainline Protestant denominations. There is a tender, loving devotion to Mary found in the writings of many Eastern Orthodox, Anglican, Methodist and Presbyterian thinkers that may seem astonishing to Catholics.

Overview of the Trilogy

In our attempt to set forth the truth about Mary, we will proceed in three phases, each phase being the subject of a standalone volume. The three volumes comprising this trilogy are **From Human Invention to the Truths Taught by Scripture**, **Mary in Scripture and the Historic Christian Faith**, and **A Response to Fundamentalist Misconceptions and a Return to Historic Christianity**.

The structure of **THE TRUTH ABOUT MARY** trilogy may be compared to a journey in search of buried treasure. Volume One is the reliable map and sturdy ship that will take us to Treasure Island. Volume Two is our journey to Treasure Island and our discovery there of the buried treasure. Volume Three is our return journey through perilous waters (infested with pirates and sharks and beset by storms) and our first efforts to expend the treasure once we have safely reached home.

In **From Human Invention to the Truths Taught by Scripture**, the launching-pad of the Trilogy, we consider the Starting Points with which we must be equipped if we wish to understand (a) the truths that God intended to communicate through Scripture and (b) the truth about Mary as this has been taught by biblical and historic Christianity.

We start with two crucial charts that give us an aerial view of some of the terrain we will pass through in the course of our journey. In Ten Portraits of Mary in Scripture we are introduced to the scriptural snapshots of Mary that were later developed and printed as doctrines. The second chart summarizes the tragic shortcomings of Fundamentalism, the chief barrier to Marian doctrine and devotion in many denominations. These charts are followed by a rapid survey of the Marian teachings of the architects of the Protestant Reformation, Luther, Calvin and Zwingli and also the English Reformers. Fundamentalists who derive their principles from the Protestant Reformation must take note of the Reformers' testimony to the truth of Marian doctrine.

In the next section we address the central starting points in the study of Mary, the questions of (a) the interpretation of Scripture (b) the relation between faith, works and salvation and (c) man's mediation of God's plan of salvation. We cannot know the truth about Mary if we have not answered these questions accurately. The Fundamentalist responses to these questions, *Sola Scriptura*, *Sola Fidei* and *Sola Christus*, have deteriorated into dangerous doctrines of private interpretation, salvation-by-predestination and de facto pantheism (i.e. God is the only actor in the play).

To recover the answers given by historic Christianity, we consider the basic issues: the origin of the canon of Scripture and the central role played here by the Apostolic Community and the Councils; the interpretation of Scripture and the obvious need for an authoritative interpretation; the affirmations of the historic Christian Faith that are recognized to be inerrant interpretations of the inerrant Word of God; and then the all-important question of faith, works and salvation and of man's mediation of God's grace. On this last question we see that the Calvinist/Fundamentalist view portrays men as preprogrammed for salvation or damnation by God with no free choice involved. Said John Calvin, "By an eternal and immutable counsel, God has once for all determined, both whom he would admit to salvation, and whom he would condemn to destruction." Those preprogrammed for damnation have been "devoted from the womb to certain death, that his name may be glorified in their destruction(!)." The historic Christian teaching, on the other hand, is that God is infinitely loving and desires the salvation of all men but has given every man the freedom to accept or reject Him. Calvinists, said John Wesley, "represent God as worse than the devil; as more false, more cruel, and more unjust."

At the end of Volume One we will have recovered the Starting Points accepted by historic Christianity, namely, the inerrant interpretation of the inerrant Word of God and the vision of a God Who invites all men to accept His free gift of salvation but gives them the freedom to reject His gift. With these Starting Points in hand, we now have the map and the ship that will take us to Treasure Island.

In **Mary in Scripture and the Historic Christian Faith**, we study both Scripture and Scripture-as-read-by-the-Apostolic-Community in our pursuit of the truth about Mary. The first section is a study of Mary in Scripture that considers the portrayal of Mary in the Gospels, the Epistles and the *Acts of the Apostles* as well as in *Genesis* and *Revelation* and the books of the Old Testament. The exaltation of Mary in Scripture and the consistent theme of her participation in her Son's mission as the New Eve and the Daughter of Zion indicates that the "biblical Mary" is incomparably more spectacular than the Mary of doctrine and devotion.

The second section is a survey of the Marian teachings of the historic Faith. These teachings simply reflect the witness of Scripture and the witness of the Fathers, Councils and Creeds. The doctrines of Mary's divine maternity, perpetual virginity, immaculate conception, assumption and mediation are inseparably linked to both her role as the New Eve and her privilege of being the Mother of the Second Person of the Holy Trinity and the Spouse of the Third Person. The doctrines also reflect the great mystery of Mary's role in the scheme of salvation: her free and total cooperation with her Creator is an integral part of the final victory of God over Satan. Many of the expositions of various Marian doctrines cited here come from Protestant authors.

At the end of this volume we will not only have reached Treasure Island but have uncovered the untold treasures awaiting us there. The truth about Mary, we find out, actually leads us to the truth about Jesus. Each Mariological doctrine is in truth a Christological doctrine. Through our understanding of Mary our minds and hearts enter into the mystery of the Holy Trinity.

The final volume in the trilogy, **A Response to Fundamentalist Misconceptions and a Return to Historic Christianity,** is initially at least a survival guide. We have brought the treasure of truth into our minds and hearts. But now we face attacks on every side. Doubt, error, fear, half-truths more dangerous than falsehoods - these are the pirates, sharks and storms that stand in our way as we head back home.

We begin the first section with a chart summarizing the principal Fundamentalist misconceptions about each Marian doctrine and the response and actual teaching of historic Christianity on the doctrine in question. In the next chapter we study the characteristics and weaknesses of Protestant Fundamentalism and then present the principal Protestant Fundamentalist critiques of Marian doctrine and devotion in great detail. The chief Fundamentalist allegations are that Marian doctrines are unscriptural and substitute Mary for Christ. These and other allegations are addressed in some detail especially by reference to Scripture. Tragically the Fundamentalists are handicapped by the doctrine of private interpretation [which shuts out the truth of Scripture] and the Calvinist denial of man's freedom and God's unconditional love for all men.

In the next chapter we show that Fundamentalism, as a result of these flaws, is in a state of collapse today. Many Fundamentalists are turning to the Charismatic movement, to Liberalism and to the cults. Within Fundamentalism itself, there is a profusion of "human traditions" that compete with each other and govern the Fundamentalist's reading of Scripture. At the root of this disarray is the Fundamentalist doctrine of private interpretation which is a formula for chaos.

The second section touches a more positive theme. We offer some suggestions whereby Fundamentalists can come to the teachings of the historic Faith thereby progressing in their Christian growth and protecting themselves from error and heresy. We also see how many modern Protestants have returned to the Marian heritage of the historic Faith.

In the final section, we turn from "survival strategies" to the joyous task of expending and investing the treasure we have graciously been given by the Holy Spirit. Here we apply the truth about Mary to our practical life as Christians. Marian devotion brings us closer to Jesus and protects us from the world, the flesh and the Devil. Those who worry about an "excess of Marian devotion" should realize that the real issue is what role the Holy Trinity has ordained for Mary in the scheme of salvation. All devotion to Mary is to be related to this role. If Mary's role is to bring us to Jesus, to form us in Jesus, to fill us with the Holy Spirit, then she is to be our model and spiritual mother. To see her and invoke her in these roles is not "excess" but an integral part of our journey to her Father, her Son and her Holy Spouse. With this final section our trilogy comes to a close and we turn from knowing about Mary to knowing Mary.

The reader should note that each volume of the Trilogy is intended to be a standalone unit. Although the ideal course of action would be to read all three volumes, it is possible to read any one of them without reference to the others. If, for instance, your only interest is in the questions of scriptural interpretation and faith, works and salvation then Volume One is all you need. The standalone nature of the individual volumes necessarily means that there is some degree of repetition and overlap across the three volumes. The question of faith and works, for instance, is of importance in each one of the volumes and so it is treated in all three. The treatment of this question is undertaken from a different angle in each volume but the use of common material in all three is inevitable.

A Journey Through the Library of Twenty Centuries

The reader will notice that the Trilogy is marked by extensive quotation from a variety of sources. In fact, more than three quarters of the three volumes is given to such citation. There is a very good reason for this.

This Trilogy is not intended simply as an apologetic for Marian doctrine. It is a journey in search of the Mary of the Christian Faith. It is a journey that seeks to re-connect our modern minds to the historical witness, to historic Christianity. To make this journey we must hear the Fathers firsthand, we must see how the great doctrines of Christianity were developed in the New Testament Church, how Scripture has been interpreted through the centuries, how Christians of different denominations have approached the question at hand and how Fundamentalism by its very nature destroys the possibility of consistent Christian doctrine. And in getting to the truth about Mary there is no substitute for hearing the testimonies and reports and studies of great Christian thinkers and leaders in their own words. What we seek is a comprehensive overview and not a simple summary.

"I Will Bless Them That Bless Thee"

This Trilogy is written from the standpoint of the historic Faith. It is written for Christians of all denominations. Its concern is the truth about Mary and not questions about the "true Church," the Papacy or the Sacraments. These latter questions are deferred not because they are unimportant but because Mary is considered here in her role as the Mother of all Christians.

In particular we seek to bring the scriptural witness to Mary to the attention of her severest critics, the Protestant Fundamentalists. If the Fundamentalist breaks free from the ideological agendas of the various "human traditions" of Fundamentalism (Dispensationalism and Calvinism for instance) then he will at least be able to appreciate the truths shown on the surface of Scripture as in *Luke* 1-2 or the Gospel of *John*. His next step could be to ponder the promise of Christ, "When he, the Spirit of truth, is come, he will guide you into all truth." The vast majority of Christians throughout history - and this includes Luther, Calvin and Zwingli - have believed that the Spirit of Truth has spoken through the Fathers and the Councils of the Apostolic Community in interpreting Scripture. It is this body of interpretation that has remained the same for 20 centuries and is called the Historic Christian Faith. This Faith is the true home of all Bible-believing Christians. The Fundamentalist who studies the teachings of the historic faith with an eye on the promise of Christ will find that he has returned to the home he unwittingly left.

In *Genesis* 12:3, God promises Abraham that "I will bless them that bless thee, and curse him that curseth thee; and in thee shall all families of the earth be blessed." It is well known among exegetes who accept the historic Faith that Abraham pre-figured Mary. As the New Testament scholar John McHugh has written:

> God made three promises to Abraham: that his children would be a great nation (Gen 12:2; 13:16; 15:5; 17:6, 19;

22:17); that his descendants would possess the land of Canaan (Gen 12:7; 13:15; 15:18-21; 17:8); and that in him all the nations of world would count themselves blessed (Gen 12:3; 22:18). In Mary's child, the last of the three promises was fulfilled, and it is not surprising that Luke draws out many parallels between Mary and Abraham. Like Abraham (Gen 18:3), Mary found favour with God (Lk 1:30); like Abraham (Gen 12:3; 18:18; 22:18), she is a source of blessing for, and is blessed by, all nations (Lk 1: 42,48); like Abraham (Gen 15:6), she is praised for her faith in the promise that, by a miracle, she would have a son (Lk 1:45).[10]

The New Testament tells us that all generations are to call Mary blessed. This is a divine instruction not a option to be exercised by private interpretation. After all why should any Christian hesitate to praise her whom God Himself has found worthy of favor for it was to her that the Angel Gabriel said "thou hast found favor with God." Let us rest assured that God will "bless them that bless" her whom all generations are to call blessed.

---

[10] John McHugh, *The Mother of Jesus in the New Testament* (New York: Doubleday, 1975), p. 78.

PREAMBLE TO VOLUME ONE

The subject of this volume has already been summarized in the introduction to the Trilogy. The first section presents charts of Marian portraits in Scripture and of Fundamentalism and a survey of the Marian doctrine of the Protestant Reformers. The second section is an extensive investigation into the Starting Points required in discerning biblical truth. Our task in this latter section is, first, to find out how to arrive at the interpretation and understanding of Scripture intended by its Author and, second, to discover the historic Christian teaching on God's plan of salvation.

Our studies here lead us to conclude that the inerrant Word of God has an inerrant interpretation preserved from the time of the New Testament Church to the present day. Concerning the divine plan of salvation, both Scripture and the historic Faith teach us that God desires the salvation of all men but that men have the freedom to reject His unconditional offer of union with Him. These are the Starting Points that emerge in this volume after comprehensive study. These same Starting Points lie at the heart of all discussions of Christian doctrine and devotion. As such they constitute a map that leads us not just to the truth about Mary but to all biblical truth.

PART I

OVERVIEW

-1-

OVERVIEW WORD PICTURES

A. MARY IN SCRIPTURE: TEN PORTRAITS

Scripture is the inerrant Word of God. The historic Christian Faith is the inerrant interpretation of the inerrant Word of God. This inerrant interpretation is the interpretation of Scripture given to us, under the inspiration of the Holy Spirit (as Jesus promised), by the early Church and by the Councils, Creeds and Fathers of the Church. This interpretation was accepted as inerrant by all Christians including the Protestant Reformers. *Martin Luther himself held that (a) no interpretation of Scripture can differ from a continuous past tradition of interpretation and (b) Tradition can contain teachings that are not in Scripture as long as these teachings do not contradict Scripture.* [**The Theology of Martin Luther**, Fortress Press, 1966]. Scripture is the architect's blueprint. The authoritative divinely guided interpretation of scripture that we call the historic Christian Faith is the house built by a divine Builder, the Holy Spirit, from the blueprint. Scripture is the conception, the historic Christian Faith is the birth.

As inerrantly interpreted within the historic Faith from the earliest days of the apostolic community, all of Scripture, from Genesis to Revelation, is ablaze with Mary. The Mary of Marian doctrine and devotion is a pale shadow of the majestic portraits of Mary given us in Scripture. Doctrine and devotion are important because they represent the believer's attempt to remain faithful to the testimony of divine revelation. Nevertheless the scriptural witness to Mary must constantly feed and nourish the body of doctrine handed down by the historic Faith.

When Christians interpret Scripture outside the bounds of the historic Christian Faith they will inevitably end up in division, confusion and error. As a result of the primacy of private interpretation, today there are over 22,000 denominations each with their own interpretation of Scripture. Moreover, again as a result of the doctrine of private interpretation, millions of Christians have joined cults that deny the divinity of Christ or embraced Liberalism, the denial of the divine inspiration and inerrancy of Scripture. None other than Martin Luther warned us about the consequences of private interpretation:

> "There are as many sects and beliefs as there are heads. This fellow will have nothing to do with baptism; another denies the sacraments; a third believes that there is another world between this and the Last Day. Some teach that Christ is not God; some say this, some say that. There is no rustic so rude but that, if he dreams or fancies anything, it must be the whisper of the Holy Ghost, and he himself a prophet."
> [**Luther** (1525), Grisar, Vol IV, p.386]

The rejection of the historic interpretation of Scripture has also led to the loss of the scriptural Mary in this modern age. Fortunately modern scriptural exegesis has enabled many scholars and laity to discover new dimensions of Mary in Scripture thereby rediscovering the lost Marian heritage of the early Church. We present here ten portraits of Mary in Scripture that lead us back to the Mary of historic Christianity. For the most part we use the King James Version of the Bible since this is the version most commonly used by Protestant Fundamentalists.

Bridge Between the Old and New Testaments

Mary is a bridge between the Old and the New Testaments because Scripture shows her representing both the people of Israel and the Church begun by her Son.

> "A very important insight of modern exegesis," reports Ignace de la Potterie, "has brought to light that the mystery of Mary forms in some way the synthesis of all the former revelation about the people of God, and of all that God by

his salvific action wishes to realize for his people. In Mary are accomplished all the important aspects of the promises of the Old Testament to the Daughter of Zion, and in her real person there is an anticipation which will be realized for the new people of God, the Church. The history of revelation on the subject of the theme of the Woman Zion, realized in the person of Mary, and continued in the Church, constitutes a doctrinal bastion, an unshakable structured ensemble for the comprehension of the history of salvation, from its origin up to its eschatology."[1]

"She is the climax of the Old Testament people," writes the Protestant theologian John de Satge, "the one to whom the cloud of witnesses from the ancient era look as their crowning glory, for it was through her response to grace that their Vindicator came to stand upon the earth. In the order of redemption she is the first fruits of her Son's saving work, the one among her Son's people who has gone all the way. And in the order of her Son's people, she is the mother."[2]

A truly biblical interpretation of Mary will see her as representing both the people of Israel and the future Church. Many of the Old Testament texts describing the Daughter of Zion are amazingly enough applied to Mary: Luke 1:26-38, John 2:1-12, John 19:25-27. "Here," writes Ignace de la Potterie, "the Old Testament texts of the 'Daughter of Zion' are applied to a definite woman... This is precisely the reason why, in the Fourth Gospel, both at Cana and at the Cross, Jesus addresses Mary calling her 'Woman.'" At the same time many of the texts on Mary are seen in terms of the Church. "It is in Mary that the Church is born; Mary is the Church at the very moment of its birth. The scene this evokes is above all that of Mary at the foot of the Cross; it is there that she is especially 'the Church in her beginning.'" Mary "is found exactly at the threshold [of the Old Testament and the New Testament], and thus can be considered from both sides at the same time."[3]

---

1   Ignace de la Potterie, *Mary in the Mystery of the Covenant* (New York: Alba House, 1992), 262.

2   *Down to Earth: The New Protestant Vision of the Virgin Mary* (Consortium, 1976), 111.

3   Ignace de la Potterie, *Mary in the Mystery of the Covenant*, xxxviii.

Mary is the bridge between the New and the Old Testaments. She has "won favor with God." She will be called blessed by "all generations" because she has "believed."

The comparison of *Zephaniah* 3:17-17 and *Luke* 1:28-33 is especially striking:

> "Rejoice, Daugher of Zion, the King of Israel, Yahweh, is IN you. Do not be afraid Zion, Yahweh your God is in your womb as a strong Savior." [*Zephaniah* 3:14-17]

> "Rejoice so highly favored. The Lord is WITH you. Do not be afraid, Mary ... Listen, you are to conceive in your womb and bear a son and you must name him "Yahweh Savior." He will reign [*Luke* 1:28-33].[4]

John McHugh notes that the passages in *Joel* and *Zechariah* are modelled on the *Zephaniah* passage which is the most ancient of the three. He describes *Zephaniah* 3:14-17 as "two short poems in which the prophet envisages the day of salvation as already begun, and calls upon the Daughter of Zion to rejoice with all her heart, not to fear, because the Lord is with her, as her king and saviour. This is exactly the message of the angel in Lk 1:28-33 ... The texts of Joel and of Zechariah carry the same message in almost the same phrases." In his commentary on the Magnificat, McHugh points out that when Mary "speaks of what God has done for her, she speaks of what God has done for Israel: that is, she speaks of herself as the Daughter of Zion."[5]

Mary's presence in the Old Testament is found at three levels: in prophecy, in prefigurings and in parallels.

The most famous Old Testament prophecies concerning the coming of the Messiah are *Genesis* 3:15, *Isaiah* 7:14 and *Micah* 5:1-4. In all three prophecies the Mother of the Messiah plays a prominent part.

---

[4]   Cited in Rene Laurentin, *A Short Treatise on the Virgin Mary* (Washington, New Jersey: AMI Press, 1991), 25.

[5]   John McHugh, *The Mother of Jesus in the New Testament* (New York: Doubleday, 1975), pp.41-2, 76.

Genesis 3:14,15:
> "And the Lord God said unto the serpent, ... I will put enmity between thee and the woman, and between thy seed and her seed; it shall bruise thy head, and thou shalt bruise his heel."

Isaiah 7:10-14:
> "The Lord spake again unto Ahaz, saying, Ask thee a sign of the Lord thy God; ask it either in the depth, or in the height above. But Ahaz said, I will not ask, neither will I tempt the Lord. And he said, Hear ye now, O house of David; Is it a small thing for you to weary men, but will ye weary my God also?
>
> "Therefore the Lord himself shall give you a sign; Behold, a virgin shall conceive, and bear a son, and shall call his name Immanuel."

Micah [5:2-4]:
> "But thou, Bethlehem Ephratah, though thou be little among the thousands of Judah, yet out of thee shall he come forth unto me that is to be ruler in Israel, whose goings forth have been from of old, from everlasting. Therefore will he give them up, until the time that she which travaileth hath brought forth: then the remnant of his brethren shall return unto the children of Israel. And he shall stand and feed in the strength of the Lord, in the majesty of the name of the Lord his God; and they shall abide: for now shall he be great unto the ends of the earth. And this man shall be the peace."

Mary is also pre-figured in many of the holy women of the Old Testament. About the influence of the Old Testament prefigurings on the New Testament, Marie Isaacs, a Baptist, writes:

> Luke portrays Mary as the supreme example of the faithful of Israel, of whom the Messiah was to be born. He does this, not only the way he structures the narrative, but also in the language he employs: language which is full of OT allusions and symbols.
>
> To read *Luke* 1-2, even superficially, is immediately to call to mind stories in the OT of women who gave birth to remarkable offspring: Sarah, old and childless and yet who

was blessed with the birth of Isaac; the mother of Samson (the last and greatest of the Judges), who like Elisabeth, had previously been barren, but to whom an angel was to announce that she would have a son. The similarities between these and the lucan Infancy Narratives are obvious: all describe miraculous conceptions, announced by angelic messengers and issuing in the birth of a great hero. John the Baptist, like Samson, is to take a nazarite vow. But it is probably to the story of the birth of Samuel that Luke is most indebted. In many ways Mary, 'the handmaid of the Lord' is patterned on Hannah, 'the handmaid' who, of all OT mothers, is the archetypal figure of maternal devotion and religious piety, dedicating her son entirely to the service of Yahweh in the temple, and there rejoicing over her son's birth with a paean of praise. Much of the thought and even the language of Hannah's song is taken up by Mary, the new Hannah, in the Magnificat. So now Mary becomes, not merely the symbol of the faithful of Israel in general, but the symbol of the faithful mother in particular."[6]

Finally we find parallels to Mary in the Old Testament. She is an intercessor and mediator like Abraham and Moses. It has often been said that Abraham pre-figured Mary for reasons explained by the exegete John McHugh:

God made three promises to Abraham: that his children would be a great nation (*Gen* 12:2; 13:16; 15:5; 17:6, 19; 22:17); that his descendants would possess the land of Canaan (*Gen* 12:7; 13:15; 15:18-21; 17:8); and that in him all the nations of world would count themselves blessed (*Gen* 12:3; 22:18). In Mary's child, the last of the three promises was fulfilled, and it is not surprising that Luke draws out many parallels between Mary and Abraham. Like Abraham (*Gen* 18:3), Mary found favour with God (*Lk* 1:30); like Abraham (*Gen* 12:3; 18:18; 22:18), she is a source of blessing for, and is blessed by, all nations (*Lk* 1: 42,48); like Abraham (*Gen* 15:6), she is praised for her faith in the promise that, by a miracle, she would have a son (*Lk* 1:45).[7]

---

6   Marie E. Isaacs, "Mary in the Lucan Infancy Narrative," *The Way*, Summer 1975, 91.
7   John McHugh, *The Mother of Jesus in the New Testament*, p.78.

The parallels to Moses and Mary and Exodus and Cana are equally remarkable as de la Potterie has shown:

> Moses then went, convoked all the elders of the people and related to them all that Yahweh had ordered him to tell them. Then the entire people, with one accord responded: '*All that Yahweh has said, we will do.*' And Moses brought back to Yahweh the response of the people." (*Ex* 19:1-8). In this text and the others that we pointed out, even though they appear with several variants, there are always two constants: the word of the mediator and the response of the people.
>
> A. Serra correctly noticed that the expression of the Covenant ("All that Yahweh has said, we will do"), closely parallels the words of Mary to the servants at Cana: "Do whatever he tells you" (*Jn* 2:5). From this one can conclude that Mary - in her very last words - uses the formula of the Covenant; she personifies in a certain manner the people of Israel in the context of the Covenant. For, as A. Serra continues, "John puts on the lips of Mary the profession of faith that the whole community of the chosen people pronounced one day in front of Sinai." Mary therefore asks of the "servants" to adopt vis-a-vis Jesus an attitude, which is in reality the attitude of the Covenant, that is an attitude of perfect submission to the will of God, expressed here in the command given by Jesus.[8]

Mary's future role in Christendom is also pre-figured in the Old Testament Queen Mother theme as shown by Mark Miravalle:

> We can see an authentic foreshadowing of the role of the Mother of Jesus as Advocate for the People of God in the Old Testament role of the *Queen Mother*, the role and office held by the mothers of the great Davidic kings of Israel ...
>
> The office and authority of the queen mother in her close relationship to the king made her the *strongest advocate to the king* for the people of the kingdom. The Old Testament understanding of an *advocate* is a person who is called in to intercede for another in need and particularly at court, and no one had more intercessory power to the king than the queen mother, who at times sat enthroned at the

---

8   Ignace de la Potterie, *Mary in the Mystery of the Covenant,* 189-190.

right side of the king (cf. 1 *Kings* 2:19-20). The queen mother also had the function of *counselor* to the king in regards to matters of the kingdom (cf. *Prov* 31:8-9; 2 *Chr* 22:2-4).

The recognized role of *advocate* of the quuen mother with the king for members of the kingdom is manifested in the immediate response of King Solomon to his mother, Bathsheba, in this queen mother's petition for a member of the kingdom: "And the king rose to meet her, and bowed down to her; then he sat on his throne, and had a seat brought for the king's mother; and she sat on his right. Then she said, 'I have one small request to make of you; do not refuse me.' And the king said to her, 'Make your request, my mother; for I will not refuse you.' (1 *Kings* 2: 19-20).

The Old Testament image and role of the queen mother, the "great Lady," as *advocate to the king for the people of the kingdom* prophetically foreshadows the role of the great *Queen Mother and Lady of the New Testament*. For it is Mary of Nazareth who becomes the Queen and Mother in the Kingdom of God, as the Mother of Christ, King of all nations. The Woman at the foot of the Cross (cf. Jn 19:26) becomes the Great Lady (*Domina*) with the Lord and King, and thereby will be the Advocate and Queen for the People of God from heaven, where she is the "woman clothed with the sun ... and on her head a crown of twelve stars" (*Rev* 12:1).[9]

The themes of Mary as the New Ark of the Covenant and the New Eve are also of great importance in considering Mary in relation to both Testaments and are separately treated.

The New Ark of the Covenant

In the Gospels of *Luke* and *John*, in the Book of *Revelation* and in the doctrine and devotion of the New Testament Church (in hymns such as the *Akathistos*), Mary was identified as the new Ark of the Covenant. The Ark lies at the center of the Old Covenant and is continued into the New Covenant in the person of Mary in whom the Holy Spirit indwells. Once we understand Mary's biblical role as the new Ark of the Covenant we cannot fail to see why

---

9   Mark I. Miravalle, *Mary: Coredemptrix, Mediatrix, Advocate* (Santa Barbara, CA: Queenship Publishing, 1993), 58-9.

Christians have always honored her so highly.

Luke and *John* introduce Mary as the Ark of the Covenant by applying to her Old Testament texts that any Jewish reader would understand and identify with the Ark.

Exodus 40:34: "The cloud covered the Tent of meeting and the glory of Yahweh filled the tabernacle."

Luke 1:35: "The power of the Most High will cover you with its shadow. And so the child will be holy and will be called Son of God."

John 1:13: "Not born of blood or of the desire of the flesh or of the desire of God."

Luke 1:34: "I do not know man."

John 1:13: "But of God."

Luke 1:35: "The power of the Most High will cover you ..."

John 1:14: "And the Word was made flesh and pitched his tent among us."

Luke 1:35-46 and 2 Samuel 6 on the theme of the Ark of the Covenant. In this passage from John there is an allusion to "the tent or tabernacle where God resided since the making of the Covenant (*Exodus* 40:34-35; cf. 25:8; 26, etc.)."[10]

The parallelism of Mary and the Ark is continued in the visitation narrative.

2 Samuel 6:9: "However can the Ark of Yahweh (= My Lord) come to me?"

Luke 1:43: "Why should I be honored with a visit from the mother of My Lord?"

2 Samuel 6:11: "The Ark of Yahweh remained for three months in the house ..."

Luke 1:56: "Mary remained about three months in the home of Elizabeth."

---

[10] Rene Laurentin, *A Short Treatise on the Virgin Mary* (Washington, New Jersey: AMI Press, 1991), 34-5.

"The two "journeys" take place in Judea; the shouts of jubilation of the people and of Elizabeth; David and John the Baptist "exult for joy"; the presence of the Ark and that of Mary are blessing for the house; the Ark and Mary remain in the house for three months."[11]

"As Jesus enters the Temple Simeon greets him as 'the glory of Israel' (Luke 2:32). This is a divine title. The glory of Yahweh that had deserted the Temple once it was bereft of the Ark of the Covenant now reenters the Temple as Mary comes there carrying Jesus. Thus it is that Simeon can die happy (Luke 2:26, 29): he now can "see death" since he has "seen the glory of the Lord." The time has been fulfilled. Here Mary, eschatalogical Daughter of Zion and new Ark of the Covenant, accomplishes her mission in a way in bringing to the Temple the one whose place it properly is. This is what Jesus himself will affirm in the very last episode of the infancy gospel, that of his being found in the Temple: 'I must be in my Father's house.' [*Luke* 2:49]."[12]

The Ark symbolism and its relationship to Mary continues in the Book of *Revelation*.

> *Revelation* 21:3: "Behold the tent of God with men; he will tent with them."

In this text (and apparently in *Revelation* 11:19 and 12:1, two closely linked verses) the 'tent' is also a 'woman':

> "I saw the holy city, the new Jerusalem, coming down from God out of heaven, as beautiful as a bride all dressed for her husband, and then I heard a loud voice call out from the throne, 'Behold the tent of God with men ...'" (21:2-3).

> "Then the sanctuary of God in heaven opened, and the Ark of the Covenant could be seen inside it ... Now a great sign appeared in heaven: a woman, adorned with the sun ... She was pregnant." (11:19-12:1).

---

[11] Stefano Manelli, *All Generations Shall Call Me Blessed* (New Bedford, Massachussetts: Academy of the Immaculate, 1995), 152.

[12] Rene Laurentin, *A Short Treatise on the Virgin Mary*, 27-30.

When the book of *Revelation* was written there were no chapter divisions and so there should be a continuous flow from 11:19 to 12:1: the revelation of the Ark of the Covenant in God's temple in Heaven is followed immediately by the vision of the woman clothed by the sun because the Ark is identified with her who is none other than Mary.

[For further information on this theme, the reader is invited to consult a superb recent study on historical and contemporary evidence for Mary's relation to the Ark of the Covenant, **A Scientist Researches Mary the Ark of the Covenant** (101 Foundation, Asbury, New Jersey, 1995) by the internationally reputed scientist Courtenay Bartholomew].

New Adam, New Eve

At the root of all Marian doctrine is the biblical revelation embraced by the early Church (as demonstrated in the writings of the earliest Church Fathers) that Mary is the New Eve just as Jesus is the New Adam. The drama of salvation begins in the book of Genesis with the prophecy of a new Adam and a new Eve and ends in the book of Revelation with the culmination of the battle between the serpent and the new Adam (Jesus) and the new Eve (Mary).

In this truth, of her role as the New Eve, is contained all other truths about Mary: by her obedience, the new Eve gave birth to her seed, the new Adam, who would "save his people from their sins." He was "Emmanuel," God with us, and she was therefore the "Mother of God" - by seeing her as Mother of God we are reminded too of His true humanity, His Adamness. If it was truly God Who was born with a human nature, He could not be generated by a human action - hence the Virgin Birth. In truly being the Mother of God who was "overshadowed" by the Holy Spirit it was unthinkable that Mary could be mother of anyone else - hence the doctrine of her perpetual virginity. If Mary was truly to be the New Eve she could not be subject to the Original Sin brought about by the first Adam - and hence the doctrine of the Immaculate Conception brought about by the redemption won by the new Adam and scripturally confirmed by the Angel's proclamation of Mary's transformation by grace. Since the corruption of the grave came from

Original Sin, and the new Eve was truly the partner of the new Adam who reversed Original Sin, she could not be subject to the consequences of Original Sin - hence the doctrine of the Assumption. Beginning with her obedience at the Annunciation and culminating with her offering up of her Son at Calvary, in fulfillment of Simeon's prophecy, the New Eve participates in the mission of the New Adam, a role which gave her the title of Coredemptrix (where "co" means "with" and not "equal to"). From the acorn of the revelation of "the new Adam and the new Eve" grew the oak tree of all other Marian doctrine.

Gen. 3:14-15	*Rev.* 12:9,13 and 17
God said to the *serpent*...	The great dragon, the *primeval serpent* known as the devil or Satan ...
I will make you enemies of each other: you and the *woman*	sprang in pursuit of the *woman* ... but she was given a huge pair of eagle's wings to fly away from the serpent into the desert.
your offspring and her *offspring*	The dragon was enraged with the woman and went away to make war on the *rest of her children*, that is, all who obey God's commandments and bear witness for Jesus.

"The word "woman" functions, as it were, as an alpha and omega term, appearing initially in *Genesis* 3:15 - the first and crucial moment of human history - and running like a thread throughout all written revelation, reappearing at four other decisive moments: in Galatians 4:4, at the human origin of Christ; at Cana of Galilee, at the "hour" of the first messianic and salvific manifestation of Christ; on Calvary, at the hour of the Passion and death for the fulfillment of the redemption; and finally, in Revelation, at the last act in the manifestation of Christ as Judge and Sovereign of the universe."[13]

---

[13] Stefano Manelli, *All Generations Shall Call Me Blessed,* 352-360.

Genesis 3:14-15:

> "And the Lord God said unto the serpent, ... I will put enmity between thee and the woman, and between thy seed and her seed; it shall bruise thy head, and thou shalt bruise his heel."

The Marian and Messianic interpretation of *Genesis* 3:15 was accepted by all Christians including Martin Luther. In his last sermon in Wittenberg in 1546, Luther said:

> "Is Christ only to be adored? Or is the holy Mother of God rather not to be honoured? This is the woman who crushed the Serpent's head. Hear us. For your Son denies you nothing."[14]

Revelation 12:

> And there appeared a great wonder in heaven; a woman clothed with the sun, and the moon under her feet, and upon her head a crown of twelve stars: And she being with child cried ... and the dragon stood before the woman which was ready to be delivered, for to devour her child as soon as it was born. And she brought forth a man child, who was to rule all nations with a rod of iron ... And when the dragon saw that he was cast unto the earth, he persecuted the woman which brought forth the man child ...

Exegete Ignace De La Potterie's commentary:

> Certain authors have remarked correctly that it is unthinkable that the apostolic Church, confronted with the description of the Woman of Revelation 12, had never thought of Mary. The fact was there: Mary was a real woman, occupying a special place in the mystery of salvation announced to the young Church by the preachers of the Gospel. Besides this, two facts should be kept in mind: first, the background for the fundamental theme which we are studying, namely, the mystery of Mary in the New Testament is a feminine figure of the Old Testament, the 'Daughter of Zion'; sec-

---

[14] Martin Luther, Weimar edition of *Martin Luther's Works,* Volume 51, 128-129.

ondly, explicitly with John but implicitly with Luke, it is precisely the word 'Woman' which is employed in order to designate Mary, the Mother of Jesus. When one considers all that has been said, notably about this Old Testament figure of a woman which provided the background thought from which several evangelical texts have spoken of Mary, it seems impossible that the first Christian generation and all the subsequent ecclesial tradition did not also give, in this broader framework, a Marian interpretation to the victorious Woman of Revelation 12. In fact, that is precisely what has happened."[15]

Mary's participation in the work of the new Adam is specifically prophesied by Simeon under the direct inspiration of the Holy Spirit: "And the Holy Ghost was upon him ... And Simeon blessed them, and said unto Mary ... A sword shall pierce through thy own soul also." [*Luke* 2:25,34-35].

This prophecy is borne out in the life and mission of the new Adam. Peter Stravinskas writes,

"At every significant juncture in our Lord's life, one finds Mary on the horizon. When God began His plan for our redemption, He sent to Nazareth an angel, who hailed a woman as 'highly favored' or 'full of grace' to be the human partner in this divine enterprise (cf. *Luke* 1:28). When the Babe was born in Bethlehem, He came forth into our world not from heaven but from the womb of the Virgin Mary (cf. *Mt* 1:25; *Lk* 2:7). As the Child was presented to the Lord in the Temple of Jerusalem on the fortieth day, the old prophet Simeon singled out His Mother Mary for special mention as a woman destined to be the Mother of Sorrows (cf. *Lk* 2:35). Twelve years later, after another temple visit, the Boy Jesus returned with His Mother and foster father to Nazareth and was subject to them (cf. *Lk* 2:51). It was Mary who prodded her Son into action at Cana to work His first miracle, launching Him on His public ministry (cf. *Jn* 2:3). And it was Mary who stood by His side at the foot of the Cross and was given to John as the Mother of the Church (cf. *Jn* 12:26f). Finally, as the Church was waiting

---

[15]   Ignace de la Potterie, *Mary in the Mystery of the Covenant*, 258.

to be born in the Upper Room, while the disciples prayed for the Pentecost gift of the Spirit, Luke tells us that Mary was in their midst (cf. *Acts* 1:14)."[16]

Chapter 12 of the *Book of Revelation* gives us the full thrust of Mary's participation in her Son's mission.

Mary's role as the New Eve was recognized by the earliest Christian Fathers:

Justin Martyr [155 A.D.]:
"Eve, a virgin and undefiled, conceived the word of the serpent and bore disobedience and death. But the Virgin Mary received faith and joy when the angel Gabriel announced to her the glad tidings that the Spirit of the Lord would come upon her and the power of the Most High would overshadow her, for which reason the Holy One being born of her is the Son of God. And she replied 'Be it done unto me according to your word.' (*Luke* 1:38)." [*Dialogue with Trypho the Jew*, 155 A.D., p. 100]

Irenaeus [189 A.D.]:
"The knot of Eve's disobedience was loosed by the obedience of Mary. What the virgin Eve had bound in unbelief, the Virgin Mary loosed through faith." [*Against Heresies*, 189 A.D., 3:22:24]

Ambrose [397 A.D.]:
"Evil came by a woman, so good has come by the Woman; for by Eve we fell, by Mary we stand; by Eve we were reduced to slavery, by Mary we were made free. Eve took from us length of days, Mary restored to us immortality; Eve caused us to be condemned by the fruit of the tree, Mary wrought our pardon by the gift of the Tree, because Christ also hung upon the Tree as Fruit. As therefore we died through a tree, so by a Tree are we brought to life. All that was done by Adam is washed out by Mary." [cited in *Virgin Wholly Marvelous*].

---

16 Peter J. Stravinskas, *The Catholic Response* (Huntington, Indiana: Our Sunday Visitor, 1985), 70-1.

Mary's role as the New Eve leads us to one of the greatest mysteries in God's salvific plan: she embodies the ultimate victory of God. By bringing about the Fall of Adam and Eve and therefore their descendants, Satan may seem to have frustrated God's plan for mankind. True, by His Death and Resurrection, Jesus re-opened Heaven to the human race. Nevertheless Jesus was a divine Person and so it may be argued that the victory of God required divine intervention in opposition not just to the Devil but to the human race that God had created with such great anticipation. But when we recognize that it was Mary's obedience at the Annunciation that reversed "the knot of Eve's disobedience" we realize that it was a human person whose cooperation enabled the Incarnation and the subsequent salvific death of Christ. Ultimately, then, the victory of God is not simply in frustrating the Devil's schemes for mankind but in having created at least one human person who would not be subject to the Devil and in using that person to bring to us the Redeemer Who necessarily had to be fully God and fully man. Since the Original Sin, like every sin, was an offense against an infinite being and therefore an infinite offense, only an infinite Person, Jesus Who is the Second Person of the Trinity, could make sufficient reparation for the sin. Moreover, the reparation, to be efficacious, had to be made by a human being since the infinite offense was committed by the human race. This is the importance of why Jesus the divine Person also had to be fully human. But for the divine Person to make the all-sufficient reparation, a human person had to first reverse "the knot" and it is here that we perceive both Mary's true glory and God's ultimate victory. Again, it was through Mary's cooperation that the divine Person could become a human being - thus laying the groundwork for the future Redemptive Act.

This is why the poet William Wordsworth called Mary "Our tainted nature's solitary boast." Or as the great ecumenist W.E. Orchard said, "For while none but Christ could open to us the gates of heaven, not only did God choose Mary to be the mother of his Son, but by her meek assent to God's will it was she who opened the gates of earth to the coming of our Lord."[17]

---

[17] C.N.R. Wallwork, "The Cult of Our Lady in the Presbyterian and Catholic Ministries of W E Orchard", ESBVM, Wallington, Surrey, 1990, 5.

Rejoice Highly Favored/Hail Full of Grace: Transformed by Grace from the Beginning

We see in the Old Testament that the prophets and messengers of God's salvation, from Abraham and Moses to the later Prophets, were given special graces to perform their mission. In certain exceptional cases, notably Jeremiah and John the Baptist, the prophets were sanctified while still in the womb. This process of pre-ordained purification reached its climax in Mary who was called to play, next to the mission of Christ, the single most important role in the history of salvation. From the announcements of the angel Gabriel and Elizabeth revealed in Scripture we are led to conclude that this preparation meant that Mary was immaculately conceived.

> *Luke* 1:28-31:
> "And the angel came in unto her, and said, Hail, thou that art highly favoured, the Lord is with thee: blessed art thou among women. And when she saw him, she was troubled at his saying, and cast in her mind what manner of salutation this should be. And the angel said unto her, Fear not, Mary: for thou hast found favour with God. And behold thou shalt conceive in thy womb, and bring forth a son, and shalt call his name JESUS.

The Angel Gabriel's greeting to Mary is of great consequence for our understanding of Mary and Marian doctrine. The greeting has been variously translated as "Rejoice highly favored" and "Hail full of grace." The object of the varied translations is the Greek word *kecharitomene* which refers to one who has been transformed by God's grace. The word is used only one other time in the New Testament and that is in the epistle to the Ephesians where Paul is addressing those who by becoming Christians are transformed by grace and receive the remission of sins. We conclude then that Mary is considered to already have been transformed by grace before the birth of Christ.

The noted exegete Ignace de la Potterie gives us a detailed study of the great text:

> The dominant translation which ancient Christianity has given is very clear: the Byzantine tradition in the East and the me-

dieval tradition in the West have seen in *"kecharitomene,"* the indication of Mary's perfect holiness ...

The verb utilized here by Luke (*charitoun*) is extremely rare in Greek. It is present only two times in the New Testament: in the text of Luke on the Annunciation (*Luke* 1:28), *"kecharitomene,"* and in the Epistle to the Ephesians (*Ephesians* 1:6), *"echaritosen."* ... These verbs, then, effect a change of something in the person or the thing affected. Thus, the radical of the verb *'charitoo'* being *'charis'* (= grace), the idea which is expressed is that of a change brought about by grace. In addition the verb used by Luke is in the past participial form. *"Kecharitomene"* signifies then, in the person to whom the verb relates, that is, Mary, that the action of the grace of God has already brought about a change. It does not tell us how that came about. What is essential here is that it affirms that Mary has been *transformed by the grace of God* ...

The perfect passive participle is used by Luke to indicate that the transformation by grace *has already taken place* in Mary, well before the moment of the Annunciation.

In what then would this transformation of grace consist? According to the parallel text of the Letter to the Ephesians 1:6 the Christians have been 'transformed by grace' in the sense that 'according to the richness of his grace, they find redemption by his blood, the *remission of sins.'* (*Ephesians* 1:7). This grace, in reality, takes away sin. This is elucidating for our particular case. Mary is 'transformed by grace,' because she has been *sanctified* by the grace of God. It is there, moreover, in the Church's tradition that we have the most customary translation. Sophronius of Jerusalem, for example, interprets the term 'full of grace' in this manner: 'No one has been fully sanctified as you ...; no one has been *purified in advance* as you.' In addition, he takes from the total context that Mary had been 'transformed by the grace' of God in view of the task which she awaits, that of becoming the Mother of the Son of God, and to do so while remaining a virgin. There we have the double announcement of the angel: as mother she brings to the world the Son of the Most High (v.33), but that will take place by the 'power of the Most High' (v.35), that is virginally. God had prepared Mary for this by inspiring in her the desire for virginity. This desire of Mary was then for her a result of her transformation by grace ...

It is true that we do not find in the text of Luke evidence that Mary is "full of grace" *from the first moment of her existence*. But what in reality does the proclamation of the dogma of the Immaculate Conception say? Grace has preserved Mary of all sin and of all consequences of sin (concupiscence). This is also the biblical understanding of the concept of "grace." Grace takes away sin (*Ephesians* 1:6-7). If it is true that Mary was entirely transformed by the grace of God, that then means that God has preserved her from sin, "purified" her, and sanctified her...

As one can notice in the schema of the structured text the theme of "being full of *grace*" is continued in the first proclamation, "You have found *grace with God*"; then follows the substance of the announcement: Mary will become the mother of the Messiah. It is apparent that Mary was "full of grace" by God in view of this maternity, and even that she was prepared, by the grace of her virginity, for her own mission, that of being the virginal mother of the Savior.[18]

Concerning Mary's sanctification before birth, Martin Luther said: "God has formed the soul and body of the Virgin Mary full of the Holy Spirit, so that she is without all sins, for she has conceived and borne the Lord Jesus."[19] The rationale for Mary's sanctification was simple, as Ulrich Zwingli saw it: "It was fitting that such a holy Son should have a holy Mother."[20]

The Ever-Virgin Spouse of the Holy Spirit
Who is the Mother of God

If there is a message of Scripture that is as textually clear-cut as it can be it is the fact that Mary is the Spouse of the Holy Spirit (see the infancy narratives in Matthew and Luke). Scripture documents six direct interventions of the Holy Spirit: the virginal conception in *Matthew*, Elizabeth's hymn to Mary under the inspiration of the Holy Spirit in *Luke*, Simeon's inspired prophecy to Mary

---

18 Ignace de la Potterie, *Mary in the Mystery of the Covenant*, 17-20.

19 Martin Luther, Weimar edition of *Martin Luther's Works* (Translation by William J. Cole) Volume 52, 39.

20 E. Stakemeier, *De Mariologia et Oecumenismo*, K. Balic, ed., (Rome, 1962), 456.

in *Luke*, the baptism of Jesus in *Matthew*, the coming of the Holy
Spirit at Pentecost in *Acts* and finally the direction of the Holy
Spirit in the laying on of hands in *Acts* 13. Of these six explicit
interventions Mary is present at four and enters into the deepest
possible intimacy with the Spirit in the first intervention. How can
we possibly comprehend what it means to be to be "overshadowed"
by the Holy Spirit? Luke draws attention to the presence of Mary
at Pentecost and this has been reflected in the traditional Christian
emphasis on the intercession of Mary.

It was the Holy Spirit Himself Who honored Mary (as no other
human person has been honored by God Himself) by speaking
through the lips of Elizabeth ("Elisabeth was filled with the Holy
Ghost"):

> "Blessed art thou amongst women and blessed is the fruit
> of thy womb ... As soon as the voice of thy salutation sounded
> in mine ears, the babe leaped in my womb for joy. And
> blessed is she that believed: for there shall be a performance
> of those things which were told her from God."

Again the Holy Spirit addresses her through Simeon ("the Holy
Ghost was upon him ... he came by the Spirit into the temple"):

> "Simeon ... said unto Mary his mother, Behold this child is
> set for the fall and rising again of many in Israel ... Yea, a
> sword shall pierce through thy own soul also."

Not only was Mary Spouse of the Holy Spirit but she was the
Mother of the Second Person of the Trinity.

> *Luke* 1:43:
> "And whence is this to me, that the mother of my Lord
> should come to me?"

"Lord" is used here in the same sense as "Yahweh" which refers to God in the Old Testament. Mary is the mother of God.

Mary's identity as the Mother of God was affirmed by the Christian community in its earliest Councils and by the Protestant Reformers as well [see **Mary and the Protestant Reformation**].

Christians from the very beginning have realized that it is unthinkable that she who is the Mother of the Second Person of the Trinity and Spouse of the Third Person could have had any other children. Mary's perpetual virginity was defined by the Third Council of Constantinople in 681 (and by earlier and later councils) and was passionately affirmed by the Protestant Reformers [see **Mary and the Protestant Reformation**].

About biblical texts that have been interpreted to deny the perpetual virginity, Calvin's Geneva Bible of 1560 had the following commentary: "When *Matthew* 1:25 and *Luke* 2:7 speak of Jesus as, respectively, her 'first borne sonne' or 'first begotten sonne,' they speak thus because she had never none before, and not in respect of any she had after. Neither yet doeth this worde (til) import alwayes a time following: wherein the contrarie may be affirmed, as our Saviour, saying that he wil be present with his disciples, til the end of the world meaneth not, that after this worlde he wil not be with them."

Even Methodist commentaries followed the same line of interpretation:

> In the **Notes on the New Testament**, which are based on the work of the German scholar J.G. Bengel, and are part of the Methodist doctrinal standards, there is this comment on Matthew 1:25: '*He knew her not till after she had brought forth* - It cannot be inferred from that expression (2 *Sam.* 6:23), "Michal had no child till the day of her death," that she had children afterward. Nor do the words that follow, "the firstborn" son, alter the case. For there are abundance of places where the terms "firstborn" is used, though there were no subsequent children.' The brethren of Jesus (Matthew 12:46 and parallels, etc.) are 'his kinsmen. They were the sons of Mary, the wife of Clophas or Alphaeus, his mother's sister.'[21]

Mary's perpetual virginity was prophesied most clearly in *Ezekiel* 44:2-3 as recognized by the early Christians: "Then said the Lord unto me: This gate shall be shut, it shall not be opened,

---

21   Gordon Wakefield, "The Mother of Jesus: The Methodist Point of View", ESBVM paper, October 11, 1967, 8.

and no man shall enter in by it; because the Lord, the God of Israel, hath entered in by it, therefore it shall be shut. It is for the prince ... he shall enter by the way of the porch of that gate, and shall go out by the way of the same."

Luke 1:34 "How shall this be, seeing I know not a man?" has traditionally been considered a reference by Mary to a vow of life-long virginity. Laurentin notes that here we must "recognize the present tense 'I do not know' as having to do with a condition rather than an instant of time. To give an example, if someone to whom a cigarette is offered replies, 'I don't smoke,' he is understood to mean 'I never smoke' and not 'I am not smoking right now.'"[22]

Eastern Christianity has always understood the unique relationship of the Holy Spirit and Mary. So much so the name given to Mary in the East - "Panagia" ("all holy" in Greek) - is the same given to the Holy Spirit - "Panagion".

The Exaltation of Mary in Scripture

Luke 1:28, 30:

> "And the angel came in unto her, and said, Hail, thou that art highly favoured, the Lord is with thee: blessed art thou among women. And when she saw him, she was troubled at his saying, and cast in her mind what manner of salutation this should be. And the angel said unto her, Fear not, Mary: for thou hast found favour with God."

Luke 2:41-44:

> "And it came to pass, that, when Elisabeth heard the salutation of Mary, the babe leaped in her womb; and Elisabeth was filled with the Holy Ghost: and she spake out with a loud voice, and said, blessed art thou among women, and blessed is the fruit of thy womb. And whence is this to me, that the mother of my Lord should come to me? For, lo, as soon as the voice of thy salutation sounded in mine ears, the babe leaped in my womb for joy."

Luke 2:48:

> "From henceforth all generations shall call me blessed."

---

[22] Rene Laurentin, *A Short Treatise on the Virgin Mary*, 285.

Says biblical scholar Rene Laurentin, "No other biblical personage has been given such strong praise":

> This [the angel Gabriel's] initial greeting of praise is prolonged throughout the accounts of the annunciation and the visitation. The Lord is with her (1:28), the Holy Spirit comes down upon her (1:35), great things are accomplished in her (1:49) thanks to her faith (1:45), and 'that is why' (as she herself recognizes) 'all generations will call [her] blessed' (1:48). No other biblical personage has been given such strong praise, and without anything said to the contrary.
>
> In Luke 1:35 the angel tells Mary, 'The Holy Spirit will come upon *you* and the power of the Most High will cover *you* with its shadow.' In the light of Isaiah 11:2 would it not have been more normal to say that the Holy Spirit was coming on the Emmanuel rather than on his Mother? In Luke 1:42 Elizabeth proclaims Mary's blessing before that of her Son and adds, 'Why should I be honoured with a visit from the *Mother of my Lord*?' even though the honour that falls to her is actually the visit of the *Lord* rather than of the Mother. She adds, 'For the moment *your greeting* reached my ears, the child in my womb leapt for joy,' even though in reality the benefit of the visitation is to be attributed to the action of Mary's child rather than to Mary's voice. That Mary should thus be placed in the forefront is most astonishing and gives food for reflection to those who fear that they do Christ some offense in exalting his Mother.[23]

According to the exegete John McHugh,

> There is nothing improbable in the suggestion that the early Christians sang hymns of praise in honour of Mary... That her special rank was acknowledged by the Church is implied by the text of the Magnificat, where Luke says that 'from this present time' (1:48b) all generations will call her blessed. Could Luke have written that phrase if, at the time when he was writing (A.D. 70-80), his own generation had not begun to call her blessed? The text of Lk 1:42 would seem conclusive proof that the early Church expressed its reverence for the mother of its Lord by singing hymns in her honour.[24]

---

23   Rene Laurentin, *A Short Treatise on the Virgin Mary*, 20-1.
24   John McHugh, *The Mother of Jesus in the New Testament*, 71.

Similarly, the exegete Manuel Miguens writes:

> The praise and veneration of Mary was a practice of the New Testament community that will be continued throughout all generations. This testimony, however is not just historical, it is "biblical," it is part of the written word of God. The veneration of Mary by God's people in "all generations" ever since the earliest Christian days is a "biblical" fact, biblical information, and biblical teaching.
>
> Mary's veneration is a "biblical" fact also from another standpoint - from the standpoint of all the "servants of the Lord." God's saving instruments were publicly venerated and praised by the biblical people as the instances of Moses, Pinhas, Debora, Yael, David, Judith, etc., serve to prove. In the New Testament we meet the example of John the Baptizer whom the Christian Community of the New Testament celebrated together with the Messiah, though of course, in second position. Mary's veneration and exaltation by "all generations" of the Christian people, ever since the very first one, is grounded on the purest and surest biblical practice of glorifying God for his saving deeds through "his servants." ...
>
> The biblical teaching and the biblical practice establish a principle... Mary deserves a very singular veneration by God's people redeemed by "the Servant of the Lord," born of "the mother of my Lord"; and for the very reason of her having borne the Messiah, the Son of David, Mary is acknowledged and greeted as "Our Lady" by the messianic community.[25]

Mary's exalted position was acknowledged by the Protestant Reformers [see **Mary and the Protestant Reformation**].

The Woman Clothed with the Sun:
Mary the First Fruit of Christ's Resurrection

Luke 2:48:
> "From henceforth all generations shall call me blessed."

---

[25] Manuel Miguens, *Mary "The Servant of the Lord": An Ecumenical Proposal* (Boston: Daughters of St. Paul, 1978), 176-7.

Revelation 12:1:
> "And there appeared a great wonder in heaven; a woman clothed with the sun, and the moon under her feet, and upon her head a crown of twelve stars."

The Old Testament has at least three instances of assumptions: Moses, Elijah and Enoch. Although Scripture shows Elijah and Enoch being taken up into Heaven, in the case of Moses it is less clear. The "proof" for Moses' assumption is the fact that both Moses and Elijah appear on the mountain during the Transfiguration of Jesus. In *Revelation* 12, when the "Woman" is identified as Mary, as the text demands, we have a clear indication of Mary's Assumption (much as the appearance of Moses and Elijah with Jesus indicated their assumption). Since the *Book of Revelation* was not accepted as part of the canon of Scripture for several centuries, it had no early tradition of interpretation. Once its canonicity was established, the identification of Mary with the Woman of *Revelation* 12 became obvious [since the Woman's Son was Jesus]. With this the scriptural basis of the Assumption was set solidly in place.

Whereas Christians around the world have ancient traditions about the tombs of each one of the Apostles, there is no place venerated as the tomb containing the remains of the greatest of Christians, Mary. This is because the earliest Christians accepted her assumption into Heaven. The absence of a tomb with Mary's remains parallels the empty tomb of her Son. From at least the third century the Eastern Orthodox have held to the universal conviction that Mary was taken up into heaven at the end of her earthly life - as have most Christians for most of Christian history.

Moreover the verse "all generations shall call me blessed" has been interpreted as an implicit prophecy of Mary's assumption.

The Protestant scholar Donald Dawe notes that "The Magnificat foretells the time when 'all generations' will call her 'blessed' (Greek: *makaria* [1, 48b]). The greek word translated 'blessed' here is more than a polite honorific term. The 'blessed' are those who stand in a special relationship to God. In the early patristic literature, it was used as a characterization of the martryrs. The highest expression of this 'blessedness' was in the possibility of their ascension into heaven to dwell in the immediate presence of God." This passage is crucial for the doctrine of the Assumption because of "the future tense of the verb in verse 1,48: 'All generations *will* call me blessed'." In this verse we can see that "Mary was related not only to her role in the Incarnation but also to the final consummation of salvation in the kingdom."[26] This consummation, in Mary's case, is her assumption into heaven.

The Assumption is related to other biblical truths about Mary as well. Since God created Mary free from Original Sin it is at least expectable that He would not let her body suffer from the fruits of Original Sin. For her sin the first Eve was punished with libido, the pains of labor and corruption of the tomb: it is perfectly coherent that Mary as the new Eve cannot be subjected to these three punishments. Equally it is unthinkable that the Spouse of the Holy Spirit who is the new Ark of the Covenant will be left by her beloved Son to decay in a grave.

Intercessor, Mediatrix

The central figures of the Old Testament, Abraham and Moses, were intercessors.

Genesis 18:22-24,26:
"Abraham stood yet before the Lord. And Abraham drew near, and said, Wilt thou also destroy the righteous with the wicked? Peradventure there be fifty righteous within the city: wilt thou also destroy and not spare the place for the fifty righteous that are therein? ... And the Lord said, If I find in Sodom fifty righteous within the city, then I will spare all the place for their sakes."

Exodus 32:30-32:
"Moses said unto the people, Ye have sinned a great sin: and now I will go up unto the Lord; peradventure I shall make an atonement for your sin. And Moses returned unto the Lord, and said, Oh, this people have sinned a great sin, and have made them gods of gold. Yet now, if thou wilt forgive their sin -; and if not, blot me, I pray thee, out of thy book which thou has written."

---

26 Donald G. Dawe, "The Assumption of the Blessed Virgin in Ecumenical Perspective," *The Way*, Summer 1982, 45.

In Old Testament times, the Queen-Mother, the Mother of the King, had the right to intercede with the King - and so Marian intercession was accepted without question by the first Christians who were Jews:

> 1 *Kings* 2: 19-20:
> "And the king rose to meet her, and bowed down to her; then he sat on his throne, and had a seat brought for the king's mother; and she sat on his right. Then she said, 'I have one small request to make of you; do not refuse me.' And the king said to her, 'Make your request, my mother; for I will not refuse you.'

The office of the Queen-Mother was particularly important in the reign of the Davidic Kings. We cannot forget that Jesus sat on the throne of "his father David."

Mary is portrayed as both intercessor and mediatrix in the gospels. The greatest grace received by all of humanity was the Incarnation of Jesus Christ and this grace came from the Holy Spirit *through His Spousal Union* with the Virgin Mary whereby she was prepared for the coming of her divine Son. *In that very act she became the mediatrix of the greatest of all graces.* In the Gospel of John we see her petition to her Son result in the grace of faith for the disciples of Jesus:

> "This beginning of miracles did Jesus in Cana of Galilee, and manifested forth his glory; and his disciples believed on him."

Like Abraham who offered up his son Isaac to God, Mary offers up her Son to God. She first offered Him up in His infancy at the Temple where Simeon prophesies under the inspiration of the Holy Spirit to Mary that "a sword shall pierce through thy own soul also." This prophecy is fulfilled on Calvary where she is present at the culmination of the offering of her Son to the Father. In making this offering, Mary became the mediatrix of Jesus' redemptive death and all the graces that came with it. It was the Holy Spirit Himself, the Source of all graces, Who honored Mary (as no other human person has been honored by God Himself) by speaking through the lips of Elizabeth ("Elisabeth was filled with the Holy

Ghost"): "Blessed art thou amongst women and blessed is the fruit of thy womb." These are not strained or recent "Catholic" interpretations of biblical texts. At the ecumenical Council of Ephesus, Cyril of Alexandria proclaimed, "Hail Mary Theotokos, venerable treasure of the whole world ... it is you through whom the Holy Trinity is glorified and adored ... through whom the tempter, the devil is cast down from heaven, through whom the fallen creature is raised up to heaven, through whom that all creation, once imprisoned by idolatry, has reached knowledge of the truth, through whom holy baptism has come to believers ... through whom nations are brought to baptism."

A striking parallel has been drawn between Mary and Old Testament mediators like Moses in recent exegesis as Ignace de la Potterie shows:

> "His mother said to the servants: 'Do whatever he tells you.'" In passing let us note that these are the final words of Mary in the Gospels ...
>
> "A. Serra having examined in depth the use of this expression in the Old Testament proposes another exegesis, which to us seems more solid and which at the same time is very attractive. He puts forth evidence that here we are dealing with an expression that is almost a technical one, which appears several times in the Old Testament in connection with the Covenant when Israel, in response to the promises which have been made to her, pledges obedience to God. It is utilized as well on the occasion of the conclusion of the Covenant at Sinai (Ex 1(;8; 24:3-7; Dt 5:27), as well as its renewal later (cf. Jos 24:24; Ex 10:12: Ne 5:12). We find it for the first time in Exodus 19:8. Situated in its context it is the following: "In the third month of their departure from the land of Egypt ... the Israelites came to the desert of Sinai ... Moses then went up the mountain to God. Yahweh called to him and said: 'Here is how you shall address the house of Jacob ... If you obey me and respect my Covenant, you shall be my special possession, dearer to me than all other people, though all the earth is mine ... That is what you must tell the Israelites.' Moses then went, convoked all the elders of the people and related to them all that Yahweh had ordered him to tell them. Then the entire people, with one accord responded: '*All that Yahweh has said, we will do.*' And Moses brought back to

Yahweh the response of the people." (Ex 19:1-8). In this text and the others that we pointed out, even though they appear with several variants, there are always two constants: the word of the mediator and the response of the people.

"A. Serra correctly noticed that the expression of the Covenant ("All that Yahweh has said, we will do"), closely parallels the words of Mary to the servants at Cana: "Do whatever he tells you" (Jn 2:5). From this one can conclude that Mary - in her very last words - uses the formula of the Covenant; she personifies in a certain manner the people of Israel in the context of the Covenant. For, as A. Serra continues, "John puts on the lips of Mary the profession of faith that the whole community of the chosen people pronounced one day in front of Sinai." Mary therefore asks of the "servants" to adopt vis-a-vis Jesus an attitude, which is in reality the attitude of the Covenant, that is an attitude of perfect submission to the will of God, expressed here in the command given by Jesus."[27]

In making Mary the Mother of all Christians (see *John* 19 and *Revelation* 12), Jesus made her also Intercessor and Mediatrix. In addressing Mary as Mediatrix we must distinguish between the unique Mediatorship of Jesus (which is unique in the same way in which God is uniquely Father) and the mediation of all servants of God. All Christians are given the opportunity to mediate God's message of salvation - that is why even Fundamentalists have preachers and missionaries and pastors. We bring people to salvation by preaching the Gospel to them: we are therefore mediators of salvation, the salvation that comes only from Jesus. Of all human persons Mary was the greatest mediator of salvation because it was her obedience to God that led to the Incarnation.

That we are all called to mediate is affirmed by the Apostle Paul in his letter to the Colossians: "I rejoice in my sufferings for your sake, and in my flesh I complete what is lacking in Christ's afflictions for the sake of his body, that is the Church." (*Colossians* 1:24) This is a startling passage because it implies that there is something "lacking in Christ's afflictions" and that Paul can "complete" what is lacking through *his suffering*. While the redemptive

---

[27] Ignace de la Potterie, **Mary in the Mystery of the Covenant** (New York: Alba House, 1992), 189-190.

sacrifice of Christ was completed on Calvary the work of redemption, the application of this redemptive sacrifice to men and women, will continue throughout history. The suffering of any person, when offered freely to God, is incorporated by Him in the salvific scheme. We can all be co-redeemers in this sense. But the co-redemptive role performed by the immaculately conceived Mother of God is qualitatively distinct. Because of her relation to her Son as Mother and because her aversion to sin in her Immaculate Conception and her love for God is far greater than that of any other human person, Mary's suffering is most intimately united to our Lord's and plays such a significant role in the divine scheme of salvation.

The first Christians accepted Mary as Mediatrix as demonstrated in the discovery of a third century document with the famous *Sub Tuum* prayer:

> We fly to thy patronage, O holy Mother of God, despise not our petitions in our necessities, but deliver us from all danger, O ever glorious and blessed Virgin.

Mother of All Christians

Genesis 3:15:
> "I will put enmity between thee and the woman, and between thy seed and her seed."

John 19:25-27:
> "Now there stood by the cross of Jesus his mother ... When Jesus therefore saw his mother, and the disciple standing by, whom he loved, he saith unto his mother, Woman, behold thy son! Then saith he to the disciple, Behold thy mother."

Revelation 12:17:
> "And the dragon was wroth with the woman, and went to make war with the remnant of her seed, which keep the commandments of God, and have the testimony of Jesus Christ."

Because Mary is the new Eve she is the Mother of all Christians. The theme of the new Eve's relationship to her seed is as clear and consistent in Scripture as the new Adam-new Eve theme.

The Marian references in the Book of Revelation are closely related to the references in the Gospel of John. In the Gospel Mary is never named: she is referred to by her Son as "Woman" - indicating that she is the "Woman" both of Genesis and Revelation. At the crucifixion when her Son entrusts her to the care of the beloved disciple, He says "Woman, behold thy son! ... Son behold thy mother!." [*John* 19:27]. By this instruction, as we see below, all Christians are placed under the spiritual motherhood of Mary. And this explains why in *Revelation* 12 we read that "the dragon was wroth with the woman, and went to make war with the remnant of her seed, which keep the commandments of God, and have the testimony of Jesus Christ." [*Revelation* 12:17]. The seed of the Woman now includes every Christian, a continuation and confirmation of the theme in *John* 19 where our Lord makes His mother the mother of all His disciples.

In his study of Calvary the French exegete F.-M. Braun shows that Jesus' words to His mother in *John* 19:25-27 are a fulfillment of the *Genesis* prophecy. It must be understood first that the number 7 plays a major role in John's Gospel: Jesus performs seven signs or miracles, the opening events take place over seven days with the culmination at Cana, the Passion begins with the verse "Six days before the Passover" (*John* 12:1) and finally Jesus has seven "I am" statements ("I am the Bread of Life," etc.). Braun shows that six separate incidents in *John* 19:17-42 are the fulfillment of prophecies [He is crucified between sinners, He is described as "the King of the Jews," the soldiers draw lots for His clothes, He asks for a drink, His bones are not broken, He is buried by Joseph of Arimathaea and Nicodemus]. From this Braun concludes (writes John McHugh):

> If every other incident described between v.17 and v.42 is a fulfilment of prophecy, then there is good ground for suspecting that the incident related in vv. 25-7 is also a fulfilment of prophecy. The fact that no text is there mentioned need cause no difficulty, for in the first two examples cited and in the last, the reference is only implied, and implicit allusion is wholly in John's manner. One could add (a point not made by Braun) that the whole gospel is permeated structurally with the idea of seven (though the word itself never occurs) - an indication of its connection with Apocalypse. The

fulfilment of seven prophecies at the death of Jesus would be wholly in line with this careful hidden structure of the Fourth Gospel...

If, then, the incident in *Jn* 19:25-7 is the fulfilment of a prophecy, to what Old Testament text does it refer? There are only three texts which refer to the mother of a saviour: *Is* 7:14, *Mic* 5:2 ('Until the time when she who is to give birth does give birth'), and *Gen* 3:15. The first two concern the birth of the Messiah, and may therefore be set aside. This leaves only *Genesis* 3:15...

Could John have had in mind *Gen* 3:15? In the Fourth Gospel, it is the devil who is the great adversary of Jesus (*Jn* 12:31; 16:11; cf. *Apoc* 12:4-6), who puts it into the mind of Judas Iscariot to betray him (*Jn* 13:2; cf. 6:70); and in *Apoc* 12:9 the devil or Satan, is openly identified with 'that serpent of old.' If the author of the Apocalypse and the evangelist were one and the same man then it is clear that in the Gospel we may legitimately look for references to *Gen* 3... The evangelist would seem to have been conscious of the importance of *Gen* 3:15, for the curious expression about 'the seed of the serpent' is taken up in *Jn* 8:41-4, where we read of 'the children of the devil,' and in 1 *Jn* 3:8-10, where the children of God are contrasted with the children of the devil. Then there is the important statement of Jesus to Pilate: 'For this I was born, for this I came into the world, to bear witness to truth' (*Jn* 18:37). Jesus' whole life was therefore a war against 'the father of lies' (*Jn* 8:44), a title clearly echoing *Gen* 3:4 and 13 ('The serpent lied to me'); and his Passion in particular was the supreme battle of this war, in which the prince of this world was stripped of his empire (*Jn* 12:27-36; 14:30). By comparing 12:23 with 12:31-2 it is evident that the victory over the prince of this world takes place at the same hour as the glorification of the son of man. It was on the cross that Jesus 'crushed the head' of that 'serpent of old' (*Gen* 3:15 with *Apoc* 12:9) and 'cast him down' (or: out) for all future time (*Jn* 12:31).

In the texts cited in the last paragraph, there has been mention of the devil and his offspring (explicit in *Jn* 8:41-4; 1 *Jn* 3:8-10; implicit in *Jn* 6:70 and 13:2), and of their enemy, Jesus. Therefore of the four figures named in *Gen* 3:15, the only one not so far mentioned is the woman, the mother of 'him who crushed the serpent's head.' Yet according to *Genesis*, she too is at war with the serpent, and one would expect her to share somehow in the victory of her offspring. In *Genesis*, of course, the woman is undoubtedly the mother of the human race, Eve. But if John, reading the text in the Septuagint, thought of the 'offspring' as an individual, i.e., Jesus the Christ, is it not likely that he would have perceived that Mary was the mother of this individual? Having found a place in his work for three of the four figures in *Genesis*, why should he not also include the mother of him who by the cross crushed the serpent to death? Jesus was descended from Eve by the fact that she was the mother of all the living (*Gen* 3:20), but he was more immediately the son of Mary. Hence her physical presence 'beside the Cross' (or even: 'beside the Crucified') associates her for ever with the *triumph* of Jesus: for in John the cross is never a gibbet, but always a royal throne. Eve, to whom the text from *Genesis* primarily refers, had been dead for thousands of years, but her enemy the serpent lived on. Eve survived only in her children, and so the place assigned to the woman was filled by 'the mother of Jesus.' ...

What, then, is the meaning of 'Woman, behold thy son'? It is usually taken as an act of filial piety, as if Jesus were anxious to provide for his mother after his death. This idea is certainly not absent, but it is hard to accept it as the primary meaning of the gospel for three reasons. First, the rest of the context is concerned with the fulfilment of prophecy. Secondly, on every other occasion when Jesus speaks during his Passion, his words are concerned with his divinely ordained mission; it would be truly astounding if these words, to his mother, constituted a solitary exception. Thirdly, if *Jn* 19:25-7 is primarily an act of solicitude for Mary, why is the disciple first entrusted to Mary, and not vice versa?

Perhaps the best way to approach the problem is to look first at the words 'the disciple whom Jesus loved.' More than once John presents an individual as representative of a group. For example, Nicodemus is a type of the learned Jew seeking after truth (*Jn* 3:1-15) ... So the disciple beside the Crucified is a figure of all who love Jesus. Jesus had promised that all who loved him and kept his commandments would in turn be loved by the Father 'and I too will love him' (14:21,23; cf. 1 *Jn* 2:5). These men would be his friends (*Jn* 15:13-15), and the disciple who followed him to Calvary seems to have been the closest friend of all (18:15ff and especially 13:25). Probably nearly all modern exegetes would agree that in 19:26-7 this disciple should be taken as a type of all who love Jesus.

'Woman, behold thy son!' In the Fourth Gospel, the words of Jesus are not merely declarative, but also causative ... Jesus is 'the Word by whom all things were made' (*Jn* 1:3). Hence his utterance changes water into wine (2:7-8), heals the ruler's son (4:51) and the paralysed man .... Mary was placed in a new relationship to 'the disciple(s) whom Jesus loved' by the words spoken from the cross.

What is Mary's new function to be, as mother of the disciples? It must be in some way bound up with the work of Jesus himself, and the best clue is in *Jn* 17. Jesus there prays that his disciples may be one (vv. 11-14) and that they may be defended from the Evil One (v.15; cf. 1 *Jn* 2:13,14; 3:12; 5:18,19). For this purpose Jesus sacrificed himself (v.19), and from Cana to the cross Mary shared by spiritual communion in this suffering and sacrifice. The fruit of this sacrifice is that the disciples are to be brought to their home in heaven. 'Father I desire that those whom thou hast given me may be where I am, together with me, that they may gaze upon my glory, which thou hast given me, because thou hast loved me, before the foundation of the world' (v.24). If Mary is the mother of all who love Jesus, then her one desire will be that all her children may never be separated from Jesus or from her, that they may all be in the end united with Jesus, to gaze upon his glory. She is charged to pray the same prayer as Jesus at the Supper, on behalf of 'all his brothers,' the disciples whom Jesus loves. And correspondingly, the disciples are charged to look upon this woman who stood faithful beside the Crucified as *their* mother, if they would be truly one with their dying Saviour.[28]

Another exegete Ralph Russell reaches the same kind of conclusion:

John records five episodes at the cross: the title, proclaiming Jesus as King of the Jews, the parting of his garments

---

[28]   John McHugh, *The Mother of Jesus in the New Testament*, 372-8.

and casting of lots on his tunic, this one, 'I thirst,' and the piercing of his side, no bone being broken. The other four fulfil prophecies which converge upon Calvary (cf. Ps. 21:19; 69:21; Exoc. 12:46; Zech. 12:10); and our passage would also appear to refer to prophecy because John continues: 'After this Jesus knowing that all was not completed' and 'completed' would ordinarily refer to the fulfilment of his Father's will expressed in prophecy. What prophecy? The key word 'Woman' takes us back to Genesis 3:15 - 'I will put enmity between you (the serpent) and the woman, and between your seed and her seed. He shall bruise your head and you shall bruise his heel.' The combat between the woman and her seed (man, and ultimately Christ) against the devil and his seed ('you are of your father the devil' [John 8:44]), culminates on the cross. Then 'the ruler of this world is cast down' and Jesus 'lifted up from the earth draws all men to himself (John 12:31 f.). Standing by the redeemer, the second Adam, is his mother, the second Eve.

'Woman, behold your son' and to the beloved disciple 'behold your mother.' Distinguished Anglican scholars (Hoskyns, Lightfoot), besides some Roman Catholics, suggest that in a text to which St. John attaches such importance on Calvary more is involved than *simply* asking the disciple to look after his mother. For one thing, it is his mother whom Jesus addresses first. Then in Genesis 3:20 we find 'Adam called the name of his wife (same word as "woman") Eve, because she was the mother of all the living,' and in a moment John's Gospel by mention of a 'garden' (John 19:41, cf. 20:15) will hint at the new creation. The beloved disciple is real, but like other figures in the Gospel (e.g. Nicodemus), he is also representative. For all the disciples are beloved, as are all who keep Jesus's commandments (14:21).[29]

Concerning *Revelation* 12, Rene Laurentin writes,

The beginning of the passage echoes the prophecy of Is. 7:14 taken up by Mi. 5:1-2. As the *almah* of Isaiah, the

---

[29] Ralph Russell, "The Blessed Virgin Mary in the Bible" in *Mary's Place in Christian Dialogue*, edited by Alberic Stacpoole (Middlegreen, Slough: St. Paul Publications, 1982), 48-9.

woman of the Apocalypse is a sign (*semeion*). But here she appears in her triumph; the moon "under her feet" seems to indicate that she is raised above the vicissitudes of which this constantly changing planet is the symbol. As with Mary in Jn. 19:25-27, this heavenly personage is repeatedly designated by the word "woman" (Apoc. 12:1,4,12,13-17). As with Mary, she is taken to be the Mother of Christ, and mother of the disciples of Christ, who are called "the rest of her children" (Apoc. 12-17). This last term is an echo of Gn. 3:14-15, where also the serpent (Apoc. 12:9 and 14) is at war against "the woman" and "her descendants."[30]

Let us not forget that for 30 years Jesus was "subject" [*Luke* 2:51] to Mary. He is now offering her to us as our Mother. And now that His "hour" has "come" she can now also be the Mediatrix for "the remnant of her seed, which ... have the testimony of Jesus Christ."

The Seven Splendors of Mary in Scripture

A study of Mary in Scripture that is true both to Scripture and to the ancient divinely-protected interpretation of Scripture reveals a seven-dimension portrait of Mary. The same Mary is shown to us from seven perspectives each one of which complements the six others. If we do not understand these seven dimensions - as Christians have from time immemorial - our understanding of the Scriptural Mary will be defective and distorted. The seven dimensions of Mary merely reflect the Splendor of God and we will call them here the Seven Splendors of Mary.

The Salvific Splendor - God's Promise of a Second Eve Whose Seed will Crush Satan

> "And the Lord God said unto the serpent, ... I will enmity between thee and the woman, and between thy seed and her seed; it shall bruise thy head, and thou shalt bruise his heel." [*Genesis* 3:14,15]

---

[30] Rene Laurentin, *A Short Treatise on the Virgin Mary*, 39-40.

The Prophetic Splendor - the Prophecy of the Virgin Birth and the Coming Messiah

"The Lord spake again unto Ahaz, saying, Ask thee a sign of the Lord thy God; ask it either in the depth, or in the height above. But Ahaz said, I will not ask, neither will I tempt the Lord. And he said, Hear ye now, O house of David; Is it a small thing for you to weary men, but will ye weary my God also?

"Therefore the Lord himself shall give you a sign; Behold, a virgin shall conceive, and bear a son, and shall call his name Immanuel." [*Isaiah* 7:10-14].

"For unto us a child is born, unto us a son is given: and the government shall be upon his shoulder: and his name shall be called Wonderful, Counsellor, The mighty God, The everlasting Father, The Prince of Peace. Of the increase of his government and peace there shall be no end, upon the throne of David, and upon his kindgdom, to order it, and to establish it with judgment and with justice from henceforth even for ever." [*Isaiah* 9:6-7].

"But thou, Bethlehem Ephratah, though thou be little among the thousands of Judah, yet out of thee shall he come forth unto me that is to be ruler in Israel, whose goings forth have been from of old, from everlasting. Therefore will he give them up, until the time that she which travaileth hath brought forth: then the remnant of his brethren shall return unto the children of Israel. And he shall stand and feed in the strength of the Lord, in the majesty of the name of the Lord his God; and they shall abide: for now shall he be great unto the ends of the earth. And this man shall be the peace." [*Micah* 5:2-4].

The Maternal Splendor - Mary, Daughter of the Father, Spouse of the Holy Spirit, Mother of the Son

"The angel Gabriel was sent from God unto a city of Galilee, named Nazareth, To a virgin espoused to a man whose name was Joseph, of the house of David; and the virgin's name was Mary. And the angel came in unto her, and said, Hail, thou that art highly favoured, the Lord is with thee:

blessed art thou among women. And when she saw him, she was troubled at his saying, and cast in her mind what manner of salutation this should be. And the angel said unto her, Fear not, Mary: for thou hast found favour with God. And behold thou shalt conceive in thy womb, and bring forth a son, and shalt call his name JESUS. He shall be great, and shall be called the Son of the Highest: and the Lord God shall give unto him the throne of his father David: And he shall reign over the house of Jacob for ever; and of his kingdom there shall be no end... The Holy Ghost shall come upon thee, and the power of the Highest shall overshadow thee: therefore also that holy thing which shall be born of thee shall be called the Son of God... And Mary said, Behold the handmaid of the Lord; be it unto me according to thy word." [*Luke* 1:26-33, 35,38].

"Now the birth of Jesus Christ was on this wise: When as his mother Mary was espoused to Joseph, before they came together, she was found with child of the Holy Ghost." [*Matthew* 1:18].

"Elisabeth was filled with the Holy Ghost: and she spake out with a loud voice, and said, blessed art thou among women, and blessed is the fruit of thy womb. And whence is this to me, that the mother of my Lord should come to me? ... *And blessed is she that believed.*" [*Luke* 2:41-43,45].

"But when the fulness of the time was come, God sent forth his Son, made of a woman, made under the law, To redeem them that were under the law, that we might receive the adoption of sons." [*Galatians* 4:4-5].

"And he went down with them, and came to Nazareth, and was subject unto them." [*Luke* 2:51],

The Merciful Splendor - Mary in the Public Ministry of Jesus

"And when they found him not, they turned back again to Jerusalem, seeking him ... And when they saw him, they were amazed: and his mother said unto him, Son why hast thou thus dealt with us? behold thy father and I have sought thee sorrowing. And he said unto them, How is it that ye sought me? wist ye not that I must be about my Father's business. And they understood not the saying which he spoke to them. And he went down with them, and came to Nazareth, and was subject unto them: but his mother kept all these sayings in her heart." [*Luke* 2:45-9].

"While he yet talked to the people, behold, his mother and his brethren stood without, desiring to speak with him. Then one said unto him, Behold, thy mother and thy brethren stand without, desiring to speak with thee." [*Matthew* 12:46-7].

"There came then his brethren and his mother, and standing without, sent unto him, calling him. And the multitude sat about him, and they said unto him, Behold thy mother and thy brethren without seek for thee." [*Mark* 3:31-2].

"Then came to him his mother and his brethren, and could not come at him for the press. And it was told him by certain which said, Thy mother and thy brethren stand without, desiring to see thee." [*Luke* 8:19, 20].

"And when they wanted wine, the mother of Jesus saith unto him, They have no wine ... His mother saith unto the servants, Whatsoever he saith unto you, do it." [*John* 2:3,5]

The Sorrowful Splendor - Mary at the Foot of the Cross Crowned as the Mother of All the Faithful

"And Simeon blessed them, and said unto Mary ... A sword shall pierce through thy own soul also." [*Luke* 2:34-35].

"In the midst of the elders, stood a Lamb as it had been slain." [*Revelation* 5:5].

"And she being with child cried." [*Revelation* 12:2].

"Now there stood by the cross of Jesus his mother ... When Jesus therefore saw his mother, and the disciple standing by, whom he loved, he saith unto his mother, Woman, behold thy son! Then saith he to the disciple, Behold thy mother." [*John* 19:25-27].

The Holy Splendor - Mary at Pentecost

> "These all continued with one accord in prayer and supplication. with the women, and Mary the mother of Jesus ... And when the day of Pentecost was fully come, they were all with one accord in one place... And there appeared unto them cloven tongues like as of fire, and it sat upon each of them. And they were all filled with the Holy Ghost." [*Acts* 1:14, 2:3-4].

The Heavenly Splendor - the Second Eve Continues Her Mission in the War with the Dragon until the Final Consummation of the Wedding Feast of the Lamb

> "And there appeared a great wonder in heaven; a woman clothed with the sun, and the moon under her feet, and upon her head a crown of twelve stars: And she being with child cried ... and the dragon stood before the woman which was ready to be delivered, for to devour her child as soon as it was born. And she brought forth a man child, who was to rule all nations with a rod of iron ... And the dragon was wroth with the woman, and went to make war with the remnant of her seed, which keep the commandments of God, and have the testimony of Jesus Christ." [*Revelation* 12].

> "The marriage of the Lamb is come, and his wife hath made herself ready ... Blessed are they which are called unto the marriage supper of the Lamb." [*Revelation* 19:7,19].

The first dimension of Mary, her first Splendor, is the Salvific Splendor. This is her role as the New Eve prophesied in Genesis and manifested throughout Scripture. This dimension of Mary was celebrated by the earliest Church Fathers and became the starting-point of all Marian doctrine and devotion.

The second dimension is the Prophetic Splendor. Mary was foreshadowed not just in *Genesis*, and not even just in *Isaiah* and *Micah*, but in a multitude of layers in the Old Testament ranging from the Daughter of Zion theme to specific individuals such as Abraham. Again this scriptural backdrop was noted by the ancient Christians.

Thirdly we have the Maternal Splendor - a dimension that manifests her both as the Spouse of the Holy Spirit and the Virgin

Mother of the Word Incarnate. We see how the Salvific and the Prophetic Splendors lead inexorably to the Maternal Splendor.

Fourth is the Merciful Splendor. It is this fourth dimension of Mary that has been entirely lost by Fundamentalists and Liberals in their reading of Scripture. As a result these Christians today disparage Mary using the same texts that drew the historic Christian community to the merciful mother. Only a recovery of this lost dimension can help the Christians of today to come to grips with the Scriptural Mary.

Fifth there is the Sorrowful Splendor which in a sense reflects both the Maternal and Merciful Splendors. Who can gauge the sorrow of a mother whose Son is humiliated and rejected by His and her people and then subjected to public torture and a cruel death? This sorrow is magnified with the spiritual death of any of the children entrusted to her by her Son.

Sixth is the Holy Splendor. Mary is the Spouse of the Holy Spirit and of the six direct interventions of the Holy Spirit in Scripture Mary is present at four and enters into the deepest possible intimacy with the Spirit in the first intervention.

The Seventh Splendor, the Heavenly, is the culmination of all the others. From "All generations shall call me blessed" to "the woman clothed with the sun" to the great "wedding feast of the Lamb," Scripture tells us of the highest honors bestowed on Mary by the Almighty. The traditional Christian doctrines of Mary's Assumption and her coronation as Queen simply echo the undeniable testimony of Scripture.

This seven-splendored story was the story of Mary that the Fathers of the Church and *all* Christians for 1600 years saw in Scripture and this is still the story grasped by *the vast majority* of Christians to this day in the Holy Bible. The glorious tapestry of Mary's mission woven in the Word of God gave rise to the great Marian titles and devotions of the centuries. The Fathers recognized in Mary a bridge between the Old and the New Testaments, a Second Eve whose cooperation with the Second Adam was foretold and fulfilled. For our part, we cannot know the truth about Mary if we do not contemplate and appropriate each one of the seven scriptural splendors of Mary. If Mary is seen in the light of only one or a few of the seven splendors, the Mary we see is not the Mary of either Scripture or the Historic Christian Faith.

B. FUNDAMENTALISM AND THE HISTORIC CHRISTIAN FAITH

Fundamentalism represents a break from the Historic Christian Faith that in turn led to various "human traditions," rejections of the doctrine of the Trinity (and other basic doctrines), Liberalism, the Cults and 22,000+ denominations.

The Historic Christian Faith

Foundations of the Body of Teaching that is the Historic Christian Faith:

- Scripture
- The Apostolic Community
- The Fathers
- The Councils
- The Creeds
- The Authorized Interpretation of Scripture
  [The Inerrant Interpretation of the Inerrant Word of God]

Teachings of the Historic Christian Faith:

- God is the Holy Trinity, Three Divine Persons Sharing One Divine Nature
- Jesus Christ is fully God and fully Man, a divine Person Who united Himself to a human nature while retaining His divine Nature
- Mary is the perpetually virgin Mother of God who was immaculately conceived, assumed body and soul into Heaven, and now intercedes for her children with her Son
- God desires the salvation of all men and has endowed all men with the freedom to accept or reject Him for all eternity. Salvation is possible for those who accept the divine invitation because, by His death on the cross, Jesus Christ made the supreme and all-sufficient Atonement for Original Sin. Men, in turn, have the freedom to participate in God's plan of salvation (through His grace) by bringing the Good News to all mankind.

The teachings of the Historic Christian Faith were accepted by the churches of the East and the West until the time of the Protestant Reformation. Although the Protestant Reformers accepted most of the teachings of the Historic Faith, with their doctrines of *sola scriptura* [scripture alone], *sola fidei* [faith alone] and *sola Christus* [Christ alone] they introduced the idea of the private interpretation of scripture and the notion that salvation comes not from man's free choice for or against God but from God's predestination of a few men to salvation and the vast majority of men to damnation; moreover those who turned to God, in this view, did not freely and therefore commendably mediate His message of salvation but were passive instruments. About the doctrine of private interpretation Luther himself later said:

> There are as many sects and beliefs as there are heads. This fellow will have nothing to do with baptism; another denies the sacraments; a third believes that there is another world between this and the Last Day. Some teach that Christ is not God; some say this, some say that. There is no rustic so rude but that, if he dreams or fancies anything, it must be the whisper of the Holy Ghost, and he himself a prophet.

About the doctrine of salvation-by-predestination, Calvin said "Eternal life is foreordained for some, and eternal damnation for others. Every man is created for one or the other of these ends ... He is predestinated either to life or to death." Of this doctrine [which he embraced through his sola fidei principle], Luther wrote: "It seems an iniquitous, cruel, intolerable thought to think of God ... I have stumbled at it myself more than once, down to the deepest pit of despair, so that I wished I had never been made a man."

The doctrines of private interpretation and salvation-by-predestination created Fundamentalism, a set of principles that led to further departures from the Historic Faith and that [especially through the principle of private interpretation] also spawned Liberalism and the Cults. An article titled "Is Evangelicalism Christian?" in *The Evangelical Journal* warns: "In reality, evangelicalism is a variant form of Christianity and one that, due to the dangerously loose lines that connected it to the heritage of the wider historic faith, could now be in danger of losing its grasp of the faith it seemingly holds dear... Evangelicalism as known in the modern world (individualistic, pietistic, missionary) is a child of the enlightenment and thus is disintegrating and dying with the passing of the world of the enlightenment."

Fundamentalism

Principles of Fundamentalism:

Private Interpretation of Scripture
The principle of *Sola Scriptura* or Scripture Alone in practice became the principle of the private interpretation of Scripture. According to this principle any man can interpret Scripture in any way he pleases as long as his feelings tell him that he is being led by the Holy Spirit: this meant there would no authoritative, certain or unified interpretation of Scripture and in practice it created (even among committed Christians) a medley of competing interpretations of the most fundamental texts.

Salvation by Predestination
The principle of *Sola Fidei* or Faith Alone became a doctrine of salvation whereby God deliberately created the vast majority of men with the specific intention of damning them. He damns them by "pre-programming" them for damnation while setting aside a minority of mankind who He will bring to salvation by pre-programming them to have faith in Him. According to this doctrine, men do not have freewill and their free choice plays no role in their salvation or damnation or even in their act of faith in God. God has already predetermined their ultimate destiny.

Pantheistic Denial of All Human Mediation
The principle of *Sola Christus* [Christ Alone] was interpreted to deny any role for human beings in God's scheme of salvation. Everything is done by God through passive instruments; Christian believers are not seen as free and responsible beings who can commendably cooperate with the plan of God ("Well done thou good and faithful servant"). God is the only actor on the stage of salvation.

Fruits of Fundamentalism:

Denial of Central Teachings of the Historic Christian Faith
Once the authoritative nature of the inerrant interpretation of the Historic Christian Faith was denied, Fundamentalists de-

nied various teachings that were considered central to the Faith even by the Reformers. The teachings that were denied include the Marian doctrines of historic Christianity. Because Fundamentalists do not believe it is possible to have any authoritative interpretation of Scripture, they discarded the inerrant scriptural teachings on Mary (and many other inerrant teachings as well). And because Fundamentalist theology portrays man as a robot without freewill, Fundamentalists fail to see the majesty of Mary's free acts of obedience in the scheme of salvation; the salvation or damnation of each and every human being is foreordained by God according to fundamentalism. Many Fundamentalists have also denied the doctrine of the Trinity and many hold views of Christ that were condemned as heresies by the Councils of the New Testament Church. *Christianity Today* (April 18 and May 2, 1980) reported that only two out of five Evangelicals (i.e., 43%) affirm that Jesus Christ is fully God and fully man!

Human Traditions

Although Fundamentalists claim to go by Scripture Alone, in practice their theologies are governed by various unscriptural traditions such as Dispensationalism and Calvinism which have no root in the historic Faith.

22,000+ Denominations

Today there are over 22,000 denominations. This multiplication was inevitable once the doctrine of private interpretation was embraced. Every difference in private interpretation which was supposedly inspired by the Holy Spirit led to the creation of new denominations, most of which have conflicting interpretations of salvation and fundamental Christian doctrines. These 22,000 denominations have promoted every possible interpretation on every theological question: baptism, the Lord's Supper, clergy, marriage and divorce, musical instruments at church, the endtimes, Original Sin, Heaven and Hell, sanctification, sin, the relevance of the Old Testament, the gifts of the Spirit, the dispensations, miracles, the Holy Trinity and on and on. Since no interpretation is authoritative or definitive, there is no possibility of certainty or finality about any aspect of the Christian revelation.

Liberalism

Fundamentalists deny the inerrant interpretation of the inerrant Word of God. Once this step has been made, the next logical step is to deny the Bible as the inerrant Word of God. This is what Liberalism has done. While Fundamentalism makes doctrinal absolutes impossible, Liberalism questions all absolutism and this conveniently means there are no moral absolutes. At the root of both Fundamentalism and Liberalism lies the principle of private interpretation. Although Liberalism came before modern American Fundamentalism, the private interpretation principle of earlier varieties of Fundamentalism was the root inspiration of Liberalism.

Cults

At the origin of every cult is an individual who developed his own interpretation of various passages in Scripture, an interpretation which he then used in attracting followers. These interpretations invariably contradicted the historic Faith. The cults emerged once the Fundamentalist doctrine of private interpration became accepted and many cultists are former Fundamentalists. Since both Fundamentalism and the cults rest on the principle of private interpretation it is obvious that Fundamentalists can be drawn into the cults once they are persuaded by ingenious cultists that their previous interpretations are flawed unlike those of the cultists. The only authority the Fundamentalist respects is his own interpretation of Scripture and not the historic interpretation. Once he sees reason to change his own interpretation he goes wherever the new interpretation takes him. All cults deny the doctrine of the Trinity and other central doctrines of the historic Faith.

Between the two extremes of Pelagianism (Liberalism) and Pantheism (Calvinistic Fundamentalism) is the teaching of the Historic Christian Faith: we are creatures made in the image of God and our Creator seeks to bring us to salvation. We cannot accept the divine invitation without the grace of God. But we can refuse this grace - and be damned. Marian doctrine and devotion preserve this great teaching of the historic Faith as well the great Christological and Trinitarian doctrines.

MARY AND THE PROTESTANT REFORMATION:
Acceptance of Fundamental Marian Doctrines by the Founding Fathers of the Reformation

Imagine that a historian uncovers documents showing Karl Marx to be a devout Christian believer. This discovery would come as a shock since Marxism and Marxists are known to be implacably hostile to all forms of religion. No such discovery has, of course, been made but there is a discovery of comparably shocking proportions that Protestant Fundamentalists have yet to make about the Founding Fathers of the Protestant Reformation. When Fundamentalists study the writings of the Reformers on Mary, the Mother of Jesus, they will find that the Reformers accepted almost every major Marian doctrine and considered these doctrines to be both scriptural and fundamental to the historic Christian Faith.

Almost all Fundamentalist scholars and leaders, on the other hand, have rejected the very same Marian doctrines that were considered fundamental to the Christian interpretation of Scripture by the fathers of the Reformation. This departure from the "faith of their fathers" will appear disturbing to any thoughtful Fundamentalist. The Reformation was spearheaded and guided by Martin Luther, John Calvin and Ulrich Zwingli. Their principles continue to be affirmed and proclaimed by today's Fundamentalists. But such affirmations are mere lipservice if they do not include any reference to what the Reformers thought about the Mother of Jesus - particularly because the Reformers, like the great Christian thinkers of the early Church, saw intrinsic links between Marian doctrines and the Chrisological doctrines. Unfortunately the Marian teachings and preachings of the Reformers have been "covered up" by their most zealous followers - with damaging theological and practical consequences. This "cover-up" can be detected even in **Chosen by God: Mary in Evangelical Perspective**, an Evangelical critique of Mariology. One of the contributors admits that "Most remarkable to modern Protestants is the Reformers' almost universal acceptance of Mary's continuing virginity, and their widespread reluctance to declare Mary a sinner." He then asks if it is "a favourable providence" that kept these Marian teachings of the Reformers from being "transmitted to the Protestant churches"![31]

At this stage the fiercer Fundamentalists may halt further discussion with the declaration that the teachings of the Reformers are entirely irrelevant. For them, they claim, neither creed nor council, neither church nor exegete carry any weight whatsoever. For them the only reliable authority in biblical interpretation is the internal testimony of the Holy Spirit. In preferring their interpretations to the interpretations of the Reformers, they will say, they are remaining true to the spirit of the Reformation. Dramatic though it sounds, this fervent affirmation merely avoids the question at issue and provides a formula for anarchy and heresy as well.

The doctrine-rejecting mindset and strategy of the Protestant Fundamentalist has dangerous consequences. If the historic Christian Faith has no authoritative role in their theological systems, then literally any traditional doctrine is up for grabs. The notion that such fundamental doctrines as the doctrine of the Trinity is "obvious" to anyone who reads Scripture turns out to be entirely false in practice - there are Fundamentalists and theological Liberals who do not accept this doctrine despite their intensive study of Scripture. Even more dangerous is the well-known fact that Fundamentalists in particular (as some of their leaders have confessed) are the easiest of prey for non-Trinitarian cults such as the Oneness Pentecostals, Jehovah's Witnesses and Mormons. Lacking any concept of authoritative interpretations of Scripture they are easily brow-beaten into the interpretation fervently pushed by the "Bible-only" Jehovah's Witness at the door.

---

[31]   David F. Wright, ed., *Chosen by God: Mary in Evangelical Perspective* (London: Marshall Pickering, 1989), 180.

We will be considering the question of the Authorized Interpretation of Scripture in the next three chapters. Here we will note that Fundamentalists usually cite the authority of the Protestant Reformers, especially Luther and Calvin, when they defend their interpretations of Scripture. Accordingly they cannot turn a deaf ear to the Reformers' understanding of Mary in Scripture. Here we will see what the first Protestants said about Mary:

Luther:

Mary the Mother of God - Throughout his life Luther maintained without change the historic Christian affirmation that Mary was the Mother of God:

> "St. Paul (Galatians 4:4) says, 'God sent his Son born of a woman.' These words which I hold for true, really sustain quite firmly that Mary is the Mother of God.'"[32]

> "The council [Ephesus] has not offered anything new to faith but has strengthened the old faith against the new arrogance of Nestorius. This article of faith - that Mary is the Mother of God - is present in the Church from the beginning and is not a new creation of the Council but the presentation of the Gospel and Scriptures."[33]

> "She is rightly called not only the mother of the man, but also the Mother of God ... It is certain that Mary is the Mother of the real and true God."[34]

Perpetual Virginity - Again throughout his life Luther held that Mary's perpetual virginity was an article of faith for all Christians - and interpreted Galatians 4:4 to mean that Christ was "born of a woman" alone.

---

[32] Martin Luther, Weimar edition of *Martin Luther's Works* (Translation by William J. Cole), 50, p. 592, line 5.

[33] Martin Luther, Weimar edition of *Martin Luther's Works*, English translation edited by J. Pelikan [Concordia: St. Louis], volume 7, 572.

[34] Martin Luther, Weimar edition of *Martin Luther's Works*, English translation edited by J. Pelikan [Concordia: St. Louis], volume 24, 107.

"It is an article of faith that Mary is Mother of the Lord and still a Virgin."[35]

Luther was a severe critic of Helvidius who questioned the perpetual virginity of Mary. Concerning the attempt of some to interpret Scriptural verses as teaching that Mary had other children, Luther explained that these were relatives.

After Mary "knew that she was the Mother of the Son of God, she did not wish to become the mother of the son of man, but remained in that gift."[36]

"Undoubtedly there is no one so powerful that, depending on his own intelligence, without Scripture, he would maintain that she did not remain a Virgin."[37]

The Immaculate Conception - Yet again the Immaculate Conception was a doctrine Luther defended to his death (as confirmed by Lutheran scholars like Arthur Piepkorn). Like Augustine, Luther saw an unbreakable link between Mary's divine maternity, perpetual virginity and Immaculate Conception. Although his formulation of the doctrine of the Immaculate Conception was not clearcut, he held that her soul was devoid of sin from the beginning:

"But the other conception, namely the infusion of the soul, it is piously and suitably believed, was without any sin, so that while the soul was being infused, she would at the same time be cleansed from original sin and adorned with the gifts of God to receive the holy soul thus infused. And thus, in the very moment in which she began to live, she was without all sin..."[38]

"God has formed the soul and body of the Virgin Mary full of the Holy Spirit, so that she is without all sins, for she has conceived and borne the Lord Jesus."[39]

---

[35] Martin Luther, op. cit., Volume 11, 319-320.
[36] Martin Luther, Weimar edition of *Martin Luther's Works* (Translation by William J. Cole), 11, p. 320.
[37] Martin Luther, Weimar edition of *Martin Luther's Works* (Translation by William J. Cole) 11, p. 320.
[38] Martin Luther, ibid., Volume 4, 694.
[39] Martin Luther, ibid., Volume 52, 39.

Assumption - Although he did not make it an article of faith, Luther said of the doctrine of the Assumption:

> "There can be no doubt that the Virgin Mary is in heaven.
> How it happened we do not know."[40]

Honor to Mary - Despite his unremitting criticism of the traditional doctrines of Marian mediation and intercession, to the end Luther continued to proclaim that Mary should be honored. He made it a point to preach on her feast days.

> "The veneration of Mary is inscribed in the very depths of the human heart."[41]

> "Is Christ only to be adored? Or is the holy Mother of God rather not to be honoured? This is the woman who crushed the Serpent's head. Hear us. For your Son denies you nothing."[42]

Luther made this statement in his last sermon at Wittenberg in January 1546.

Images of Mary

> "One cannot grasp spiritual things unless images are made of them."[43]

> "Nothing else can be drawn from the words: 'Thou shalt have no strange gods before me' except what relates to idolatry. But where pictures or sculptures are made without idolatry, the making of such things is not forbidden."[44]

---

40 [Martin Luther, Weimar edition of *Martin Luther's Works* (Translation by William J. Cole) 10, p. 268.

41 [Martin Luther, Weimar edition of *Martin Luther's Works* (Translation by William J. Cole) 10, III, p.313.

42 Martin Luther, ibid., Volume 51, 128-129.

43 Martin Luther, Weimar edition of *Martin Luther's Works* (Translation by William J. Cole) 46, p.308.

44 Martin Luther, Weimar edition of *Martin Luther's Works* (Translation by William J. Cole) 18, p. 69.

"If I have a painted picture on the wall and I look upon it without idolatry, that is not forbidden to me and should not be taken away from me."[45]

Luther was, in fact, buried in a tomb with a sculpture of the coronation of Mary in Heaven by the Holy Trinity.

Mother of All Christians

"Mary is the Mother of Jesus and the mother of us all. If Christ is ours, we must be where he is; and all that he has must be ours, and his mother is therefore also ours."[46]

"We are the children of Mary."[47]

Calvin:

It has been said that John Calvin belonged to the second generation of the Reformers and certainly his theology of double predestination governed his views on Marian and all other Christian doctrine . Although Calvin was not as profuse in his praise of Mary as Martin Luther he did not deny her perpetual virginity. The term he used most commonly in referring to Mary was "Holy Virgin."

"Elizabeth called Mary Mother of the Lord because the unity of the person in the two natures of Christ was such that she could have said that the mortal man engendered in the womb of Mary was at the same time the eternal God."[48]

"Helvidius has shown himself too ignorant, in saying that Mary had several sons, because mention is made in some passages of the brothers of Christ."[49]

---

[45] Martin Luther, Weimar edition of *Martin Luther's Works* (Translation by William J. Cole) 28, p.677.

[46] *Luther's Works* (Weimar), 29:655:26-656:7.

[47] *Luther's Works* (Weimar), 11:224:8.

[48] John Calvin, *Calvini Opera* [Braunshweig-Berlin, 1863-1900], Volume 45, 35.

[49] Bernard Leeming, "Protestants and Our Lady", *Marian Library Studies*, January 1967, p.9.

Calvin translated "brothers" in this context to mean cousins or relatives.

> "It cannot be denied that God in choosing and destining Mary to be the Mother of his Son, granted her the highest honor."[50]

> "To this day we cannot enjoy the blessing brought to us in Christ without thinking at the same time of that which God gave as adornment and honour to Mary, in willing her to be the mother of his only-begotten Son."[51]

> "Let us act as did the Virgin Mary and say 'Lord let it be done unto me according to your word' ... We see then the instruction that is given to us here by the Virgin Mary who will be to us a good teacher, provided that we take advantage of her lessons as it becomes us."[52]

Zwingli:

> "It was given to her what belongs to no creature, that in the flesh she should bring forth the Son of God."[53]

> "I firmly believe that Mary, according to the words of the gospel as a pure Virgin brought forth for us the Son of God and in childbirth and after childbirth forever remained a pure, intact Virgin."[54]

Zwingli used *Exodus* 44:2 to defend the doctrine of Mary's perpetual virginity.

> "I esteem immensely the Mother of God, the ever chaste, immaculate Virgin Mary."[55]

---

50 John Calvin, *Calvini Opera* [Braunshweig-Berlin, 1863-1900], Volume 45, 348.
51 John Calvin, *A Harmony of Matthew, Mark and Luke* (St. Andrew's Press, Edinburgh, 1972), p.32.
52 John Calvin, *Calvini Opera*, op. cit., Volume 1, 320 ff).
53 Ulrich Zwingli, *In Evang. Luc., Opera Completa* [Zurich, 1828-42], Volume 6, I, 639
54 Ulrich Zwingli, *Zwingli Opera, Corpus Reformatorum*, Volume 1, 424.
55 E. Stakemeier, *De Mariologia et Oecumenismo*, K. Balic, ed., (Rome, 1962), 456.

"Christ ... was born of a most undefiled Virgin.[56]

"It was fitting that such a holy Son should have a holy Mother."[57]

"The more the honor and love of Christ increases among men, so much the esteem and honor given to Mary should grow."[58]

Bullinger [Cranmer's brother-in-law and successor of Zwingli]:

Mary's "sacrosanct body was borne by angels into heaven."[59]

"She can hardly be compared with any of the other saints, but should by rights be elevated above all of them."[60]

It must not be thought that all the Reformers shared the same views on Mary or that there was no change in their later thought. For this reason we cite here only statements on the positions they consistently held in their post-Reformation writings. The most drastic Mariological differences between the Reformers and the Historic Christian Faith centered on the participation of Mary in God's plan of salvation - but these differences sprang from the Reformers' position on salvation and not from Mary as such. These differences on Marian mediation will be spotlighted in the chapter **Once Saved Always Saved**.

We should also cite here the views of Reformers in England on Mary. Hughes Latimer, Miles Coverdale and Robert Barnes accepted the doctrine of Mary's perpetual virginity using *Exodus* 44. Latimer was a defender of the Immaculate Conception.[61]

---

56 Ibid.
57 Ibid.
58 Ulrich Zwingli, *Zwingli Opera, Corpus Reformatorum*, Volume 1, 427-428.
59 Thomas O'Meara, *Mary in Protestant and Catholic Theology* (New York: Sheed and Ward, 1965), p.178-9.
60 Max Thurian, *Mary, Mother of All Christians* (New York: Herder and Herder, 1964), p. 89.
61 Peter Stravinskas, "The Place of Mary in Classical Fundamentalism", *Faith and Reason*, Spring 1994, p.15].

The Anglican Chancellor of Chichester Cathedral has written that,

> "In the great sermons and meditations of these men, Lancelot
> Andrewes, Jeremy Taylor, Mark Frank and their contempo-
> raries, a tender devotion to Mary and a deep appreciation
> for her role in the mystery of redemption are expressed. So
> many of the classic themes of Catholic mariology are also
> articulated here: Mary is Mother of God, Ever Virgin, the
> Second Eve, (even Star of the Sea!), Full of Grace, Free
> from Sin and the Model of all Christian virtues, especially
> of faith, humility and obedience."[62]

We quote below some of the major statements of the English Reformers:

Perpetual Virginity

Jeremy Taylor:

And He that came from His grave fast tied with a stone and a
signature, and into the college of the apostles 'the doors being
shut,' and into the glories of His Father through the solid orbs
of all the firmament, came also (as the Church piously believes)
into the world so without doing violence to the virginal and
pure body of His mother, that He did also leave her virginity
entire, to be a seal, that none might open the gate of that sanctuary; that it might be fulfilled which was spoken of the Lord
by the prophet 'This gate shall be shut, it shall not be opened,
and no man shall enter in by it; because the Lord God of Israel
hath entered by it, therefore it shall be shut.' (Ezek 44:2.).[63]

George Bull:

Now the necessary consequence of this dignity of the blessed
Virgin [viz., that she was the Mother of God] is that she re-

---

[62] Roger Greenacre, "Mother Out of Sight" (Wallington, Surrey: Ecumenical
Society for the Blessed Virgin Mary, 1990), 8.

[63] Quoted in A.M. Allchin, "Seventeenth Century Anglican Theology," in *The
Blessed Virgin Mary: Essays by Anglican Writers*, E.L. Mascall and H.S. Box,
eds. (London: Darton, Longman & Todd Ltd, 1963), 61.

mained for ever a virgin, as the catholic church hath always held and maintained. For it cannot with decency be imagined, that the most holy vessel, which was thus once consecrated to be a receptacle of the Deity, should afterwards be desecrated and profaned by human use.[64]

John Wesley:

"I believe that he (the Son of God) was made man, joining the human nature with the divine in one person, being conceived by the singular operation of the Holy Ghost and born of the Blessed Virgin Mary, who, as well after as when she brought him forth, continued a pure and unspotted virgin."[65]

Immaculate Conception

Thomas Ken, Bishop of Bath and Wells [1637-1711]:

The Holy Ghost his temple in her built,
Cleansed from congenial, kept from mortal guilt,
And from the moment that her blood was fired,
Into her heart Celestial Love inspired.[66]

Francis Quarles (1592-1644) and Abraham Cowley (1618-1667):

Hail, Blessed Virgin, full of heavenly grace,
Blest above all that sprang from human race.[67]

Mark Frank (1613-1664):

He is not with her, as he is with any else. *Tecum* in mente, tecum *in ventre* as the Fathers gloss it; *Tecum* in spiritu, *tecum in carne,* with her he was, or would be presently, as well in her body as in her soul, personally, essentially, nay bodily with her, and take a body from her - a way of being with any never

---

[64] Ibid., 61.
[65] John Wesley, *Letter to a Roman Catholic.*
[66] Quoted in D. Nicholson, "The Caroline Divines and the Blessed Virgin Mary" (Wallington, Surrey: Ecumenical Society for the Blessed Virgin Mary, 1969), 12.
[67] Ibid., 12.

heard before or since - a being with her beyond any expression or conception whatsoever. And the Lord thus being with her, all good must needs be with her: all the gracious ways of his being with us are comprehended in it; so the salutation no way to be exceeded. And well may he choose to be with her - even make haste and prevent the Angel, as St Bernard speaks, to be with her. He is with 'the pure of heart,' with the humble spirit, and piously retired soul, and she is all...

Maria is *maris stella* says St Bede: 'the star of the sea'; a fit name for the mother of the bright Morning Star that rises out of the vast sea of God's infinite and endless love. Maria, the Syriac inteprets Domina, 'a lady,' a name yet retained and given to her by all Christians; our lady, or the Lady Mother of our Lord. Maria, rendered by Petrus Damiani, *de monte et altitudine Dei*, highly exalted, as you would say, like the mountain of God, in which he would vouchsafe to dwell, after a more miraculous manner than in very Sion, his 'own holy mount.' St Ambrose interprets it, *Deus ex genere meo*, 'God of my kin'; as if by her very name she was designed to have God born of her, to be Deipara, as the Church, against all heretics, has ever styled her, the Mother of God.

'Thou that art highly favoured' so our new translation renders it; 'full of grace,' so our old one hath it, from the Latin *gratia plena*; and both right ... Grace is favour; God's grace is divine favour; high in grace, high in his favour; full of his grace, full of his favour; all comes to one.

Created grace is either sanctifying or edifying; the gifts of the Holy Spirit that sanctify and make us holy; or the gifts that make us serviceable to make others so ... Of each kind she had her fullness according to her measure, and the designation that God appointed her. For sanctifying graces, none fuller, *solo Deo excepto*, 'God only excepted,' saith Epiphanius. And it is fit enough to believe that she who was so highly honoured to have her womb filled with the body of the Lord, and her soul as fully filled by the Holy Ghost.[68]

---

68 Quoted in A.M. Allchin, "Seventeenth Century Anglican Theology," op. cit.,70-1.

Alexander Nowells (Dean of St Paul's in the latter part of the sixteenth century):

In the serpent's head lieth all his venom, and the whole of his life and force. Therefore do I take the serpent's head to betoken the whole power and kingdom, or more truly the tyranny, of the old serpent the devil. The seed... is Jesus Christ, the Son of God, very God and very man: conceived of the Holy Ghost: engendered of the womb and substance of Mary, the blessed, pure and undefiled maid: and was so born and fostered by her as other babes be, saving that he was most far from all infection of sin.[69]

William Fulke (Puritan Master of Pembroke Hall, Cambridge, in the 1570s):

The salutation of the Virgin may be said still, either in Latin or in English ... 'Hail Mary, freely beloved' ... 'that art high in favour' denies not that the Virgin Mary, of God's special goodness without her merits, as she confesseth, was filled with all gracious gifts of the Holy Spirit, as much as any mortal creature might be, except our Saviour Christ.[70]

William Wordsworth:

Woman! above all women glorified,
Our tainted nature's solitary boast.[71]

Assumption

Thomas Ken, Anglican Bishop of Bath and Wells [1637-1711]:

Heaven with transcendent joys her entrance graced
Next to his throne, her Son his mother placed
And here below, now she's of heaven posssess'd
All generations are to call her bless'd.[72]

---

[69] Quoted in Ralph Townsend, "The Place of Mary in Early Anglican Thought" (Wallington, Surrey: Ecumenical Society for the Blessed Virgin Mary, 1983), 3.
[70] Ibid., 5.
[71] Quoted in D. Nicholson, "The Caroline Divines and the Blessed Virgin Mary," op. cit., 13.
[72] Ibid., 13.

Veneration

Pearson of Chester [17th century]:

We cannot bear too reverend a regard unto the Mother of our Lord, so long as we give her not that worship which is due unto the Lord himself. Let us keep the language of the primitive Church; let her be honoured and esteemed, let him be worshipped and adored.[73]

Miles Coverdale (16th century; at the end of his life Bishop of Exeter and leader of the Puritan party):

Call her as God's word teacheth you, full of grace, blessed, immaculate virgin etc. Pray to God that ye may follow the steps of her constant faith, her fervent charity, and godly love, her most meek and humble behaviour, her unfeigned truth.[74]

Mark Frank:

Thou that art highly favoured, but why *thou* without a name? He forbears it out of reverence to her. We use not to salute great persons by their names but by their titles. We must not be too familiar with those whom God so highly favours: that is our lesson hence. We are not to speak of the Blessed Virgin, the Apostles and Saints as if we were speaking to our servants: Peter, Paul, Mary or the like. It is a new fashion of religion to unsaint the saints, to deny them their proper titles, to level them with the meanest of our servants. We might learn better manners from the angel here, manners, I say, if it were nothing else![75]

We might wonder why the Marian affirmations of the Reformers did not survive in the teaching of their heirs - particularly the Fundamentalists. This break with the past did not come through any new discovery or revelation. The Reformers themselves [see above] took a benign even positive view of Marian doctrine - although they did reject Marian mediation because of their rejection of all

---

73 Ibid., 10.
74 Quoted in Ralph Townsend, "The Place of Mary in Early Anglican Thought", op. cit., 3.
75 Quoted in D. Nicholson, "The Caroline Divines and the Blessed Virgin Mary," op. cit., 11.

human mediation. Moreover, while there were some excesses in popular Marian piety, Marian doctrine as taught in the pre-Reformation era drew its inspiration from the witness of Scripture and was rooted in Christology. The real reason for the break with the past must be attributed to the iconoclastic passion of the followers of the Reformation and the consequences of some Reformation principles. The Reformation formulas of *sola scriptura* [Scripture Alone], *sola fidei* [Faith Alone] and *sola Christus* [Christ Alone] were relentlessly applied to every traditional Christian doctrine by the followers of Luther, Calvin and Zwingli. In practice *sola scriptura* resulted in a doctrine of private interpretation which resulted in the splintering of the unified body of Christian doctrine. And *sola fidei* and *sola Christus* ended up as doctrines denying all human response to God thus giving a "puppet" view of man. Even doctrines certified as authentically Christian by the first Protestants were dropped by the next generation. Since there were no checks and balances to this process and it was simply a matter of one man's interpretation against another's, there was no hope of retaining the traditional interpretations and declarations of the Historic Christian Faith. Hence, along with numerous other ancient teachings and insights, Marian doctrine and devotion were cast aside by many Protestants in the post-Reformation era.

We must not minimize here the significance of the Reformers own break with the ancient doctrine of Marian mediation. The assertions of *sola fidei* and *sola Christus* essentially ended any idea that human beings are capable of free actions. Since the time of the earliest Fathers, it was believed that Mary's greatest and most commendable act was her acceptance of the divine invitation to bear the Son of God, a free act of obedience that made her the New Eve. As a result of her obedience, she became the Mother of God and, subsequently, the spiritual Mother of all Christians interceding on their behalf. The Reformers accepted one "effect" [that Mary was the Mother of God] but not the "cause" [her free act of obedience]. Neither did they accept the second "effect" [her intercession - although Luther admitted that she was the spiritual mother of Christians and may have retained a minimal idea of Marian intercession]. According to both Luther and Calvin, God had "preprogrammed" all the choices and actions of all human beings. Thus there is no freedom, responsibility or merit. The unfortunate consequences of this particular view of God and man are explored in great detail in **Once Saved Always Saved**. But it cannot be denied that the elimination of freedom had a negative effect on the post-Reformation understanding of Marian doctrine - although the Reformers themselves upheld Mary's personal holiness, perpetual virginity and divine maternity.

Even more influential in the break with Mary was the influence of the Enlightenment Era which essentially questioned or denied the mysteries of faith. A famous Lutheran theologian Friedrich Heiler has written that the Marian doctrines were lost by later Protestants because of "the spirit of the enlightenment with its lack of understanding of mystery, and especially of the mystery of the Incarnation, which in the 18th century began the work of destruction."[76] Another Lutheran scholar, Basilea Schlink, holds that "the majority of us [Protestants] have drifted away from the proper attitude towards her [Mary], which Martin Luther had indicated to us on the basis of Holy Scripture ... [partially due to the rise of Rationalism which] has lost the sense of the sacred. In Rationalism man sought to comprehend everything, and that which he could not comprehend he rejected. Because Rationalism accepted only that which could be explained rationally, Church festivals in honor of Mary and everything else reminiscent of her were done away with in the Protestant Church. All biblical relationship to the Mother Mary was lost, and we are still suffering from this heritage."[77]

---

[76] "Die Gottesmutter im Glauben und Beten der Jahrhunderte," *Hochkirche* 13 (1931), p. 200.

[77] Basilea Schlink, *Mary, the Mother of Jesus* (London: Marshall Pickering, 1986), 114-115.

PART II

STARTING POINTS

-1-

THE ORIGIN OF THE NEW TESTAMENT

What is the basis of Marian doctrine and devotion? Christians who accept Marian doctrine see its foundations in Scripture and the historic Christian Faith while Protestant Fundamentalists reject it as unscriptural. In approaching this question our first task is to determine what can be called "scriptural." This takes us to the question of how we got Scripture and how Scripture is to be interpreted [so as to determine "scriptural teaching"].

Our starting-points in this study are five: first, there is *Holy Scripture* itself and here we refer primarily to the 27 New Testament books; second, there is the *Authorized Interpretation* of Holy Scripture, the interpretation of Scripture given us in Councils and Creeds that Christians from the beginning have believed to be inspired by the Holy Spirit and therefore binding; third, there is the *Apostolic Community*, what Catholic, Protestant and Orthodox Christians agree is the "early Church" under the leadership of the Apostles and their successors; fourth, there is the *Historic Christian Faith*, the body of teaching and Christian doctrine that developed over centuries through the Authorized Interpretation and the witness of the Apostolic Community; fifth, there is the *Doctrine of Private Interpretation* often inaccurately called the Sola Scriptura principle, the idea that any man can interpret Scripture in any way he wants.

Almost all Fundamentalists accept the New Testament as the Word of God. On the question of how we got the New Testament and why we believe it to be the Word of God there seems to be widespread ignorance and confusion among Fundamentalists. The situation is even worse when we come to the interpretation of Scripture. Fundamentalists believe that the Bible is self-interpreting and that anyone who asks for the direction of the Holy Spirit can interpret the Bible for himself without reference to any other interpretation. The consequences of this approach will be laid out here.

The prime issue in the Fundamentalist criticism of Marian doctrine is the relationship between the Bible and the divinely guaranteed and preserved interpretation of the Bible that is given us in the historic Christian Faith. The vital role of this divinely protected interpretation of Scripture becomes especially obvious when we examine the source of the "fundamentals" that give Fundamentalists their name: the Bible and in particular the New Testament.

It has often been said that the New Testament did not drop down from Heaven. Nor was it a work of a single human author believed by his followers to be divinely inspired and playing a special role between God and mankind (as is the case with the Koran and Mohammed in the Moslem religion). On the contrary, the New Testament is a collection of writings that came from a variety of authors. Moreover those who hold that the New Testament is divinely inspired are not "followers" of the human authors in the sense of giving them pride of place as the only chosen channels of God who are unique prophets (as is the case with Moslems and Mormons for instance).

It is a fact of history that the books comprising the New Testament were chosen by the Councils of Hippo, Carthage and Florence and that these Councils were authorized and directed by the Apostolic Community, the Church. These books were chosen in preference to a wide variety of other books that claimed to be gospels and lives of Christ and the like. Not only were the Councils recognized as having the authority to decide which of the available gospels were to be incorporated into the canon of Scripture - i.e., to be proclaimed as books inspired by God - but the Councils were also perceived as having the stupendous authority to determine which of the books were divinely inspired. The authority of the Councils was therefore invoked in setting the canon, in discerning the authoritativeness of the various New Testament writings.

Some Fundamentalists may argue that neither the Councils nor the Apostolic Community did the selecting but that it was the Holy

Spirit Who set the canon. This argument misses the point because the question here is not *whether* the Holy Spirit is operative in this activity of selection but *how* the Holy Spirit chose to act. The question here is: *what or who was the chosen instrument of the Holy Spirit in defining the canon of Scripture, in deciding which books were inspired by God and therefore without error.* There is simply no denying the historical fact that the Councils set the canon and this in turn implied that *they - the Councils under the direction of the Apostolic Community - had an authority comparable to that of the content of the canon itself.*

This point of authority must be clearly understood. If a man tells you that he is an authority on paintings by the artist Rembrandt and if you take a collection of false and genuine Rembrandts to him seeking his assistance in screening the fakes, then you are committing yourself to belief in his authority. When he makes a judgment as to whether a painting is genuine or false, the accuracy of his judgment will depend entirely on whether or not he has the authority he claimed. It would be entirely irrational to accept a painting as genuine on the basis of his authority and then later deny his authority while also continuing to hold that the painting is genuine. As with all analogies this is not an exact parallel to the connection between the New Testament and the Councils of the Apostolic Community but there are remarkable similarities. There is no way to avoid the parallel by pointing to the Holy Spirit as being active then but not so now. The issue is whether the Apostolic Community and the Councils it authorized were instruments of the Holy Spirit at the time they made their judgment on the canon. If you do not accept the Community and the Councils as having had that authority, you cannot accept the divine inspiration of the New Testament. If you accept the Community and the Councils as having the authority at that time but claim that they lost this authority subsequently, the question becomes, how do you know this to be the case? What kind of authority does your judgment on this matter have?

The Fundamentalist may be surprised to know that it was only toward the end of the fourth century - in 397 A.D. - that a Church-directed Council, the Council of Carthage, approved the canon of Scripture. The Evangelical scholar F.F. Bruce documents the historical background:

The Council of Hippo (393) was probably the first church council to lay down the limits of the canon of scripture: its enactments are not extant, but its statement on the canon was repeated as Canon 47 of the Third Council of Carthage (397). The relevant words are these:

> And further it was resolved that nothing should be read in church under the name of the divine scriptures except the canonical writings. The canonical writings, then, are these: Of the New Testament:
> The four books of the gospels,
> the one book of the Acts of the Apostles,
> the thirteen epistles of the apostle Paul,
> the one [epistle] to the Hebrews, by the same,
> two of the apostle Peter,
> three of John, one of James, one of Jude,
> John's Apocalypse - one book.
> ... Let it be permitted, however, that the passions of martyrs be read when their anniversaries are celebrated.

The Sixth Council of Carthage (419) repromulgated in Canon 24 the resolution of the Third Council regarding the canon of scripture, and added a note directing that the resolution be sent to the bishop of Rome (Boniface I) and other bishops:

> Let this be made known also to our brother and fellow-priest Boniface, or to other bishops of those parts, for the purpose of confirming that Canon [Canon 47 of the Third Council], because we have received from our fathers that these are the books which are to be read in church.

In his list of canonical books addressed to Exuperius, bishop of Toulouse, in 405, Pope Innocent I specifies the books of the New Testament (after those of the Old Testament) ....

The sixth-century compilation commonly called the 'Gelasian decree' continues as follows after its list of Old Testament books:

> The order of the scriptures of the New Testament, which the holy and catholic Roman church accepts and venerates:
> Of the gospels four books [etc.] ....

The Gelasian decree follows its lists of books which are to be received with a long catalogue of books which are not to be received, comprising a variety of apocryphal, spurious and heretical writings.[1]

The divine inspiration of Scripture was articulated in its fullness only in 1441 A.D. at the Council of Florence: "One same God is author of Old Testament and New, that is of the Law and the Prophets and the Gospel, since the Holy Men of each Testament spoke under the inspiration of the same Holy Spirit." Through all the years prior to these proclamations, nevertheless, the Christian faithful received the historic Christian Faith and the message of the Gospel from the same body that later proclaimed the canon and inspiration of Scripture. It is also fundamentally important to understand that *conformity to the then-existing body of Christian Teaching authorized by the Apostolic Community* was a major criterion for inclusion of a book in the canon of the New Testament. Thus a gospel or an epistle would not be included in the canon if its message conflicted with the oral and credal teaching of the Apostolic Community.

Like it or not, the Fundamentalist must accept the central role played by the Apostolic Community and the Councils, with their divinely guaranteed authority to discern and interpret Scripture, in giving us the canon. Their authority extended to all their theological decisions. We can see three obvious areas where their authority was unquestioned: (1) decisions relating to the setting of the canon, determining which books constitute Scripture; (2) decisions affirming the divine inspiration of Scripture; (3) teachings that were affirmed as binding interpretations of Scripture.

On the third of the categories listed above, we note that the Councils made certain fundamental interpretations of Scripture. These included the doctrines of God as Three Persons in One Divine Nature, of the Divine Person of Christ acting through a human and a divine nature and of Mary as the Perpetually Virgin Mother of God. To accept the authority of the Apostolic Community and its Councils is to accept these definitions. The Fundamentalist cannot enjoy the fruits of the Community and the Councils while denying the existence of the tree from which these fruits

---

1   F.F. Bruce, *The Canon of Scripture* (Downers Grove, Illinois: Inter Varsity Press, 1988), 232.

sprang forth. The effect cannot be greater than the cause: if the Bible is divinely inspired then the body making the judgment that it is divinely inspired must also be divinely inspired. Fundamentalists who protest that they do not want to put Councils or creeds at the same level as Scripture are missing the point. If they undermine the authority of the Councils then they undermine the authoritativeness of decisions made by the Councils. To sever Scripture from the divinely guaranteed authority granted to the Apostolic Community and Councils that preceded and discerned Scripture is quite literally to cut off the branch on which you are sitting. Another Evangelical theologian admits the connection:

> Who made these decisions and on what grounds? Here we enter a minefield of controversy which goes back at least to the Reformation. Roman Catholics (and Eastern Orthodox) believe that the Church acting through its bishops and synods, fixed the canon. There is no doubt that there is some truth in this assertion, since the precise limits of the New Testament were in dispute for some centuries and common agreement of this kind was the only possible answer.[2]

The Protestant **Interpreter's Bible Commentary** again shows the link between traditional teaching and the authority of Scripture:

> The question of the authority of scripture and its relation to ecclesiastical authority was central to the Reformation. It is a drastic and misleading over-simplification, however, to assert that only at long last was the authority of the Bible being enunciated. Its authority is presupposed throughout the history of biblical interpretation sketched above. Nevertheless it is true that Augustine stated he would not believe the gospel were he not moved to do so by the authority of the Catholic Church. In the conflicts with heretics the orthodox maintained that the sense extracted from the text of scripture must be controlled by the tradition of catholic teaching.[3]

---

[2] John H. Leith, ed., *Creeds of the Churches* (Chicago: Aldine Publishing Company, 1963), 46, 48.

[3] George W. Anderson, "The History of Interpretation," *The Interpreter's One-Volume Commentary on the Bible* edited by Charles M. Laymon (Nashville: Abingdon Press, 1971), 975.

Once we get into the actual details of the history of the transmission of the books of the Bible and the rejection of counterfeits, the indispensable role played by the Apostolic Community and the Councils becomes obvious. Paul Sternhouse, an authority on Fundamentalism, makes some critical points here:

> We offer the following list of only a few of the important questions to which Bible Christians who genuinely seek the truth must find an answer ...

1. **How does one know which books of the New Testament, if any, are inspired?**

> This is a mammoth problem for bible Christians. Scripture cannot testify to its own veracity and authenticity. When the bible Christians reply that the New Testament was written by the apostles of Jesus and his disciples, one must enquire how the bible Christians know that the apostles and disciples of Christ always or even ever wrote under the inspiration of the Holy Spirit. They were fishermen, tax-gatherers, artisans, uneducated for the most part, and even if they claim to be inspired, what reason have we to believe them? St Paul, in his second letter to Timothy (3,16) simply says that 'all inspired scripture has its use for teaching the truth and refuting error.' But how are we to know what scripture is inspired and what is not...

2. **Christians accept two gospels written by non-apostles: the Gospels of St. Mark and St. Luke. Why don't they accept the epistle written by the Apostle Barnabas? Or the gospels of St. Peter and St Thomas?**

> St Barnabas was certainly an apostle (Acts 14,24) and is described as being 'full of the Holy Spirit.' So why do bible Christians not accept his epistle? For that matter, why do they not accept the gospel of St Peter, the founder of the Church and head of the apostles? Or the gospel of St Thomas? Or the acts of St Andrew?
>
> By what authority do bible Christians know that the works attributed to certain apostles and disciples, are actually written by those whose names they bear?
>
> In the early centuries of the Church's history numerous spurious books of Prophecies, Apocalypses, Gospels and

Epistles were circulating, written by pious or disturbed or heretical people; and at the same time quite a few of the books which we have today in our New Testament were rejected, or their authenticity doubted.

The 'canon' of scriptures (i.e., the list of genuine works, approved as written by those to whom they are attributed, and inspired by God) was fixed for all orthodox Christians by the tradition and authority of the Catholic Church, in a decree of Pope Innocent I (401-417 A.D.) contained in a letter written in 405 A.D. to Exuperius bishop of Toulouse (died in 411) advising him which books were to be held as 'canonical,' and which ones were authorised to be read at Mass. The Council held at Carthage in North Africa in 419 A.D. [the Sixth Council of Carthage] attended by St Augustine (354-430 A.D.), confirmed by Pope St Boniface I (418-422 A.D.), successor to Pope St Innocent I, declared the 27 books known to us as the 'New' Testament to be the 'Canonical Scriptures,' and forbade anything else to be read as 'Holy Scripture'.

Well-informed bible Christians cannot be unaware of the words of the Protestant reformer, Martin Luther, who in his *Commentary on St John* (c.16) admits, 'We are obliged to yield many things to the Catholics - (for example) that they possess the Word of God which we received from them, otherwise we should have known nothing at all about it.'...

3. **Even supposing the scriptures to be inspired and written by those to whom they are attributed, how do bible Christians now that what was originally written is what we have in our texts?**

How do bible Christians know, for example, that what St Paul wrote to the Romans was not changed by Phoebe, to whom he gave it (Romans 16, 1-2) to be carried by her to Rome and given to the Church there? Or, if she didn't change anything, how do they know that the endless copying that went on did not result in modifications, omissions or additions?

How can the bible Christians be sure that what St Paul wrote to the Christians of Ephesus was not changed by Tychicus to whom he entrusted it (Ephesians, 6,21) to be taken to Ephesus? ...

4. How does a bible Christian know that the translation of the bible he is reading is correct?

> The fundamental weakness of their position becomes even more apparent when we consider the translations available to bible Christians.
>
> The famous Protestant theologian Simon Bisschop wanted everybody, before being given a bible to read, to be made to learn Hebrew and Greek because of the poor, corrupt and often deliberately misleading translations thtat abounded in his day. They abound, still, in ours.
>
> The faults in the English translations of both Old and New Testaments in the early days of the consolidation of Protestanism in England were notorious. William Tyndale (1484-1536) and Miles Coverdale (1488-1568) as well as Queen Elizabeth's bishops all tried their hands at translating, but met with trenchant criticism from Protestants and Catholics alike... Even King James lamented the errors and falsifications, and the 'King James Version' resulted from the outcry that the earlier, misleading translations provoked...
>
> [Today] There are numerous differing versions of the bible in circulation - many of them quite excellent, but some of which bolster up doctrines peculiar to various sects and 'evangelical' fundamentalists. The genuine seeker after biblical truth must decide between them - but how? On what basis?[4]

The Evangelical scholar Gerald Bray admits that the early Church had an accepted tradition of apostolic succession which is why the teaching of the Apostolic Community was considered authoritative:

> In favour of a doctrine of apostolic succession it can be said that the Apostles ordained men to succeed them in the care of churches. Paul left elders behind in the churches he founded, and both Timothy and Titus were specially commissioned to carry on his work. At the same time, their commission was to guard the deposit, to hold fast the form of

---

4   Paul Sternhouse, *Catholic Answers to Bible Christians* (Kensington, N.S.W.: Chevalier Press, 1993), 32-3.

sound words which they had received from Paul (2 Timothy 1:13-14).[5]

This account of the fixing of the New Testament canon would
be incomplete without reference to the attempts of Martin Luther
to change the canon. F.F. Bruce admits that Luther, the promoter of
sola scriptura, played pick-and-choose with the books of the New
Testament [for those who reverence the authority and inspiration
of Sacred Scripture this attitude is nothing less than scandalous]:

> Luther's own views on the New Testament canon gained
> wide currency with the publication of his German New Tes-
> tament in 1522. (The Greek basis for his translation was
> Erasmus's second edition of 1519.) The table of contents
> suggested that he distinguished two levels of canonicity in
> the New Testament: the names of the first twenty-three books
> (Matthew - 3 John) are preceded by serial numbers 1-23;
> the remaining four books - Hebrews, James, Jude and Rev-
> elation - are separated from those by a space and are given
> no serial number. Luther did not exclude the last four books
> from the canon, but he did not recognize in them the high
> quality of 'the right certain capital books,' and expressed
> his opinion forthrightly in his individual prefaces to these
> books. In his preface to Hebrews it is plain that he had given
> up the traditional Pauline authorship: it was written, he says,
> by 'an excellent man of learning, who had been a disciple
> of the apostles and had learned from them, and who was
> very well versed in scripture.' (By 1537 he was sure that
> this 'excellent man of learning' was Apollos.) It is in his
> preface to James in his 1522 New Testament that he calls it
> 'an epistle of straw.' He finds that it contradicts Paul and
> the other scriptures on justification by faith, and, while it
> promotes law, it does not promote Christ. Jude is a super-
> fluous document: it is an abstract of 2 Peter. (Nowadays it
> would be generally agreed that 2 Peter is based on Jude, not
> vice versa.) Moreover, Jude is suspect because it contains
> history and teaching nowhere found in scripture (this is a
> reference to the Enoch quotation and the dispute about the

---

5   Gerald Bray, *Creeds, Councils and Christ* (Downers Grove, Illinois: Inter
     Varsity Press, 1984), 48.

body of Moses). As for Revelation, it 'lacks everything that I hold as apostolic or prophetic'...

If one asked for Luther's criterion of canonicity (or at least primary canonicity), it is here. 'That which does not teach Christ is still not apostolic, even if it were the teaching of Peter or Paul. On the other hand, that which preaches Christ, that would be apostolic even if Judas, Annas, Pilate or Herod did it. '

"The conclusion," says Roland H. Bainton, "was a hierarchy of values within the New Testament. First Luther would place the Gospel of John, then the Pauline epistles and First Peter, after them the three other Gospels, and in a subordinate place Hebrews, James, Jude and Revelation. He mistrusted Revelation because of its obscurity." ...

The recognition of an 'inner canon' within the wider canon has persisted in the Lutheran tradition to the present day: the 'inner canon' is a Pauline canon. As Bainton goes on to say, 'the New Testament was for Luther a Pauline book.' So it was for Marcion [an influential heretic of the early Church; despite Luther's dangerous tendency to sit in judgment on the Bible, he did not reject the Old Testament altogether as Marcion did].[6]

The **Interpreter's Bible Commentary** notes,

Though Luther sometimes seems to equate God's word with the written text of the Bible, the true Word for him is Christ, to whom both OT and NT witness. It is this witness to Christ which constitutes the unity of the Bible... Luther therefore does not hesitate to express his preference for some books (notably Pss., John, Rom., Gal., Eph.) and a lower estimate for others (e.g. Jas., Rev.). A theological systematizer reading the Bible as a doctrinal source book might find such varying estimates embarassing. But Luther was not a systematizer.[7]

---

6   F.F. Bruce, *The Canon of Scripture*, op cit., 243.
7   George W. Anderson, "The History of Interpretation," op. cit., 976.

-2-

THE INTERPRETATION
OF THE NEW TESTAMENT

To say that Scripture interprets itself is to ignore the fact that every written text needs a person to understand and interpret it. The Anglican scholar Richard Hanson shows this:

> The development of doctrine is inevitable. The idea, dear to the hearts of many Protestants since the sixteenth century and still voiced by the more mindless among them today, that there is such a thing as a 'bible without notes,' a 'bible without interpretation,' a purely scriptural doctrine completely independent of human elaboration, is not only bad theology, it is pure illusion. Countless sects have established themselves on the basis of a pure, creedless, traditionless, biblical doctrine, attempting to distinguish themselves from past tradition and interpretation; all they have succeeded in doing is to start a series of diverse christian bodies who have a lively tradition of not having a tradition, or of imagining that they do not have a tradition. They have not been able to emancipate themselves from the necessity of interpreting the bible and thereby creating tradition. Such an emancipation is a flat impossibility. The bible does not interpret itself; it is not a self-expounding cassette. Not only does it need copying and circulating, but it needs actually turning into doctrine. All the bible provides is raw material for doctrine, not ready-made prefabricated theology ripe for incorporating wholesale, unaltered, into theological treatises or stirring sermons...

The very concept of a New Testament assumes the concept of an interpreting and expounding Church.[8]

A Reformed scholar writes in the same vein:

> Protestants have always been tempted to believe that they could somehow omit all the centuries of Christian history and read the Bible without either the help or hindrances of those who have gone before. In actual fact those who have refused to read the Bible in the light of the church traditions have always read it in the light of the traditions of their own history and culture. Karl Barth, the great Reformed theologian of the twentieth century, has written,
>
> > In actual fact, there has never been a Biblicist who for all his grandiloquent appeal directly to Scripture against the fathers and tradition has proved himself so independent of the spirit and philosophy of his age and especially of his favourite religious ideas that in his teaching he has actually allowed the Bible and the Bible alone to speak reliably by means or in spite of his anti-traditionalism.[9]

The role played by the Authorized Interpretation given us by the Apostolic Community and its Councils is as important in the exegesis and interpretation of the New Testament as it is in the very origin of the New Testament. We know from experience that any statement, any written document, can be interpreted to mean almost anything, and the Bible, being a written document, is similarly susceptible to diverse interpretations, most of them contradicting each other. The message which Christians believe to be divine revelation, the message of salvation essential to all men at all times and all places is then at the mercy of judgments which vary with background and era and culture. One unified consistent message soon becomes a medley of discordant messages. The truth that all men at all times have sought as to who they are and why

---

8   Richard Hanson, "The Cult of Mary as Development of Doctrine," *The Month*, Autumn 1984, pp.23-4.

9   John H. Leith, *Introduction to the Reformed Tradition* (John Knox Press, 1981), p. 21.

they are here will remain as obscure and unknown as it was before God became man. The Christian revelation will die the death of a thousand interpretations if every interpretation of Scripture is equally authoritative: to say that every interpretation is authoritative is to say that no interpretation is authoritative.

Did Christ then mean to leave His followers uncertain, undecided, on His fundamental message, on His teachings about God's purpose for the human race, on the nature of God and of Himself? Are we to hope to know no more from the Bible than what our limited intellects, moulded by our cultural and intellectual backgrounds, tell us differently and dare we call contradictory interpretations equally true? What does Scripture teach about salvation and sanctification, the Lord's Supper and the Second Coming? Even those who accept the divine inspiration of Scripture give widely varying answers to these and other basic questions. And even the most learned exegetes and theologians change their answers in each generation so that there is no continuity or certainty in their pronouncements.

The task and duty of biblical interpretation cannot be taken lightly. From a theological standpoint, the Protestant Fundamentalist is one who relies only on Scripture and takes the Holy Spirit as his authority in the interpretation of Scripture. But conflicting and contradictory interpretations of the same verse or verses among Bible-believing Christians and Christian denominations raises the problem of determining who indeed is truly inspired by the Holy Spirit. It is possible to address this problem by turning to additional reliable sources of guidance in discerning the direction of the Spirit. But which sources are reliable in such matters of biblical interpretation? The "founding fathers" of the Protestant Reformation? The current consensus of Fundamentalist scholars - if there is a consensus? Televangelists? Denominational confessions of faith? The biblical interpretation chosen by the majority of Christians around the world? The Church Fathers? The Councils? The historic Christian Faith? The claim that the Holy Spirit guides every individual who reads the Bible to make the right interpretation is fatally flawed because equally devout Christians make contradictory or drastically divergent interpretations of the most fundamental texts. Since two or more contradictory interpretations of Scripture cannot both or all be true, we cannot talk of the Holy

Spirit guiding every reader in his interpretation for this would be to say that God leads one into error. The Holy Spirit guides men in interpretation of the Bible - but only through one and not many channels: the divinely inspired inerrant body of intepretation that we call the historic Christian Faith.

The denial of the Authorized Interpretation, the divinely inspired inerrant interpretation of Scripture, has led to the formation of more than 22,000 different traditions, each one of which is embodied in a denomination and each one of which has a different interpretation of the teachings of Scripture. The champions of the "Sola Scriptura" [Scripture alone] slogan assumed during the Reformation that they were liberating Scripture from the dead hand of Tradition and opening it up to the unrestricted direction of the Holy Spirit. They could hardly have foreseen that their action would lead to the creation of 22,000 Christian denominations. There are dramatic differences of interpretation even among the Fundamentalists.

Bob Jones III, one of America's best known Fundamentalists, said of the evangelist Billy Graham that Graham "has done more harm to the cause of Christ than any other living man."[10] Dispensationalists say Charismatics are under the inspiration of the Devil and Charismatics say the same of Dispensationalists (this is not to say that all Dispensationalists or all Charismatics make such charges but it's every man for himself). Fundamentalists even have various views among themselves on what is meant by the divine inspiration of Scripture.

Some of the incredible interpretations made by champions of private interpretation are cited by Paul Sternhouse:

> [The principle of the private interpretation of Scripture] sprang up first in the early part of the second century A.D. with Montanus, a priest, and with Maximilla and Priscilla and their followers who believed in private interpretation of the scriptures, and the imminent end of the world. The strictness and apparent sanctity of their lives deceived many - until the Spirit that led them revealed itself, and the first two hanged themselves. (Eusebius, Ecc. Hist.v. 6) ...

---

[10] *Time*, November 15, 1993 cover story on Billy Graham.

[Five years after the Reformation] a sect called the Anabaptists arose in Germany, Belgium and Holland - ancestors of modern Baptists. They claimed to have immediate communication wich God, and to be ordered by him to kill the wicked and to establish a kingdom of the just - who had to be rebaptised.

The leader of this movement was a tailor of Leiden John Bockhold who proclaimed himself king of Sion. He committed the most extraordinary excesses, married eleven wives and put them and numberless followers to deatch. Declaring that he 'knew' that God had given him Amsterdam, he sent his followers to take it by force. Before being executed with some of his followers for their many murders and violence, he and they danced on the scaffold exulting in the 'light' of the spirit that possessed them.

Herman, another Anabaptist, declared himself the Messiah after poring over the scriptures, and told his followers, 'Kill the priests, kill all the magistrates in the world.' One of the chief preachers of the sect, David George, persuaded his followers that the Old and New Testament were imperfect, but that his teaching was perfect and that he was 'the true Son of God'...

Agricola, one of Luther's first disciples, is considered to be the founder of the Antinomians...

The Antinomians, following Luther first of all, and then following the 'Spirit,' held that the faithful are bound by no law, either of God or man, and that good works are quite useless for salvation. Amsdorf, a drinking-companion of Luther, taught that good works are actually an impediment to salvation!

In the midst of the unprecedented religious and civil upheaval that followed in the train of these and many others like them, George Fox, a shoemaker from Leicestershire proclaimed the logical consequence of private interpretation of the scriptures: 'The Scriptures are not the adequate, Primary Rule of Faith and Manners - but a Secondary Rule subordinate to the Spirit.' For Fox and the early Quakers, his followers, 'The testimony of the Spirit is that alone by which the true knowledge of God hath been, is, and can be revealed.' Fox tells in his journal of various 'Friends' who went about naked and barefoot, including one who went to the door of Parliament with a sword saying that 'he was inspired by the Spirit to kill every man who sat in the House'.

Other sects followed in the train of evangelical liberty and private interpretation - Muggletonians, Labbadists, the Moravian Brethren and many others. Baron Swedenborg (founder of the Swedenborgians) declared that he had a revelation while sitting in an eating house in London about the year 1745. 'After I had dined a man appeared to me sitting in the corner of the room, who cried out to me, with a terrible voice: "Don't eat so much." The following night the same man appeared to me and said to me: "I am the Lord, your Creator and Redeemer. I have chosen you to explain to men the interior and spiritual sense of the Scriptures: I will dictate to you what you are to write."

Swedenborg's God is a mere man; his angels are male and female; they marry and follow various trades and professions. His New Jerusalem is so like the old world we all know that the entrance to it is 'imperceptible'...

[The Antinomian] Richard Hill persisted in saying that 'adultery and murder do not hurt the pleasant children, but rather work for their good.' (Works, vol.iii, p.50) Hill maintained also that 'God sees no sin in believers whatever sin they commit, . . adultery, incest and murder shall, upon the whole, make me holier on earth and merrier in heaven.'

In our age of alleged universal literacy, with Bible Societies proliferating ... we have the unhappy spectacle of the proliferation of sects and esoteric religions ... the unleashing of literally thousands of individualistic religions, all posing as 'Christian,' no matter how contradictory their doctrines, and how unbiblical their views.

On the basis of Protestant Fundamentalist and 'biblical' premises, viewed in the light of private interpretation of the Scriptures, how can one possibly choose between the many thousands of 'biblical' Christian Churches in the centres of Protestantism - Britain, Germany, Switzerland and America and now spreading throughout the Third World? What can a reasonable person make of the differences between the more than 25 branches of the Lutheran Church in America, the 16 kinds of Mennonites, the 9 versions of Presbyterianism, the 17 versions of Baptists, the 20 kinds of Methodists, the various forms of Anglicanism, Mormonism, the Disciples of Christ, the Churches of Christ, the 5 kinds of Seventh Day Adventists, 6 versions of Plymouth

Brethren, 3 kinds of Moravians, 5 kinds of Dunkers, 4 kinds of Quakers, Jehovah's Witnesses, Swedenborgians (Church of London), Universalists, United Brethren etc? The list is as endless as the possibilities of the human imagination feeding on private biblical 'lights,' and led by the 'spirit' into statements of belief...

Many of the tens of thousands of 'Christian' Churches and sects do not baptise (despite Mt 28,19) ... The list of beliefs and disbeliefs is endless. And all claim to be 'Bible' Christians. All claim, as a 'right' to be 'interpreters,' of the Word of God...

If we are to assume, against all the evidence, that our Lord intended the *written Scripture* to be the sole rule of faith ... and, at the same time, gave each 'believer' the right to interpret them as he or she thinks fit, this would mean that Jesus established a Rule of Faith, without appointing any authority to decide on the inevitable controversies that would arise from a written text.

The absurdity of the hypothesis is self-evident. It is as improbable as claiming that a Parliament would pass laws of vital importance to its citizens, and allow each person to arbitrate on his or her own behalf - each interpretation to be as valid as the next - no matter how contradictory.

Law would fall apart if individuals were allowed to interpret it according to their 'lights,' feelings and perceived needs. And the New Testament is of far greater consequence than any human law. That Jesus would act so is unthinkable...

No sooner had Luther set up his own criterion of private interpretation of the Scriptures ... than his followers, acting logically enough on this same principle, set out to prove from the same texts of the Bible that Luther himself was in error: thus Carlstad (who attacked Luther in 1521); Zwingli (who took the reformation into Switzerland: Luther called him a 'pagan'); Oecolampadius (Luther said he was strangled by the devil); Muncer (one of the founders of the Anabaptists) and dozens more of his followers wrote and preached against him and each other: each claiming to base his doctrine on the text of the Bible! ...

Calvin, (1509-1564) wrote to Melanchthon: 'It is of great importance that the divisions, which subsist among us, should not be known to future ages; for nothing can be more ridiculous than that we, who have broken off from the whole world, should have agreed so ill among ourselves from the very beginning of the reformation.'[11]

In practice no one can possibly separate Scripture from the interpretation of Scripture. The choice is not between Scripture and Scripture + Tradition. The choice, rather, is between Scripture and its historic, authoritative interpretation, on the one hand, and Scripture and a multitude of possible interpretations on the other. The question before us is whose interpretation of Scripture do we trust and not whether or not we should accept Tradition. *We have seen that Martin Luther, the inventor of the Sola Scriptura theory, himself held that (a) no interpretation of Scripture can differ from a continuous past tradition of interpretation and (b) Tradition can contain teachings that are not in Scripture as long as these teachings do not contradict Scripture.*[12]

The choice is between one historic, consistent, and authoritative interpretation protected by the Holy Spirit and an endless succession of contradictory interpretations. These are the only two options. The Fundamentalist rejects the first option and so he has to say that no interpretation is final or certain. The Fundamentalist may claim that every doctrine must be "measured against" Scripture. But this simply means that every interpretation of Scripture must be measured against *his* interpretation of Scripture. The problem with this is that there is no standard against which his own interpretation can be measured since he rejects the possibility of "standards" (Councils, etc.). *He cannot say that his interpretation is "measured" against Scripture because then he would simply be saying that his interpretation of Scripture must be measured against his (or someone else's) interpretation - which leaves him where he began.* Thus Fundamentalism locks the believer in his own world with all its limitations, prejudices and misconceptions.

Proof-texts cannot be used in settling disputes between Fundamentalists because it is possible to have multiple interpretations of the same texts and there can thus be no certainty on the right

---

[11] Paul Sternhouse, *Catholic Answers to Bible Christians* (Kensington, N.S.W.: Chevalier Press, 1993), 8-12.

[12] cf. *The Theology of Martin Luther*, Fortress Press, 1966.

interpretation. When the same text is interpreted in a thousand ways it is no longer serves the function of a *proof*-text.

The principle of private interpretation ultimately ends up not in Sola Scriptura but in Scripture + human traditions based on changing interpretations. Fundamentalists tell us that we should rely only on the Bible. They quote the Bible to support all their beliefs and actions and claim to "test everything against Scripture." They distrust all "human" traditions as unreliable and say that the only sure guide is the Holy Bible. Certainly "human" traditions are unreliable. But this does not address the real problem which is the interpretation of Holy Writ. Yes, the Bible is reliable, authoritative and normative. But how do we know what is the right interpretation of the Bible. Not having the right interpretation of the Bible is as bad as not having the Bible at all. There is only one claimant to the authoritative interpretation of the Bible which is both inerrant and historically continuous, the Authorized Interpretation of the historic Christian Faith. This Interpretation is not "human tradition" but Scripture-interpreted-with-Divine-guidance.

THE INERRANT INTERPRETATION OF THE INERRANT WORD OF GOD

"There are as many sects and beliefs as there are heads. This fellow will have nothing to do with baptism; another denies the sacraments; a third believes that there is another world between this and the Last Day. Some teach that Christ is not God; some say this, some say that. There is no rustic so rude but that, if he dreams or fancies anything, it must be the whisper of the Holy Ghost, and he himself a prophet." - Martin Luther

"Now we see the people becoming more infamous, more avaricious, more unmerciful, more unchaste, and in every way worse than they were under Popery." - Martin Luther[13]

Calvin, (1509-1564) wrote to Melanchthon: 'It is of great importance that the divisions, which subsist among us, should not be known to future ages; for nothing can be more ridiculous than that we, who have broken off from the whole world, should have agreed so ill among ourselves from the very beginning of the reformation.'[14]

We see in the Gospels that Jesus taught as "One with authority" and had definite teachings which He wanted those who heard

---

[13] Grisar, *Luther*, Vol IV, 386, 407 (1525).
[14] Paul Sternhouse, *Catholic Answers to Bible Christians* (Kensington, N.S.W.: Chevalier Press, 1993), 12.

Him to accept as true and true in the sense He taught them. So important did He consider these teachings that He taught them as essential for salvation and gave up His life in order to proclaim them. It is simply not conceivable that He Who is Truth - and Who promised that His followers would be led "into all truth" - would have left those words of His which were more ultimate than heaven and earth to the mercy of minds darkened by the Fall or to the manipulation of the one He called "the father of lies." Nowhere does Jesus say that His teachings were to be left to individual interpretation or private inspiration or "conscience." In addition, nowhere in Scripture is the principle of "*sola scriptura*" (Scripture alone) proclaimed. The "scripture" to which there are references in the New Testament is the Old Testament because the New Testament itself was not compiled as one entity at the time when its individual texts were composed. Thus, the principle of "Scripture alone" is non- or extra- Scriptural! When Fundamentalists say that the teachings of the historic Faith must stay purely within the perimeter of the Bible, they must be reminded that the very act of teaching what constitutes the New Testament is itself an extra-Biblical teaching. Nowhere in the New Testament are we told which books belong to it.

Moreover we saw in the previous chapter that Luther himself did not intend his "Sola Scriptura" principle to rule out the teachings of the Apostolic Community that were not explicitly taught in Scripture. John Calvin, too, was attentive to the teachings of the historic Faith and "always read and heard the Bible in terms of the traditions."[15]

The New Testament Gives No Systematic Structure of the Teachings of Jesus

This brings us to a fact missed by most Fundamentalists. Neither the Gospels nor the Epistles give us the teachings of Jesus in a systematic structure. Frank Sheed writes, "Where, in the New Testament, should we look for any full and formal statement of the totality of Christ's teaching? Not in the Gospels, if we consider

---

[15]   John H. Leith, *Introduction to the Reformed Tradition* (John Knox Press: 1981), 20-1.

what they are - four accounts of the Redeemer, all four building up to the climax of the redeeming act, Passion and Death and Resurrection ... That is the Good News. That is their topic... If we were to group together all the doctrinal teaching recorded in the Gospels as given by Christ, it could be written out in very few pages."[16]

The epistles too are not manuals of doctrine: "The Epistles Paul has left us are 'occasional writings, not theological treatises but responses to concrete situations.' He writes of elements in the doctrine which had been misunderstood or even denied in this place or that ... But there is no synthesis stated, no general framework - these he assumes, just as John does, and Peter, and the rest: they were not writing to be read apart from the synthesis, outside the framework."[17]

New Testament Readers Assumed to Have Heard the Gospel Message from the Apostolic Community

The Gospels and the Epistles assume that the Christian believer receives his basic instruction, the Gospel message, from the Christian Faith taught by the Apostolic Community. "Now we command you, brethren, in the name of our Lord Jesus Christ, that ye withdraw yourselves from every brother that walketh disorderly, *and not after the tradition which he received of us.*" [II *Thessalonians* 3:6]. "Therefore, brethren, stand fast, and *hold the traditions which ye have been taught*, whether by word, or our epistle." [II *Thessalonians* 2:15] "Now I praise you, brethren, that ye remember me in all things, and *keep the ordinances, as I delivered them to you.*" [I *Corinthians* 11:2]. The Gospel of *Luke* is introduced with the statement "It seemed good to me also, ... to write unto thee in order, ... that thou mightest know the certainty of those things, *wherein thou hast been instructed.*" [*Luke* 1:3,4].

In the New Testament we notice too that references are made to traditions not contained in the Old Testament Scriptures as shown by David Palm:

---

16 F.J. Sheed, *God and the Human Condition* (London: Sheed and Ward, 1966), 74.

17 Ibid., 79.

The doctrine of the apostles came to them in oral form from Jesus. In one sense the entire Christian message is based on oral tradition and is only augmented by using the written revelation of the Old Testament. From this perspective, perhaps 90 percent of the New Testament is based on authoritative oral tradition (from Jesus), and the remaining ten percent is from written sources...

The authors of the New Testament do draw on oral Tradition in addition to Old Testament Scripture. In several instances, they explicitly cite oral Tradition to support Christian doctrine...

First, we find passages in the New Testament in which oral Tradition is cited in support of doctrine. This evidence is particularly significant because it shows that, for the apostles, oral Tradition was trustworthy when formulating and developing elements of the Christian faith...

In a second category of passages, the New Testament authors draw on oral Tradition, but not so explicitly in support of doctrine ... [These passages] are significant in that they show the extent to which the earliest Christians, including the apostles themselves, reckoned with the twin witnesses of Scripture and Tradition when they expounded the faith.

Doctrinal examples

Matthew 2:23

Scripture says that Joseph and Mary returned to Nazareth after their sojourn in Egypt, "that what was spoken by the prophets might be fulfilled, 'He shall be called a Nazarene'." (Matt. 2:23). All commentators admit that the phrase "He shall be called a Nazarene" is not found anywhere in the Old Testament. Yet Matthew tells us that the Holy Family fulfilled this prophecy, which had been passed on "by the prophets." ...

The failed attempts to locate the Old Testament background to this prophecy, coupled with this unique introduction, suggest to me that the simplest solution is probably the correct one: Matthew is drawing on oral Tradition for this saying. If this is the case, it is significant that he places this prophecy on the same level as ones he attributes to specific authors of the Old Testament. This then would be an example of God's own Word being passed on via oral Tradition and not through written Scripture.

Matthew 23:2

Just before launching into a blistering denunciation of the scribes and Pharisees, Jesus delivers this command to the crowds: "The scribes and Pharisees sit on Moses' seat; so practice and observe whatever they tell you, but not what they do; for they preach, but do not practice" (Matt. 23:2-3).

Although Jesus strongly indicts his opponents of hypocrisy for not following their own teaching, he nevertheless insists that the scribes and Pharisees hold a position of legitimate authority, which he characterizes as sitting "on Moses' seat".

One searches in vain for any reference to this seat of Moses in the Old Testament. But it was commonly understood in ancient Israel that there was an authoritative teaching office, passed on by Moses to successors.

As the first verse of the **Mishna tractate Abìte** indicates, the Jews understood that God's revelation, received by Moses, had been handed down from him in uninterrupted succession, through Joshua, the elders, the prophets, and the great Sanhedrin (Acts 15:21). The scribes and Pharisees participated in this authoritative line and as such their teaching deserved to be respected.

Jesus here draws on oral Tradition to uphold the legitimacy of this teaching office in Israel.

After citing additional examples of oral tradition, 1 *Corinthians* 10:4, 1 *Peter* 3:19 and *Jude* 9, Palm concludes

The passages that I cited demonstrate that the New Testament authors drew on oral Tradition as they expounded the Christian faith. This fact spells real trouble for any Christian who asserts that we must find all of our doctrine in written Scripture. We know that the apostles did not teach the doctrine of *sola scriptura* explicitly in Scripture, and we know through their use of oral Tradition that they did not intend to teach it implicitly by their example either. The conclusion is that they simply did not hold to a principle of sola scriptura - and neither should we.[18]

"The Spirit of Truth ... will guide you into all truth"

In the Gospel of *John*, Our Lord lays the foundations of the authoritative teachings of the historic Christian Faith: "These things have I spoken unto you, being yet present with you. But the Comforter, which is the Holy Spirit, whom the Father will send in my name, he shall teach you all things, and bring all things to your remembrance, whatsoever I have said unto you." [*John* 14: 25-26]. "I have yet many things to say unto you, but ye cannot bear them now. Howbeit when he, the Spirit of truth, is come, he will guide you into all truth." [*John* 16:12,13]. It would seem that Jesus is talking here of Divine guidance in the interpretation and understanding of His teachings after the completion of His earthly ministry. The Apostolic Community was very conscious that in its teachings it was guided and preserved by the Holy Spirit: "For *it seemed good to the Holy Ghost, and to us*, to lay upon you no greater burden than these necessary things." [*Acts* 15:28.]

Long before the canon of the New Testament was established, the initial version of the Apostles Creed was developed in Rome by the Apostolic Community in the middle of the Second Century. This is an early instance of the process of discerning the Christian revelation under the influence of the Holy Spirit. Sheed points out that the Creed "goes straight from the Holy Ghost to the Holy Catholic Church, without mention of Scripture."[19]

Canon Established Only After All the Apostles Died

Although the canon of Scripture was formally defined only towards the end of the fourth century, the inspired nature of the Gospels and Epistles was recognized by Church Fathers by the end of the second century. Proof of divine inspiration of the New Testament books, however, lay in conformity to the historic Faith

---

[18] David Palm, "Oral Tradition in the New Testament", *This Rock*, May 1995, 7-12.

[19] F.J. Sheed, *God and the Human Condition*, op. cit., 87.

along with two other criteria, acceptance by the Apostolic Community and apostolic origin. It is clear that the teaching authority of the Apostolic Community and its Councils did not depend on the Apostles themselves being alive: *the canon was established only centuries after the death of the last Apostle and fundamental doctrines were defined during and after the time of the Apostles.*

Christian Faith and Doctrine Preceded the Canon of Scripture

There was, in fact, no possibility of *selecting* the inspired books or *interpreting* them if there was no pre-existing body of teaching that could serve as the starting-point for the activities of selection and interpretation. Many texts in Scripture would contradict each other - for instance, texts on the Trinity and other texts cited later in this chapter - if there was no framework of historic teaching within which they could be interpreted. When Christ is called "the first-born of all creation" in Colossians 1:15, the text is interpreted by Tradition as meaning "begotten of the Father before all worlds" and not "created" or "created in time." Clearly this interpretation cannot be reached independent of the historic Christian Faith - and any other interpretation would be a departure from that Faith.

What becomes clear from the history of the Christian Faith is that there is a body of teaching which Christians through the ages have considered to be the divinely inspired inerrant intepretation of the divinely inspired inerrant Word of God - what we call the Authorized Interpretation of the Apostolic Community. This was recognized even by the Protestant Reformers like Martin Luther.

22,000 Denominations vs. One Authorized Interpretation

Perhaps the best argument for the need for the stable, consistent body of authorized Christian teaching dating back to the first century is the existence today of over 22,000 denominations: each denomination sprang from a new interpretation of Scripture and each gives us a competing interpretation. There is no point brandishing one's credentials as a Bible-believing Christian committed to the Sola Scriptura principle if one cannot give an authoritative account of what it means to believe the Bible. Does the Bible advocate Arminianism or Calvinism, dispensationalism or the amillenial position, infant or adult baptism, speaking in tongues or a prohibition on speaking in tongues, divorce or a prohibition on divorce? Devout non-Catholic Bible-believing Christians have given dramatically different answers to these and hundreds of other questions.

Jesus was the Way, the Truth and the Life: not 22,000 different Ways, Truths and Lives. The same Holy Spirit Who inspired and guaranteed Scripture likewise inspired and guaranteed the binding and authoritative interpretation of Scripture accepted by the vast majority of Christians throughout the history of Christendom. To reject this binding and authoritative interpretation (the historic Christian Faith) is to reject all possibility of a coherent Christian faith. Once this point hits home it becomes clear that the real issue in objections to Marian doctrine is the question of the authoritativeness of the historic Christian Faith: if the historic Faith is true then Marian doctrine that is a part of that Faith is true as well. The truth of Marian doctrine ultimately rests on the truth of the claim that there is an authoritative interpretation of Scripture that has been consistently handed down to us from the days of the Apostles.

Not Just a Teaching but a Teacher

To be sure, as we saw at the beginning of this section, the fundamental framework of the Christian Faith is not given to us in a cut-and-dry, black-and-white formula format in Scripture. This is what the Fundamentalists want but they just will not find it there. Instead Christ promised the Apostles that "the Spirit of truth ... will guide you into all truth" and the Authorized Interpretation of the historic Christian Faith grew out of the divinely-guided-and-protected reflection on the Gospel message of the Fathers, the Councils and the Apostolic Community. Through the centuries the Apostolic Community ponders the significance of the mysteries revealed in Scripture to develop an organic, coherent body of doctrine. Everything "fits" together but only the body of teaching of the historic Christian Faith is qualified (by virtue of the promise of Christ) to point out and develop the connections and the implications. And this is a gradual, progressive process.

The Teaching of the Divinity of Jesus

Even in the Gospels we see that Jesus did not simply announce His Divinity at the beginning of His life or even at the beginning of His ministry. Once He had prepared the minds of His apostles appropriately, He gradually let them see that He was indeed God incarnate. Once this mystery was understood by the apostles, they had the task of first expounding and explaining it and then drawing further conclusions from this mystery. It was only in the fourth century that the Church through the Council of Nicea issued an explicit formulation of the truth of Christ being a Divine Person with a human and a Divine nature. Other explicit formulations on the content of Christian doctrine could only come after this fundamental doctrine had been fully formulated and further formulations including the Marian doctrines came at different times through the centuries. The acorn of Scripture becomes the oak of historic Christianity. Although the oak is implicitly present in the acorn, the actual growth takes place over time.

Scripture as a Software Program

If Scripture is thought of as a huge software program with millions of encoded instruction sets, the doctrines that comprise the historic Faith must then be perceived as actions generated by the software program when it is in operation. When a software program is running, it activates operations that affect the real world: it is the medium through which the airlines can make millions of reservations, through which the cash machines interact with bank accounts and the like. The operations carried out using the software program may bear no physical resemblance to the program itself: nevertheless these operations are activated and directed by the program. The fact that we cannot "see" the process of interaction involved when an airline agent makes a reservation in the external code of a program does not mean that the code does not carry out this operation. Similarly, Christian doctrines may not be explicitly visible in Scripture but these doctrines are created and set in motion by the irresistible dynamic of Scripture.

Scripture Not a Textbook of Dogma

The question is not whether the Bible explicitly defines a specific dogma, such as the doctrine of the Assumption, but whether any dogma is defined in Scripture. The answer is that Scripture is not a textbook of dogma just as it is not a textbook of science. Dogma - even in Christology - develops through the Apostolic Community's reflection on Scripture and the pre-existing body of teaching in the historic Faith. Fundamentalists may fail to see "the remotest connection" between an acorn and the oak tree or between a caterpillar and a butterfly or between a software program and the operation it effects but this is a problem with their powers of inference and not with the entities in question.

The Fundamentalist who ignores the teachings of the historic Faith on Mary usually does not base his Christology on the teachings of the Faith either because he does not recognize the possibility of an Authorized Interpretation. Inevitably, a Christology based on purely subjective and arbitrary criteria with no anchor in the historic Faith will slip into heresy and chaos.

Just as they do not clearly spell out the Marian doctrines, the Gospels do not give us the doctrine of the Incarnation in terms of an explicit formula specifying that Jesus Christ is One Divine Person with two natures, human and Divine. The Fundamentalist who relies only on his own interpretation of every verse will be puzzled by such verses in Scripture as:

> "He [Jesus] was setting out on a journey when a man ran up, knelt before him and put this question to him, 'Good master, what must I do to inherit eternal life?' Jesus said to him, 'Why do you call me good? No one is good but God alone.'" [Mark 10:17-18].

> "If you loved me you would have been glad to know that I am going to the Father, for the Father is greater than I." [John 14:28].

Some will conclude that Jesus is denying His divinity in the first verse or that Jesus is saying that one Divine Person is inferior to another in the second verse. In neither case is such an interpretation justifiable. In the first case, as Leslie Rumble and Charles Carty point out, Jesus is not saying that He was not God because "He would not contradict Himself. He knew, however, that those around Him saw only His human nature or created humanity, and that they had not yet attained the faith to see beyond merely human appearances to His Divinity. And He once more tried to lift their thoughts to God as the Source of all created goodness. It was a warning that we must not stop at any created goodness which is but a reflection of the infinite goodness of God and meant to lead us to Him. On another occasion, when Philip said to Him, 'Lord, show us the Father,' Christ rebuked him also for not rising above thoughts of His merely human characteristics, and said, 'To have seen me is to have seen the Father, so how can you say, 'Let us see the Father?' Do you not believe that I am in the Father and the Father is in me?' [John 14:8-11]."[20]

Regarding the second verse quoted above, Rumble and Carty write, "The Eternal Son of God, after the Incarnation, possessed two natures, the uncreated Divine Nature, and the created human nature, born of the Virgin Mary. When He said, 'I and the Father are one,' He referred to His Divine Nature. When He said, 'The Father is greater than I,' He referred to the created visible human nature which appeared before the eyes of those to whom He was speaking."[21]

We find a similarly historic interpretation of *John* 14:28 in *This Rock*:

> If you read the whole of that chapter and understand the context, it will be clear what is being said. In John 14:7-10 Christ says, 'If you know me, then you will also know my Father. From now on you do know him and have seen him.' Philip said to him, 'Master, show us the Father, and that will be enough for us.' Jesus replied, 'Have I been with you for so long a time and you still do not know me, Philip? Whoever has seen me has seen the Father. How can you say, Show us The Father? Do you not believe that I am in the Father and the Father is in me? The words that I speak to you I do not speak on my own. The Father who dwells in me is doing his works.'

---

20 *Radio Replies (Volume II).*
21 Ibid.

This identification of Christ with God is emphatic in this chapter and throughout John. John 1:1 explains, "In the beginning was the Word and the Word was with God, and the Word was God." In John 11:30 Christ says, "The Father and I are one." In John 14:28 we are reaching a climax. Jesus is soon to be arrested and crucified. He is reassuring the apostles about himself. Yes, they are going to see him suffer in the flesh and die, but Jesus reminds them there is more to himself than just the human. He and the Father are one. His statement is a reassurance to them, and it should be to you as well.[22]

But we can know the true meaning of these passages only if we are aware of the reflection on them that receives the authentic guidance and protection of the Holy Spirit. The teaching of the historic Faith takes into account the context of the Gospels as a whole and the experience of the faithful and is, above all, led by the Spirit "into all truth." It is only through this teaching that the Christian can hope to understand the content of Christianity. When the Christian divorces himself from the divinely directed wisdom of the historic Faith by adopting the superstition of Private Interpretation, then the content of his faith suffers decline because it conflicts with the apostolic Faith.

Without the Authorized Interpretation Fundamentalists Join Cults

A popular Fundamentalist radio show once noted that on the average the equivalent of one "Bible-believing" [i.e., Private Interpretation] church congregation is lost to Mormons and Jehovah's Witnesses each week. Like Fundamentalists, cultists such as the Mormons and the Jehovah's Witnesses do not accept the authority of the historic Faith. Because all three groups proceed on the assumption that beliefs should be based on "proof-texts" that appear plausible, the cultists merely have to undermine a few of the Fundamentalist's favorite proof-texts to entice the Fundamentalist into one cult or the other. For instance, the cultists could misuse the verses cited above [*Mark* 10:17-18 and *John* 14:28] to draw

---

[22] "Is the Father greater than Jesus?", *This Rock*, April 1992, 30.

the Fundamentalist away from recognition of the divinity of Christ. Without the Authorized Interpretation of the Christian Faith, the gift of the Holy Spirit to believers, the Christian has no protection against error and deception. Even when the Fundamentalist tries to be orthodox he could still stray into perilous waters if he does not recognize the authority of the historic interpretations. Several conservative Fundamentalist thinkers, for example, say that it is possible that Jesus could have sinned (although they admit that He did not actually do so). This position, of course, undermines the divinity of Christ: since it is inconceivable that God could sin, we wonder how it is possible to continue to believe that Jesus is a Divine Person (united, of course, with a human nature) if we also believe that He could have sinned. Only the historic Faith consistently proclaims without hesitation or compromise that Jesus Christ is a Divine Person and not a human person although He was united with a human and a Divine nature.

Re-inventing the Wheel

In a nutshell, the Fundamentalist slogan of Private Interpretation is merely a program of re-inventing the wheel. History shows that all attempts to re-invent the wheel merely result in wasted energy and effort that could have been better utilized in putting the already-invented wheel to new and useful applications. The Fundamentalist re-invention program not only suffers from these usual problems but some other unique ones as well. In their attempts to re-invent the wheel Fundamentalists often end up with instruments that bear no resemblance at all to wheels (this happens when they gradually part company with orthodox Christology). At other times, the wheels they construct cannot bear any weight (because Fundamentalist extrapolations often contradict honest science or sound philosophy). The bottom line is this: the Fundamentalists must be shown two things, that the wheel already exists and that what they are doing is merely a futile attempt to re-invent the wheel. The choice, we have said, is between the one divinely inspired inerrant interpretation of the Word of God and 22,000 other comparatively recent speculative interpretations.

Miracles in the History of Doctrine

The full significance of the promise of Jesus that the Holy Spirit would guide the Apostolic Community is seen when we survey the history of Christian doctrine. Dave Armstrong writes:

> Like many Christian doctrines, the idea of doctrinal development is based on much implicit or indirect scriptural evidence. The best indications are perhaps *Mt* 5:17, 13:31-32, *Jn* 14:26, 16:13, I *Cor* 2:9-16; *Gal* 4:4, and *Eph* 1:10, 4:12-15.
>
> Furthermore doctrine clearly develops within Scripture ("progressive revelation"). Examples of this process include: doctrines of the afterlife; the Trinity, the Messiah (eventually revealed as God the Son), the Holy Spirit (Divine Person in the New Testament), the equality of Jews and Gentiles, bodily resurrection, and sacrifice of lambs evolving into the sacrifice of Christ. Not a single doctrine initially emerges in the Bible complete with no further need of development.
>
> In general, whenever Scripture refers to the increasing knowledge and maturity of Christians and the Church, an idea very similar to doctrinal development is present. Holy Scripture, then, is in no way hostile to development...
>
> The canon of Scripture itself is an example of developing doctrine. The New Testament never informs us which books comprise itself, and its Canon (the final list of books) took about 360 years to reach its definitive form (at the Council of Carthage in A.D 397).
>
> For instance the books of Hebrews, James, 2 Peter 2, and 3 John, Jude and Revelation were not widely accepted by the Church until 350. And books such as Barnabas and 2 Clement were considered Scripture by many at the same time (for example, the manuscripts Codex Sinaiticus and Codex Alexandrinus). Of the 27 New Testament books, 14 were not mentioned at all until circa 200, including Acts, 2 Corinthians, Galatians and Colossians. On what grounds, then, can we receive the Canon today except on the authority of the Church in the fifth century? ...
>
> Tradition, Church authority and development were all crucial elements in the very human process of selection of the biblical canon. It is impossible to maintain as did Luther

and especially Calvin, that the knowledge of what books constitute Scripture can be attained by a Holy Spirit-produced subjective intuition within each Christian: If the early Church had such a difficult time determining what was and was not Scripture, how could Calvin 15 centuries later plausibly claim that it was simple for him and every other sincere Christian without the help of the Catholic Church?

It is very difficult to argue that no development occurred in Church history or that it ceased after the first, second, third or fifth century, etc. (all arbitrary human traditions). The Bible is not absolutely clear in every part, and requires the developing wisdom of the Church.

Doctrines agreed upon by all develop, too. The Divinity or Godhood of Christ was only finalized in 325, and the full doctrine of the Trinity in 381. The dogma of the two natures of Christ (true God and true man) was proclaimed in 451. These decisions of General Councils of the Church were in response to challenging heresies...

Although understanding increases, the essential elements of doctrines exist from the beginning.[23]

In his famous *An Essay on the Development of Doctrine*, John Henry Newman shows from history that only the protection of the Holy Spirit could have enabled the Apostolic Community to uphold and teach orthodox Christian doctrine:

> Nor was the development of dogmatic theology, which was then taking place, a silent and spontaneous process. It was wrought out and carried through under the fiercest controversies and the most fearful risks. The Catholic faith was placed in a succession of perils, and rocked to and fro like a vessel at sea. Large portions of Christendom were, one after another, in heresy or in schism; the leading churches and the most authoritative schools fell from time to time into serious error; three Popes, Liberius, Vigilius, Honorius, have left to posterity the burden of their defence: but these disorders were no interruption to the sustained and steady march of the sacred science from implicit belief to formal statement. The series of ecclesiastical decisions, in which its

---

23 Dave Armstrong, "Is Development of Doctrine a Corruption of Biblical Teaching," *The Catholic Answer*, September/October 1995, 8-9.

progress was ever and anon signified, alternate between the one and the other side of the theological dogma especially in question, as if fashioning it into shape by opposite strokes. The controversy began in Apollinaris, who confused or denied the Two Natures in Christ, and was condemned by Pope Damasus. A reaction followed, and Theodore of Mopsuestia ventured to teach, the doctrine of Two Persons. After Nestorius had brought that heresy into public view, and had incurred in consequence the anathema of the Third Ecumenical Council, the current of controversy again shifted its direction; for Eutyches appeared, maintained the One Nature, and was condemned at Chalcedon. Something however was still wanting to the overthrow of the Nestorian doctrine of Two Persons, and the Fifth Council was formally directed against the writings of Theodore and his party. Then followed the Monothelite heresy, which was a revival of the Eutychian or Monophysite, and was condemned in the Sixth. Lastly, Nestorianism once more showed itself in the Adoptionists of Spain, and gave occasion to the great Council of Frankfort. Any one false step would have thrown the whole theory of the doctrine into irretrievable confusion; but it was as if some one individual and perspicacious intellect, to speak humanly, ruled the theological discussion from first to last. That in the long course of centuries, and in spite of the failure, in points of detail, of the most gifted fathers and saints, the Church thus wrought out the one and only consistent theory which can be taken on the great doctrine in dispute, proves how clear, simple, and exact her vision of that doctrine was. But it proves more than this. Is it not utterly incredible, that with this thorough comprehension of so great a mystery, as far as the human mind can know it, she should be at that very time in the commission of the grossest errors in religious worship, and should be hiding the God and Mediator, whose Incarnation she contemplated with so clear an intellect, behind a crowd of idols? [IN OTHER WORDS, IT IS NOT POSSIBLE TO SAY THAT THE HISTORIC FAITH WAS RIGHT IN ITS MOST FUNDAMENTAL TEACHING AND WRONG IN ITS OTHER TEACHINGS].[24]

---

[24]   John Henry Newman, *An Essay on the Development of Christian Doctrine* (Baltimore, Maryland: Penguin Books), 444-5.

A Greater Awareness of Historic Interpretations Among Fundamentalists and Evangelicals

Today Fundamentalists and Evangelicals are beginning to realize that the truth of the historic teaching must be affirmed if we wish to hold a consistent Faith. For instance the Evangelical Gerald Bray writes in **Creeds, Councils and Christ**:

> There was great diversity in the Early Church, and there were many disagreements about what it meant to lead a Christian life in an essentially pagan society; but there is no sign anywhere that any kind of theological pluralism was tolerated. Those who differed from the Apostles were anathematized and excluded from the fellowship. From the start there was only one way and one recognized truth, however imprecisely it may have been formulated in the apostolic writings... The purpose of dogmatic definition is to establish the framework which will define the limits of what is essential and put the isolated truths of Scripture in proper perspective, so as to avoid distortions and false emphases. Orthodox theologians would argue that the Bible itself makes this task necessary as a means to understand its message.
>
> This brings us to the third and final point we must consider in relation to the interpretation of Scripture. Is it true that the New Testament invites us to engage in theological speculation and dogmatic construction? There are many who would argue that it does not. Protestantism, they say, maintains that the Scriptures contain everything necessary for salvation. They are the Word of God in a way that creeds and doctrinal statements are not. Christianity is the religion of a person and preaches a relationship with God based on mutual love. Yet doctrine sets up barriers and has caused untold harm to the body of Christ, by splitting it into countless fragments. 'The letter kills, but the Spirit gives life,' a Pauline statement which some have taken to mean that the true Church consists of men and women who have shared a common experience, however they may choose to define it. Words are limited and limiting; only the power of the Spirit, moving beyond language into strange tongues or other forms of mystical experience, can authenticate Christian experience in a convincing way. These attitudes are widespread in

the anti-intellectual climate of today, so much so that even those who held to traditional beliefs are reluctant to suggest that an understanding of Christian doctrine is an indispensable aid to learning from the Scriptures.

Modern thinking of this kind appears to be a long way from the historical liberalism of the nineteenth century, but in fact it is very closely linked to it. The great liberals also believed that religion was a matter of feeling rather than the intellect, and were prepared to accept the superstructure of Christian worship and doctrine as a channel along which these thoughts could be directed. They propounded, with great learning, a thesis which has now penetrated to the popular level and become very influential, even in conservative evangelical circles. Antidogmatism is a feature of the age we live in, and it affects us all whether we like it or not.

In response to this mood, the orthodox theologian must say that it runs counter to the biblical witness to God and his saving work in Christ. The Bible is a revelation in writing - Scripture - and this fact is of supreme importance. Writing is fixed, objective, definable communication to an extent that no other means is. Of course it can be unclear; it may also be obscured or corrupted by faulty transmission. Textual criticism of the Bible has shown that this has sometimes been the case, and its task is to put right what has gone wrong. But the assumption on which textual criticism is based is that the original text did make sense, and that it is possible, given enough evidence, to recover that sense. It is a work of restoration similar to that carried out on old buildings and paintings. The underlying intelligible harmony is the incentive which gives textual criticism a purpose and a goal.

The task of the dogmatician is somewhat similar to that of the textual critic, but at a different level. When the two disciplines are functioning properly they feed each other in the accomplishment of their respective tasks. The textual critic is concerned with the detail of the documents in his care, whilst the dogmatician is concerned to elucidate the principles which govern the thought they contain and which led to their compilation in the form in which we now have them... The dogmatician's task is to lay bare the foundations on which the teaching of Scripture is built, both as an aid to Christian growth and as a means of evangelizing those who do not share the same principles...

It can be said that the Epistles of the New Testament are ad hoc compositions, designed to meet specific situations. They are not, and were never intended to be, manuals of theology. This is true, but so what? They may not be manuals of theology, but they very clearly operate on the assumption that the readers already possess a clear theological understanding. When Paul writes to correct or upbraid his congregations, he does so on the assumption that they have forgotten and turned away from his teaching. In some cases they have accepted the words but not drawn the logical conclusions for behaviour and worship. In this sense, the Epistles are supplements to a theological teaching which had been given orally and which is assumed in the documents we possess. It is the task of the dogmatician to uncover what that teaching was.

The relationship between the Bible and classical dogmatics is not simple, in the sense that the one does not simply contain the other, but in principle it is quite clear. Dogmatics is the study of the fundamental prinriples on which the teaching of Scripture is based *and which are necessary for a proper understanding of God's plan of salvation* in Christ...

Their [the Creeds developed by the Councils and ancient theologians] achievement, however, should not be underestimated. Whatever one may think of them today, the great creeds of Christendom established themselves as the authoritative expressions of biblical faith. Every Christian church accepts their teaching, explicitly or implicitly, in spite of all the criticisms which have been levelled against them. As such, their enduring power is unequalled by any subsequent theological thought.[25]

Under the entry on "Tradition," the *Evangelical Dictionary* has a remarkable passage:

[Tradition is] the entire process by which normative religious truths are passed on from one generation to another. As such, tradition is found in all religious communities, whether its form be oral or written, its contents embodied in

---

[25] Gerald Bray, *Creeds, Councils and Christ* (Downers Grove, Illinois: Inter Varsity Press, 1984), 63-4.

a closed canon or a living organism. Even Evangelical Protestants, inclined though they may still be to overlook it, must recognize that oral tradition preceded and shaped the canon of written Scripture and that their own understanding of Scripture and consequently their own community life have been molded, consciously or unconsciously, by particular traditions...

Even before the NT canon was fixed, early church fathers appealed to its individual books and to sayings of Christ (a lost exegesis of them by Papias). But they likewise saw the original apostolic tradition preserved in other ways. They often appealed to an orthodox "rule of faith," a kind of summary of the gospel possibly related to early baptismal creeds and later issuing in full-fledged creedal documents; this rule was not originally fixed in writing or anything contrary to or wholly outside of Scripture. They also appealed to "apostolic succession," the public teaching (as distinguished from the Gnostics' secret wisdom) in those churches where bishops stood in direct line with their apostolic founders, especially the see of Rome "founded" by Peter and Paul. And they prepared, between the first and fourth centuries, a whole series of anonymous manuals (Didache) that claimed to contain the apostles' teachings, especially on cultic and ethical matters. These were not set over against Scripture, but they rather constituted the means by which the living church carried forward its witness.

Once the NT canon was fixed and the whole Bible complete, the great church fathers of the fourth and fifth centuries distinguished tradition and Scripture more clearly, but not antithetically. Tradition was understood as the church's enriching and interpretative reflection on the original deposit of faith contained in Scripture. This pertained preeminently to Christological interpretation of the OT. But it included as well the writings of earlier "fathers," considered a product of the Spirit's guidance and used to buttress the true faith; the decisions of bishops met in council under the Spirit's aegis; and various rites which had become central to the practice of the faith. A few fathers (notably Basil) recognized that certain matters were not clearly, or even remotely, prescribed in Scripture and ascribed these separately to apostolic tradition: e.g., to pray facing East, to baptize infants, to immerse three times, to fast on certain days, and the like. To count as authentic apostolic tradition, the fathers (Augustine and Vincent of Lerins in the West, e.g.) required that these be recognized and practiced throughout the whole church...

Protestants have nearly always rejected tradition in principle, while necessarily allowing it to reappear in practice in some other form. Luther rejected ecclesiastical traditions as distortions of the true gospel found in Scripture alone, and he thus, and for nearly all Protestants ever since, radically sundered apostolic authority from ecclesiastical tradition, now rendered merely human. Calvin confronted the question of interpretation squarely and insisted that the Spirit interacts with the word to illuminate believers...

In practice, most Protestant groups formed traditions nearly as binding as the Catholics and established similar sets of authorities: ecumenical councils, confessional creeds, synodical legislation, church orders, and theologians (esp. founders) of a particular church. *Those free churches, particularly in America, that claim to stand on Scripture alone and to recognize no traditional authorities are in some sense the least free because they are not even conscious of what traditions have molded their understanding of Scripture.* [emphasis added] ...

In recent years, scholarly research into the formation of Scripture and the course of church history has inspired greater thoughtfulness and honesty among Protestants on the subject of tradition. The word of God does not and cannot operate in a vacuum, as an isolated text; it comes alive through the Spirit in the context of gathered believers who make up Christ's church. Preaching is in fact the chief Protestant form of perpetuating tradition, i.e., authoritative interpretations and applications of the word.[26]

Objectives and Achievements of New Testament Scholars

On another front the decisive interpretations of the historic Faith have been challenged by the step-children of Sola Scriptura/ Private Interpretation Fundamentalism, the Liberal New Testament

---

[26] Walter A. Elwell, ed., *Evangelical Dictionary of Theology* (Grand Rapids, Michigan: Baker Book House, 1984), 1104.

scholars. These scholars have provided us with much valuable background information on the New Testament writings. With different degrees of agreement among themselves, they have identified the *possible* dates of composition of the various writings, the *possible* cultural, theological and other influences on the various writers and the *possible* linguistic and semantic connotations of various texts. There is no consensus on any of these matters among these scholars and the only certainty is that the reigning view of the moment will be replaced frequently and rapidly by a different if not contradictory view. The New Testament scholars attempt to determine (1) what if any of the New Testament writings authentically reflect the actual beliefs of the Apostles, (2) what the authors of the texts intended to say in their writings and (3) what relationship exists between the New Testament writings and other writings such as the Old Testament. In all three areas they have nothing to offer but speculation and guess work. And in all three areas their conclusions often deny the interpretations of the historic Faith. It goes without saying that these interpretations are in no sense authoritative because the reigning views are rapidly replaced over very short periods.

New Testament Scholars Have No Certain or Permanent Views

Now no New Testament scholar claims to be inspired by the Holy Spirit in his presuppositions or conclusions. He bases his views on his own scholarship and the scholarship of his colleagues. But when pressed he will admit that his views are at best speculative and reflect a fleeting trend of the time. He cannot know with certainty what indeed were the beliefs of the Apostolic Community and therefore which writings reflect these beliefs. He cannot know with certainty what the intentions of the New Testament writers were in writing their various texts. He cannot know with certainty what other documents influenced the New Testament writings or whether a certain event in the New Testament is actually a fulfillment of an Old Testament prophecy. Most important he will gladly admit that he does not know what truth God intended to teach through the various texts of the New Testament.

The Truth Intended by God

This last area is entirely beyond the grasp of speculative scholarship and linguistic prowess. If we want to know what God intended when He inspired a writer to generate a certain text, God will have to tell us. It is possible that the scriptural writer himself will not know what God intended when he wrote a text under divine inspiration. For instance many of the Old Testament prophecies about Jesus were made without the prophets knowing how these would be fulfilled. Thus even if a scholar could find out (which he cannot) what a New Testament writer intended when he wrote a text this still may not comprise the entire truth that *God* intended to convey through the text.

Rejection of the Authorized Interpretation Leads to Liberalism and the Cults

The question is whether or not God has chosen to tell us what truths He intended to teach when He inspired the New Testament writers to produce their works. The Apostolic Community and the Fathers, the Councils and the Creeds testify without hesitation or uncertainty that God speaks through them in interpreting and explaining the Sacred Scriptures. In the Creeds and the affirmations of the Councils and in the liturgy of the ancient Church we are given the binding interpretations of Scripture that come to us from "the Spirit of truth" Who will lead us "into all truth." These authoritative interpretations, and the teachings of the Apostolic Community and its Councils, constitute the historic Christian faith. Some of these interpretations may not have been grasped even by the authors of the texts but the same Spirit Who inspired the texts also inspires their interpretation. If we reject the faith given to us by the Fathers - from the Holy Spirit - we will either sink into the New Testament scholars' swamp of ever-changing interpretations or slide down the slippery slope of arbitrary Fundamentalist interpretations into the waiting hands of the cults.

Picking and Choosing the Sayings of Jesus

The best illustration of the folly of looking to New Testament scholars for the definitive interpretation of Scripture is the so-called Jesus Seminar. In this "Seminar" a group of New Testament scholars vote on the different sayings of Jesus to decide which of them can be truly attributed to Jesus. In some respects the Seminar is a degenerate version of the process by which the Apostolic Community and the Councils selected the books that belong to the canon and the interpretations of these books. The criteria used by the Seminar for its selection process are the speculative principles of New Testament studies and the majority beliefs of the participants. Neither of these criteria can give us any degree of certainty as to which sayings can be attributed to Jesus and what He intended when He spoke. The Apostolic Community and the Councils, on the other hand, made their selections and interpretations on the basis of the apostolic teaching handed to them and with the clear awareness that they were protected from error by the Holy Spirit.

Deleting the Divine Database

Both the Fundamentalists and liberal New Testament scholars have adopted a procedure of discarding the interpretations of the historic faith and starting from scratch. Their procedure can be compared to that of a scientist who decides to ignore the collective insights of modern science and wants to start from scratch with only the knowledge available in the Stone Age. The output from this endeavor will inevitably seem naive and preposterous if compared to the results of later science. Similarly the output of the Fundamentalists and the liberal scholars has succeeded simply in deleting a divine database revealed over centuries and replacing it with programs created by infants.

Not a Textbook of Dogma but a Teacher

The cul-de-sacs of the Fundamentalists and their Liberal counterparts can be safely avoided by those who remain faithful to the treasury of scriptural truth inspired and safeguarded by the Holy Spirit in the historic Christian Faith. The truths of the historic Faith are the truths God intended to teach through Scripture. Some might ask why Scripture does not explicitly (in so many words) define the Marian doctrines, say the Immaculate Conception or the Assumption. We might as well ask why Scripture does not explicitly define the Christological doctrines. It would have been much simpler for us if Jesus said in so many words "I am the God-man, the Second Person of the Holy Trinity." But we never see Him as a teacher of dogma either about Himself or His Mother. God did not give Scripture to us as a textbook of dogma. Instead Jesus promised us that the Holy Spirit "shall teach you all things" - that we would receive a Teacher of dogma. "I have yet many things to say unto you," said Jesus, "but ye cannot bear them now. Howbeit when he, the Spirit of truth, is come, he will guide you into all truth." Let us take Him at His word and embrace the authoritative interpretations of Scripture shown to us over the centuries by the Holy Spirit.

A recent review of biblical interpretation in the Evangelical magazine *Christianity Today* has words of wisdom on this matter for Fundamentalists and all Christians:

> The massive consensus of thoughtful Christian interpretation of the Word down the ages (and on most matters of importance there is such a thing) is not likely to be wrong... The Enlightenment model of the Bible student as a Lone Ranger, out on his own away from the church as he seeks truth, inevitably leads to distorted if not heretical, conclusions.[27]

---

27 Kenneth S.Kantzer, "The Doctrine Wars," *Christianity Today*, October 5, 1992, 32

ONCE SAVED ALWAYS SAVED, ONCE PREDESTINED FOR DAMNATION ALWAYS DAMNED:
Why Faith Without Works Does Not Work

A. OVERVIEW

Although the Protestant Reformers accepted the teaching of the historic Christian Faith on the various Marian titles and attributes [Mother of God, Perpetual Virginity, Immaculate Conception, Assumption], they rejected the ancient doctrine of Mary's participation in the divine scheme of salvation. The Reformers' rejection of Marian participation was motivated more by their newly developed interpretation of salvation than by any particular doctrine of Mary.

At the top of the Reformation agenda was the thesis of Luther and Calvin that we are saved by faith alone and grace alone - believers have no part to play in their salvation through their choices or actions and they are saved entirely by the grace of God and faith in Christ. Of course this thesis of salvation through faith alone and without human cooperation is based on a particular interpretation of Scripture. Since this interpretation touches on the most important question of human life - salvation - all Christians must carefully study the interpretation in the light of Scriptural passages, the historic Christian Faith and the kind of vision of God and human nature that it projects.

It is often said that the fundamental difference between Catholicism and Protestantism concerns their respective teachings on the relationship between faith, works and salvation. Whereas, it is said, Catholics teach salvation through faith and works, Protestants (inspired by the Reformers) believe in salvation by faith alone. Now this popular understanding is both superficial and misleading. The real issue at stake is not the difference in interpretation on faith and works between Luther and Calvin, on the one hand, and the Catholic Church on the other. The real issue concerns the teaching of the historic Christian Faith on God, man and salvation. Every interpretation of Scripture assumes a certain view of God and man. It is this underlying view that should be the focus of our attention. According to historic Christianity, God desires the salvation of all men and offers them all the grace to freely choose or reject the salvation made available through the death of Jesus Christ. According to the interpretation of Scripture popularized by Luther and Calvin, God deliberately created the vast majority of mankind with the specific intention of damning them and then damns them by "pre-programming" them for damnation while setting aside a minority of mankind who He will bring to salvation by pre-programming them to have faith in Him. Unbelievable as this may sound, this description of the theology of Luther and Calvin can be easily confirmed by reading the extensive excerpts from Calvin's writings cited below [in fact the chilling title of one of his chapters is "Eternal Election, or God's Predestination of Some to Salvation, and of Others to Destruction"].

When we talk of faith, works and salvation, we are simply scratching the surface of a much larger debate on God, man and the divine plan of salvation. What is authoritative in the final analysis is the witness of Scripture and the inerrant interpretation of Scripture given us in the historic Faith. The interpretations of Luther and Calvin must be measured against Scripture and the historic interpretation of Scripture. This is not a Catholic-Protestant debate. On the one side of the discussion we have Catholics, Orthodox and many Protestant scholars and denominations. On the other side we have the interpretation of salvation given by Luther and Calvin and adopted by their modern followers, primarily the Fundamentalists.

Protestant rejection of the positions of Luther and Calvin on this issue is not often recognized. For instance, many modern Protestant exegetes reject the exegetical method used by Luther in developing his theology from the epistles of Paul. And perhaps the most powerful [and yet unanswered] critique of Calvinism is John Wesley's "Predestination Calmly Considered."

In the view of Luther and Calvin salvation actually does not come from "faith alone" except at a secondary level: salvation for any particular believer comes *from the fact that he has been pre-programmed for salvation* by God: "faith" is just a magic carpet supplied to the lucky few who have been selected for salvation and who have been pre-programmed to leap on to the rug that will take them to their pre-ordained destination. Even at this initial stage we can see that this view of God and man faces major obstacles:

i. There are numerous passages in the New Testament which decisively contradict the thesis that man's free actions have nothing to do with his salvation. Faith-alone Fundamentalists have tried to devise ingenious escape-routes to run away from the hard facts of Scripture and Luther even tried to excise the Epistle of James from the canon of Scripture because it refuted his thesis!

ii. The historic Christian Faith - the inerrant interpretation of the inerrant Word of God - has affirmed without compromise the clear teaching of Our Lord on the importance of the "obedience of faith" in salvation ["Not every one that saith unto me, Lord, Lord, shall enter into the kingdom of heaven; but he that doeth the will of my Father which is in heaven." *Matthew* 7:21.]

iii. The salvation-through-preprogrammed-faith thesis projects a monstrous vision of human beings as puppets without freedom who are manipulated by a god who arbitrarily decides to save a few and to damn the vast majority without any regard to the kind of lives they lead or the choices they make. Neither Luther nor Calvin denied this consequence. The Calvinist view ultimately projects a god who is the author of evil as John Wesley and many other Protestants recognized.

As with all interpretations that departed from the historic Christian faith, the new thesis of salvation-without-human-freedom too subsequently splintered into a dizzying array of other interpretations on the vital question of faith, works and salvation. For Christians who wish to know how to be saved, confusion of this kind is cruel and intolerable. Only the divinely protected treasury of the historic Faith continues to teach the consistent message preached by Christ and the Apostles. In what follows we will explore further the basic issues inevitably involved in all discussions of faith, works and salvation while keeping the teaching of the historic Christian Faith as a point of reference. The main sources cited here in defense of the historic Christian teaching on salvation will be Protestant thinkers.

Among the main differences between the doctrine taught by Luther and Calvin and the historic teaching are the following:

(a) According to Luther and Calvin, salvation or damnation is predetermined by God for each person regardless of his choices or actions; according to the historic faith, God gives every person the grace to choose salvation but he has the freedom to refuse God's offer and choose damnation. Moreover, contrary to Calvin and Luther, Scripture tells us that God desires the salvation of all. ["God our Savior. . . will have all men to be saved, and to come unto the knowledge of the truth." (I *Timothy* 2:3-4)]. And Jesus died for us all not just for the Elect ["He that spared not his own Son, but delivered him up for us all." *Romans* 8:32].

(b) According to Luther and Calvin there is no merit in the act of faith which justifies us because those who make the act are already pre-programmed to do so by God; the historic Faith teaches, on the contrary, that the act of faith is the act that makes salvation possible and is therefore meritorious [although this act is made only because of the grace given by God: nevertheless we have the option to reject this grace and the decision not to reject the grace is meritorious]. Many Arminians who reject the Calvinist view that God pre-programs us from eternity nevertheless hold to the view that there is no merit in the act of faith because it is entirely from God. This view is a contradiction in terms. Is the act of faith a free act although it is possible only because of God's grace? Yes. Does salvation depend on the free act of faith? Yes. Is it possible to freely choose to not make the act of faith by rejecting the grace given by God? Yes. Then is it not beneficial, worthwhile, praiseworthy to freely make the act of faith? Yes. Is it not a su-

premely important and commendable act because your
salvation depends on it? Yes. If you answer "Yes" to
the initial questions, as most Arminians will, then you
have to answer "Yes" to the last two - which is to say
that the act of accepting God's offer is meritorious.

(c) Luther and Calvin taught that justification does not bring
about any change in a person and that the righteousness of Christ is imputed to him without any real change
in the kind of person he is; the historic Faith teaches
that justification by faith introduces the grace of God
into the soul and this gradually helps it to turn from
evil toward holiness (believers become "partakers of
the divine nature" as we are told in 2 Peter 1:4).

All discussions on faith and works must come back to the issue of what kind of God we believe in. A doctrine of "faith alone"
with no role for man's freedom ultimately ends up with a Calvinist picture of God. It cannot be repeated enough that the Calvinist
god deliberately creates most men simply in order to damn them:
the specific purpose of creating them was to damn them. The reverse side of the "once saved always saved" belief is "once damned
always damned." At the bottom of all the debates about works,
justification and salvation are the questions of freedom and God's
infinite love. Faith and grace bring about salvation. But the grace
must be accepted, the act of faith must be made. Only then is salvation possible.

The consistent teaching of the historic Christian Faith is that
we are justified by faith which comes from God's grace alone. [Faith
in the New Testament is not simply an intellectual activity but involves a response of the whole person and includes "the obedience
of faith." For instance, see *Romans* 1:5 ("By whom you have received grace and apostleship, for obedience to the faith") and *Romans* 16:26 ("made known to all nations for the obedience of
faith").] This justification which comes from grace and faith results in a real change in us whereby we can begin to grow in sanctification through good works. We can also choose to defile ourselves and thereby damn ourselves even after we initially accept
God's offer of salvation. All men are in different stages of the journey towards either salvation or damnation and in different ways

and through different agents God attempts to draw us in the direction that leads to Him. This is the teaching of the historic Faith.

The possibility of our participation in Christ's work of redemption is very clearly highlighted in *Colossians* 1:24: "I Paul ... rejoice in my sufferings for you, and fill up that which is behind of the afflictions of Christ in my flesh for his body's sake, which is the church." About this latter verse, Frank Sheed writes: "The sentence is doubly stunning, for Paul not only speaks of something lacking in Christ's sufferings but says that he, Paul (and presumably other Christians), will 'complete' them for the sake of Christ's body, the Church. Whatever the God-man could do, Christ did. What was lacking could only be something which in the nature of the case could not be done by the God-man for men but must be done by men for themselves. Men are not merely to be spectators of their own redemption. Purely human love, yours and mine, is not to be denied all place in the expiation of human sin."[28] From the time of the Reformation this passage from *Colossians* has been a major obstacle to the perverse theory that denies all value and merit to good works and sees human beings simply as puppets.

This introduction to the question of faith, works and salvation highlights the indispensability of authoritative interpretation. By cutting themselves off from the interpretation of the historic Christian Faith on the relation of faith and works the Reformers condemned their followers to chaos and ambiguity on this crucial question. Luther and Calvin interpreted several Scriptural verses on God's sovereignty to mean that human beings have no freedom to accept or reject God and that salvation comes purely from God's arbitrary decision to save a few and damn the vast majority. Their system of doctrine in this area was unscriptural on the one hand and, on the other, presents a deformed view of both God and man. Post-Reformation history shows that any departure from the inerrant interpretation of the historic Faith on salvation would inevitably result in further departures. Calvinism has been followed by a plethora of contradictory views on justification and sanctification - Arminian, Pentecostal, Dispensationalist and numerous others. Proponents of each view interpret various Scriptural verses to support their particular position while ignoring contradictory verses.

---

[28] F.J. Sheed, *What Difference Does Jesus Make?* (Sheed and Ward), 219-220.

The ordinary believer is left with no certainty or authoritative direction. It is obviously no solution to say that we should study Scripture to get the right answer because the proponents of the various views each claim to have studied Scripture and yet come up with contradictory interpretations. Ultimately we have to choose either the position of the historic Faith or condemn ourselves to continuous cycles of confusion on a question that is of the most vital importance for every one of us.

B. THE CHRISTIAN GOD

The teaching of the historic Faith on salvation was memorably set forth by the Council of Orange in 529. While stating clearly that "in every good work it is not we who take the initiative and are then assisted by the mercy of God, but God himself first inspires in us both faith in him and love for him without any previous good works of our own that deserve reward ", the Council is emphatic that that any doctrine of "once damned always damned" is anathema:

> We not only do not believe that any are foreordained to evil
> by the power of God, but even state with utter abhorence
> that if there are those who want to believe **so evil a thing**,
> they are anathema.

Moreover, once a person has come to Christ, his salvation is not guaranteed but depends on his continuing cooperation with Christ and His grace:

> After grace has been received through baptism, all baptized
> persons have the ability and responsibility, if they desire to
> labor faithfully, to perform with the aid and cooperation of
> Christ what is of essential importance in regard to the sal-
> vation of their soul.[29]

About the Calvinist view of God, John Wesley said, "This is not the God of the Christians." The Christian God, said Wesley, "is

---

[29]   John H. Leith, *Creeds of the Churches* (Chicago, Illinois: Aldine Publishing Company, 1963), 45.

just in all his ways ... He requireth only according to what he hath given; and where he hath given little, little is required. The glory of his justice is this, to 'reward every man according to his works.'" [cf. 2 Tm. 4:14].[30]

The scriptural revelation of salvation history is really a story of man's free choices and its consequences and it is hard to see how anyone can understand it from a Calvinist point of view. Salvation history begins with a choice made by Adam and Eve and the punishment which follows. The rest of Scripture tells us of choices, both good and bad, that all have consequences and also of God's constant offer of the grace to do His Will and to make the right choices. According to C.S. Lewis the Christian view is that "There are only two kinds of people in the end: those who say to God, 'Thy will be done,' and those to whom God says, in the end, 'Thy will be done.' All that are in Hell, choose it. Without that self-choice there could be no Hell."[31]

In the teaching of Jesus the emphasis is first on accepting Him as Lord and, secondly, on doing the will of God, on avoiding sin and growing in holiness. In fact there can be no distinction between the two: "Not every one that saith unto me, Lord, Lord, shall enter into the kingdom of heaven; but he that doeth the will of my Father which is in heaven." *Matthew* 7:21. All that He teaches assumes that we have the freedom to choose right and wrong and therefore bear responsibility for our choices. This is the same, as we shall see, in the teaching of Paul.

Now there can be no doubt that our justification is purely a gift of God. There is no theological difference between Catholics and most Protestants on this matter as shown in a joint Lutheran-Catholic report on justification: "Catholics can speak of justification by faith or even of justification by faith alone insofar as they teach, as do Lutherans, that nothing prior to the free gift of faith merits justification and that all of God's saving gifts come through Christ alone."[32]

---

[30] John Wesley, "Predestination Calmly Considered" in Albert C. Outler, ed. *John Wesley* (New York: Oxford University Press, 1964), p.451.

[31] C.S. Lewis, *The Great Divorce* (New York: Macmillan, 1945), p.69.

[32] Joseph A. Burgess and Jeffrey Gros, eds., *Building Unity* (New York: Paulist Press, 1989), 217ff.

The difference between the historic Faith and the view of Luther and Calvin turns on whether or not we can freely accept or reject God's grace and the gift of faith. Christianity from the beginning has taught that we can accept or reject God's free gift by our own freewill and that we are responsible for this choice. Paul says Abraham was justified by his faith: but he could be justified by his faith only because he freely accepted the grace of God and made the act of faith: "Abraham believed God, and it was accounted to him for righteousness." [*Galatians* 3:6]. The whole of *Hebrews* 11 is a commentary on the Old Testament saints who freely chose faith - and the meritoriousness of their choice. Luther and Calvin, however, said that God had already programmed those who would accept the gift of faith to accept it and that they accepted it only because they were so programmed; similarly, those who reject the gift do so because they were pre-programmed to reject it.

The doctrine of faith without freedom is contrary to Christianity not only because of the deformed picture of God and man it gives us but also because it corrupts us. It smells of wishful thinking. Against the clear teaching of Christ and the Apostle Paul we claim that the lives we lead, the moral choices we make, the kind of people we become has no bearing whatsoever on our decision for or against God. We can sin all we want [as Luther, in fact, advised: see below] because we will never lose our salvation. There is no need to be holy and pure because our sins are covered under the righteousness imputed to us by Christ.

On the level of Scripture alone, we can show that this doctrine is contrary to Christian teaching. There are numerous passages in the New Testament that make it unmistakably clear that we are responsible for accepting or rejecting God's offer of salvation by our choices and actions:

"And why call ye me, Lord, Lord, and do not the things which I say." *Luke* 6:46.

"Verily I say unto you, Inasmuch as ye have done it unto one of the least of these my brethren, ye have done it unto me... Verily I say unto you, Inasmuch as ye did it not to one of the least of these, ye did it not unto me. And these shall go away into everlasting punishment: but the righteous into life eternal." *Matthew* 25:40,45,46.

"But be ye doers of the word, and not hearers only, deceiving your own selves." *James* 1:22.

"What doth it profit, my brethren, though a man say he hath faith, and have not works? can faith save him?... Even so faith, if it hath not works, is dead, being alone." *James* 2:14, 17.

"Ye see then how that by works a man is justified, and not by faith only." *James* 2:24.

"Be not deceived; God is not mocked: for whatsoever a man soweth, that shall he also reap. For he that soweth to his flesh shall of the flesh reap corruption; but he that soweth to the Spirit shall of the Spirit reap life everlasting. And let us not be weary in well doing; for in due season we shall reap, if we faint not. As we have therefore opportunity, let us do good unto all men." *Galatians* 6:7-10.

"But after thy hardness and impenitent heart treasurest up unto thyself wrath against the day of wrath and revelation of the righteous judgment of God; who will render to every man according to his deeds. To them who by patient continuance in well doing seek for glory and honour and immortality, eternal life: But unto them that are contentious, and do not obey the truth, but obey unrighteousness, indignation and wrath." *Romans* 2:5-8.

"And hereby we do know that we know him, if we keep his commandments. He that saith, I know him, and keepeth not his commandments, is a liar, and the truth is not in him." 1 *John* 2:3-4.

"For we must all appear before the judgment seat of Christ; that every one may receive the things done in his body, according to that he hath done, whether it be good or bad." 2 *Corinthians* 5:10.

"Wherefore, my beloved, as ye have always obeyed, not as in my presence only, but now much more in my absence, work out your own salvation with fear and trembling." *Philippians* 2:12.

"Follow peace with all men, *and holiness*, without which no man shall see God." *Hebrews* 12:14.

God's grace is not irresistible contrary to what Calvinists claim. As we see in these verses, our freedom allows us to reject God:

> "Ye stiffnecked and uncircumcised in heart and ears, ye do always resist the Holy Ghost: as your fathers did, so do ye." *Acts* 7:51.

> "For if we sin wilfully after that we have received the knowledge of the truth, there remaineth no more sacrifice for sins, But a certain fearful looking for of judgment and fiery indignation which shall devour the adversaries. He that despised Moses' law died without mercy under two or three witnesses. Of how much sorer punishment, suppose ye shall he be thought worthy, who hath trodden under foot the Son of God, and hath counted the blood of the covenant, wherewith he was sanctified an unholy thing, and hath done despite unto the Spirit of grace?" *Hebrews* 10:26-9.

> "But there were false prophets also among the people, even as there shall be false teachers among you, who privily shall bring damnable heresies, even denying the Lord that bought them, and bring upon themselves swift destruction." *2 Peter* 2:1.

Scripture tells us that it is possible for a believer to reject God and be lost even after initially accepting the divine offer of salvation. Thus the Word of God contradicts the Calvinist doctrine of "the perseverance of the saints" and the popular Fundamentalist doctrines of "eternal security" and "once saved always saved." 2 *Peter* 2:1 cited above is an example because this passage talks of Christian believers who are later damned ("even denying the Lord that *bought* them, and bring upon themselves swift *destruction*"). 2 *Peter* 1:10 says "Wherefore the rather, brethren, give diligence to make your calling and election sure: for if ye do these things, ye shall never fall" - thus implying that it is possible to fall. In **Life in the Son** [Minneapolis: Bethany House, 1989], the Baptist author Robert Shank cites eighty five passages in Scripture that teach the possibility of damnation for Christians who fall away. Some of these texts are cited below:

> "I am the true vine, and my Father is the husbandman. Every branch in me that beareth not fruit he taketh away; and

every branch that beareth fruit, he purgeth it, that it may bring forth more fruit... If a man abide not in me, he is cast forth as a branch, and is withered; and men gather them, and cast them in to the fire, and they are burned." (*John* 15:1-6).

"Therefore, brethren, we are debtors, not to the flesh, to live after the flesh. For if ye live after the flesh, ye shall die: but if ye through the Spirit do mortify the deeds of the body, ye shall live." (*Romans* 8:10,11). This epistle is written to believers and warns them that they could "die" spiritually if they "live after the flesh".

"Because of unbelief they were broken off ... Behold therefore the goodness and severity of God: on them which fell, severity; but toward thee, goodness, if thou continue in his goodness: otherwise thou also shalt be cut off." (*Romans* 11:20,22).

"But if thy brother be grieved with thy meat, now walkest thou not charitably. Destroy not him with thy meat, for whom Christ died." (*Romans* 14:15).

Like **Life in the Son**, another well known Protestant book, **Christian Theology** [3 volumes] by H.O. Wiley, shows that the doctrine of eternal security is contradicted by Scripture.

The passages from Scripture cited above as well as others leave little room for doubt that faith-without-freedom and predetermined-salvation are false and unscriptural doctrines. We may ask then what caused Martin Luther and his followers to misread Scripture and consequently mislead millions of Christians. Let us understand first that salvation is a free gift of God and not something that can be earned by any human being. Scripture specifically teaches that good works cannot earn salvation. But salvation is a gift that we can accept or reject and we can accept salvation only because of the grace of God. We cannot earn Heaven but we certainly can earn Hell. The possibility of damnation hangs over us all through our choices in this life as Our Lord Himself warns in unmistakable terms: "He that shall endure unto the end, the same shall be saved." *Matthew* 24: 13. This calling to persevere in holiness is echoed throughout the New Testament as we see from this verse in *Hebrews*: "For we are made partakers of Christ, if we hold the beginning of our confidence stedfast unto the end." *Hebrews* 3:14. And Paul warns: "But I keep under my body, and bring it into subjection: lest that by any means, when I have preached to others, I myself should be a castaway." 1 *Corinthians* 9:27.

The importance of performing right choices and actions and avoiding all evil is a persistent theme in Scripture. "For this is the love of God, that we keep his commandments." [1 *John* 5:3]. There is even a hierarchy of evil and of consequences for sins: "Sin no more, lest a worse thing come unto thee." [*John* 5:14]. "If any man see his brother sin a sin which is not unto death, he shall ask, and he shall give him life for them that sin not unto death. There is a sin unto death: I do not say that he shall pray for it. All unrighteousness is sin: and there is a sin not unto death." [1 *John* 5:16-6]. We cannot avoid either the consequences of sins: "Thou shalt not depart thence, till thou hast paid the very last mite." [*Matthew* 12:59]. No verse in Scripture could be clearer than *James* 2:24 on the prime importance of a holy life: "You must perceive that a person is justified by his works and not by faith alone." This was so obviously a refutation of Luther's interpretation of Paul's epistles that he wanted to excise the Epistle of *James* (which he shockingly called an "epistle of straw") from the Bible.

We have seen that Paul too emphatically preaches our participation in God's scheme of salvation. *Colossians* 1:24 is just one of many examples. But this verse is particularly significant because it highlights the importance of our choices and actions in God's work of salvation as we seen in a standard Protestant commentary:

> It is the destiny of the 'corporate Christ' the Church - to fulfil a certain tale of afflictions and that thus the apostle's hardships and privations, incurred in his calling, are a contribution made for the sake of the whole body, towards the discharge of this quota.[33]

This theme is continued in 1 *Corinthians* where Paul tells us "For we are labourers together with God." This should hardly be a surprise for those who remember the commandment of Christ: "If any man will come after me, let him deny himself, and take up his

---

[33] Matthew Black, ed., *Peake's Commentary on the Bible* (London: Thomas Nelson, 1962), 992.

cross and follow me." [*Matthew* 16:24]. In Romans 8:17 Paul tells us "We suffer with him, that we may be also glorified together."

C. THE DENIAL OF MAN'S FREEDOM AND THE AFFIRMATION OF A GOD WHO CREATES MEN SPECIFICALLY TO DAMN THEM

The doctrines of God and man ascribed to Calvin and Luther in the previous sections may seem unbelievable to some readers. It may be thought that no Christian could ever say that God creates the majority of men solely in order to damn them. It is best at this juncture to let Calvin and Luther speak for themselves. We cite below lengthy excerpts from their works concerning these issues. We begin with Calvin's exposition of God's "Predestination of Some to Salvation, and of Others to Destruction" in his **Institutes of the Christian Religion**:

> Predestination we call the eternal decree of God, by which he has determined in himself, what he would have to become of every individual of mankind. For they are not all created with a similar destiny; but eternal life is foreordained for some, and eternal damnation for others. Every man, therefore, being created for one or the other of these ends, we say, he is predestinated either to life or to death...
>
> By an eternal and immutable counsel, God has once for all determined, both whom he would admit to salvation, and whom he would condemn to destruction. We affirm that this counsel, as far as concerns the elect, is founded on his gratuitous mercy, totally irrespective of human merit; but that to those whom he devotes to condemnation, the gate of life is closed by a just and irreprehensible, but *incomprehensible*, judgment...
>
> All things being at God's disposal, and the decision of salvation or death belonging to him, he orders all things by his counsel and decree in such a manner, that *some men are born devoted from the womb to certain death, that his name may be glorified in their destruction*. If any one pleads, that no necessity was imposed on them by the providence of

God, but rather that they were created by him in such a state in consequence of his foresight of their future depravity; it will amount to nothing...

It is an awful decree, I confess; but no one can deny that God foreknew the future final fate of man before he created him, and that he did foreknow it because *it was appointed by his own decree.* If any one here attacks God's foreknowledge, he rashly and inconsiderately stumbles...

Nor should it be thought absurd to affirm, that God not only foresaw the fall of the first man, and the ruin of his posterity in him, but also *arranged all by the determination of his own will.* For as it belongs to his wisdom to foreknow every thing future, so it belongs to his power to rule and govern all things by his hand...

The reprobate wish to be thought excusable in sinning, because they cannot avoid a necessity of sinning; especially since this necessity is laid upon them by the ordination of God. But we deny this to be a just excuse; because the ordination of God, by which they complain that they are destined to destruction, is guided by equity, *unknown indeed to us,* but indubitably certain...

Those, therefore, whom he has created to a life of shame and a death of destruction, that they might be instruments of his wrath, and examples of his severity, he causes to reach their appointed end, *sometimes depriving them of the opportunity of hearing the word,* sometimes, by the preaching of it, *increasing their blindness and stupidity...*

It is a fact not to he doubted, that God sends his word to many whose blindness *he determines* shall be increased...

When the impious hear these things, they loudly complain that God, by a wanton exercise of power, abuses his wretched creatures for the sport of his cruelty. But we ... confess that the reprobate suffer nothing but what is consistent with the most righteous judgment of God. Though *we cannot comprehend the reason of this, let us be content with some degree of ignorance* where the wisdom of God soars into its own sublimity.[34]

---

[34] John Calvin, *Institutes of the Christian Religion*, Volume II, Translated from Latin by John Allen, Introduction by Benjamin B. Warfield (Philadelphia: Presbyterian Board of Christian Education, 1936), 176, 181, 206-9, 232-3, 236.

In his Commentary on Romans, Calvin writes:

> The wicked themselves have been created for *this* very end
> - *that they may perish.*[35]

Calvin's terrifying doctrine of a god whose will is to damn the majority of men was espoused by Martin Luther. Although Luther recognized that both Scripture and historic Christianity opposed such a view of God he developed a loophole by distinguishing between the will of God revealed in the Bible and the "hidden will of God" that was revealed to Calvin, Luther and their followers. In describing Luther's position, a contemporary Calvinist admits that Luther "appealed to a 'hidden will of God' that was distinct from the revealed will of God. The revealed will was that all men be saved, but the hidden will was that the greater part of mankind be damned." Again, "Luther at this point made a distinction that was important to his theology: There is the revealed will of God. On the one hand, God pleads with the sinner to believe; yet, on the other hand, he plans the damnation of many. This secret will is not to be inquired into but to be reverently adored. We should not ask why it is so but rather stand in awe of God." Concerning 1 Timothy 2:4 "God desires all men to be saved," "Luther would say that God may desire the salvation of all men but had chosen to forgo those desires for a higher, hidden purpose."[36]

Luther admitted that his picture of God was disturbing:

> Doubtless it gives the greatest possible offence to common sense or natural reason, that God, Who is proclaimed as being full of mercy and goodness, and so on, should of His own mere will abandon, harden, and damn men, as though He delighted in the sins and great eternal torments of such poor wretches. It seems an iniquitous, cruel, intolerable thought to think of God; and it is this that has been a stumbling block to so many great men down the ages. And who would not stumble at it? I have stumbled at it myself more

---

[35] Quoted in John Murray, *Calvin on Scripture and Divine Sovereignty* (Michigan: Baker Book House, 1960), 61.

[36] Erwin W. Lutzer, *All One Body - Why Don't We Agree?* (Wheaton, Illinois: Tyndale House Publishers, 1989), 171,

than once, down to the deepest pit of despair, so that I wished
I had never been made a man.[37]

Despite these reservations, Luther was totally committed to
the rejection of human freedom: "Everything we do, everything
that happens, even if it seems to us to happen mutably and contin-
gently, happens in fact nonetheless necessarily and immutably, if
you have regard to the will of God. For the will of God is effectual
and cannot be hindered."[38] "God's foreknowledge and omnipotence are diametrically opposed to our free choice."[39]

In the theology of Calvin and Luther there is no significant
human freedom whatsoever: God has predestined some humans
for Heaven and some for Hell. The Elect (who are predestined for
Heaven) have "saving faith" in Christ not because they made a
free act of the will but because they were "chosen" to have faith
beforehand; the Reprobate (who God has predestined for Hell) will
be damned eternally regardless of the choices they make in this
life. In the Calvinist world God is seen as the creator of evil (since
everything in the universe is determined by Him). In the words of
John Wesley, this doctrine of determinism represented 'God as
worse than the devil; more false, more cruel, and more unjust.'[40]
Calvin himself called God's predestination of some to Hell for no
fault of their own as His 'horrible decree.'[41]

We must remember here that the theology of Calvin and Luther
is a novel interpretation of Scripture developed by two individuals
16 centuries after the founding of Christianity. There is no authority supporting this theology save the prestige of its inventors. The
greatest arguments against the theology of faith-without-freedom
and pre-determined-damnation are the plain testimony of Scripture, the teaching of historic Christianity and our own moral sense.

Calvin recognized that numerous scriptural verses contradict
his theology. His method of dealing with such verses is to explain
away the obvious:

---

[37] Martin Luther, *Bondage of the Will*, translated J.I Packer and O.R. Johnston
(Revell: 1957), p.217.
[38] Martin Luther, *Luther's Works*, Volume 33, translated and edited by Philip S.
Watson [Philadelphia: Fortress, 1972], p. 37.
[39] Ibid., 189.
[40] John Wesley, *Works* (Grand Rapids: Baker, 1979), 7:382.
[41] *Institutes* 3:23.

The same reasoning applies to the exception lately cited, where Christ says, that "none of them is lost, but the son of perdition." (e) *Here is, indeed, some inaccuracy of expression* (!)...

I will not deny, that the Spirit sometimes accommodates his language to the limited extent of our capacity...

But as objections are frequently raised from some passages of Scripture, in which God *seems* to deny that the destruction of the wicked is caused by his decree, but that, in opposition to his remonstrances, they voluntarily bring ruin upon themselves; *let us show by a brief explanation* that they are not at all inconsistent with the foregoing doctrine. A passage is produced from Ezekiel, where God says, "I have no pleasure in the death of the wicked, but that the wicked turn from his way and live."

[Calvin's "brief explanation":]

Let us observe, therefore, the design of the prophet in saying that God has no pleasure in the death of a sinner; it is to assure the pious of God's readiness to pardon them immediately on their repentance, and to show the impious the aggravation of their sin in rejecting such great compassion and kindness of God. Repentance, therefore, will always be met by Divine mercy; *but on whom repentance is bestowed* [i.e., this passage only applies to the Elect. Of course the text itself makes no distinction of this sort. Calvin merely attempts to paint it with his colors.]...

Another passage adduced is from Paul, where he states that "God will have all men to be saved" which, though somewhat different frnm the passage just considered, yet is very similar to it. I reply, in the first place, that it is evident from the context, how God wills the salvation of all; for Paul connects these two things together, that he "will have all men to be saved, and to come unto the knowledge of the truth." *If it was fixed in the eternal counsel of God, that they should receive the doctrine of salvation ...*

"This is good and acceptable in the sight of God, who will have all men to be saved" which only imports, that God has not closed the way of salvation against any order of men, but has diffused his mercy in such a manner that he would have no rank to be destitute of it. [Calvin reinterprets "all" to mean "all orders of men" instead of "all men" as the text plainly says.] ...

There is more *apparent plausibility* in their objection, from the declaration of Peter, that "the Lord is not willing that any should perish, but that all should come to repentance." (2 Peter iii.9) But the second clause *furnishes an immediate solution of this difficulty* (?); for the willingness that they should come to repentance *must be understood in consistence with the general tenor of Scripture.* Conversion is certainly in the power of God; let him be asked, whether he wills the conversion of all, when he promises a few individuals to give them "a heart of flesh," while he leaves others with "a heart of stone. [Calvin regards the clear citation of Scripture that God wants "all" to come to repentance to be a "difficulty." He then reinteprets the passage to fit Calvinist theology by claiming that it *"must be understood in consistence with the general tenor of Scripture,"* i.e., with his particular interpretation of the "tenor of Scripture".][42]

Luther, we saw, even wanted to take out parts of Scripture that contradicted his theology.

In defending his theory Calvin claims that the "mystery" of [Calvinist] predestination and reprobation is a mystery like that of the Holy Trinity. This claim is simply false because the Trinity is a doctrine clearly assumed by Scripture and then explicitly proclaimed by Church Councils. The theory of Calvin and Luther has no other basis than their own exegetical authority.

Calvin recognized the importance of finding support for his theology in historic Christianity. On several occasions he cites Augustine in support of his theology. There is no question that Augustine developed a theory of predestination. But, equally, it is clear that Augustine did not believe that God predetermined the damnation of the majority of the human race. He even held that well-intentioned non-believers might be saved by a "baptism of desire." Calvin refers to a passage from Augustine to support his thesis that God is the creator of evil:

> And this question also, as well as others, is judiciously discussed by Augustine. "We most wholesomely confess, what we most rightly believe, that the God and Lord of all things, who created every thing very good, and foreknew that evil would arise out of good, and knew that it was more suitable

---

42 John Calvin, *Institutes of the Christian Religion*, 228-9, 236-8.

to his almighty goodness to bring good out of evil than not to suffer evil to exist, ordained the life of angels and men in such a manner as to exhibit in it, first, what free-will was capable of doing, and afterwards, what could be effected by the blessings of his grace, and the sentence of his justice." [43]

It should be clear to the reader that Augustine's statement in no way suggests that God ordains evil. It merely asserts that God *permits* evil because He can bring good even out of evil. Augustine expressly states that "the God and Lord of all things ... created every thing very good." Calvin, on the other hand, teaches that God expressly created the wicked (i.e., the vast majority of the human race) "for *this* very end - *that they may perish.*" As we saw, the view of God and man taught by Luther and Calvin was already condemned by the sixth century Council of Orange:

> We not only do not believe that any are foreordained to evil by the power of God, but even state with utter abhorence that if there are those who want to believe **so evil a thing**, they are anathema.

Ten centuries before Luther and Calvin devised their theology of a God Who ordained that "*some men are born devoted from the womb to certain death, that his name may be glorified in their destruction,*" historic Christianity recoiled (with "utter abhorence") from this view because it is "**so evil a thing**".

Calvin's theology may not be as promising as it sounds to those Fundamentalists who wishfully (but unbiblically) yearn for "eternal security." According to Calvin only true Christians belong to the Elect and those Christians who fall away from the faith or live in sin are clearly not true Christians and therefore not part of the Elect. Since it is possible for any Christian to fall away later in life, he has to live with the terrifying thought that he may not be one of the Elect and may actually have been predestined for damnation. This possibility is not denied by Calvin:

> But *it daily happens*, that they who *appeared to belong to Christ*, fall away from him again, and sink into ruin. Even in that very place, *where he asserts that none perish of those who were given to him* by the Father, *he excepts the son of*

---

[43] Ibid., 208.

perdition. This is true; but it is equally certain, that *such persons never adhered to Christ with that confidence of heart* which, we say, gives us an assurance of our election. "They went out from us," says John, "but they were not of us; for if they had been of us, they would no doubt have continued with us." [1 John ii. 19]. I dispute not their having similar signs of calling with the elect; but I am far from admitting them to possess that certain assurance of election which I enjoin believers to seek from the word of the gospel. [Here Calvin reduces "assurance of our election" to a mere "confidence of heart." Feelings are a poor basis for being certain of salvation.] ...

God acts like a good master of a feast, walking round the tables, courteously receiving his guests; but that if he finds any one not adorned with a nuptial garment, he suffers not the meanness of such a person to disgrace the festivity of the banquet. I confess, this part is to be understood of *those who enter into the Church by a profession of faith, but are not invested with the santification of Christ.* Such blemishes, and, as it were, cankers of his Church, God will not always suffer, but will cast them out of it, as their turpitude deserves. [In other words those Christians who "are not invested with the sanctification of Christ" do not belong to the Elect. Any Christian, it must be admitted, could fall away at some point in his life - so he can have no assurance that he is one of the Elect.][44]

In the next section of this chapter we consider scriptural and theological arguments against Calvinism developed by fellow Protestants.

D. "THIS IS NOT THE GOD OF THE CHRISTIANS" [JOHN WESLEY]: PROTESTANT CRITIQUES OF THE "ONCE PREDESTINED FOR DAMNATION ALWAYS DAMNED" THEORY

The most powerful critiques of Calvinism have come from Protestants. The most important of these is the critique of John Wesley which has yet to be adequately answered. "Predestination Calmly Considered" by Wesley is the classic refutation of Calvinism. "Now

---

[44] Ibid., 226-8.

if man be capable of choosing good or evil," writes Wesley,

> then is he a proper object of the justice of God, acquitting or condemning, rewarding or punishing. But otherwise he is not. A mere machine is not capable of being either acquitted or condemned. Justice cannot punish a stone for falling to the ground; nor (on *your* scheme) a man for falling into sin. For he can no more help it than the stone. If he be (in *your* sense) "foreordained to this condemnation." Why does this man sin? "He cannot cease from sin." Why can't he cease from sin? "Because he has no saving grace?" Why has he no saving grace? "Because God of his own good pleasure, hath eternally decreed not to give it to him." Is he then under an unavoidable necessity of sinning? "Yes, as much as a stone is of falling. He never had any more power to cease from evil than a stone has to hang in the air." And shall this man, for not doing what he never could do, and for doing what he never could avoid, be sentenced to depart into everlasting fire, prepared for the devil and his angels [cf. Mt. 25:41]? "Yes, because it is the sovereign will of God." Then you either found a new God, or *made* one! This is not the God of the Christians. Our God is just in all his ways ... He requireth only according to what he hath given; and where he hath given little, little is required. The glory of his justice is this, to "reward every man according to his works" [cf. 2 Tm. 4:14].[45]

We cite major portions of Wesley's essay below:

> Without any extenuation on the one hand or exaggeration on the other, let us look upon this doctrine, call it what you please, naked and in its native colour. Before the foundations of the world were laid, God, of his own mere will and pleasure, fixed a decree concerning all the children of men who should be born unto the end of the world. This decree was unchangeable with regard to God and irresistible with regard to man. And herein it was ordained that one part of mankind should be saved from sin and hell and all the rest left to perish for ever and ever, without hope. That none of these should have that grace which alone could prevent their

---

[45]   John Wesley, "Predestination Calmly Considered", op. cit., 451.

dwelling with everlasting burnings, God decreed for this cause alone, "because it was his good pleasure," and for this end, "to show forth his glorious power and his sovereignty over all the earth." ...

"But do not the Scriptures speak of 'election'? They say, St. Paul was an elected, or chosen, vessel; nay, and speak of great numbers of men as 'elect' according to the foreknowledge of God? You cannot, therefore, deny there is such a thing as 'election.' And, if there is, what do you mean by it?"

I will tell you, in all plainness and simplicity. I believe it commonly means one of these two things. First, a divine appointment of some particular men to do some particular work in the world. And this election I believe to be not only personal but absolute and unconditional. Thus Cyrus was "elected" to rebuild the temple, and St. Paul, with the Twelve, to preach the gospel. But I do not find this to have any necessary connexion with eternal happiness. Nay, it is plain it has not; for one who is "elected" in this sense may yet be lost eternally. "Have I not chosen" (elected) "you twelve?" saith our Lord, "yet one of you hath a devil" [cf. Jn. 6:70]? Judas, you see, was "elected" as well as the rest, yet is his lot with the devil and his angels.

I believe "election" means, secondly, a divine appointment of some men to eternal happiness. But I believe this election to be conditional, as well as the reprobation opposite thereto. I believe the eternal decree concerning both is expressed in those words: "He that believeth shall be saved; he that believeth not shall be damned" [Mk. 16: 16]. And this decree, without doubt, God will not change and man cannot resist. According to this, all true *believers* are in Scripture termed "elect," as all who continue *in unbelief* are so long properly "reprobates," that is, *unapproved* of God and "without discernment" touching the things of the Spirit.

Now, God, to whom all things are present at once, who sees all eternity at one view, "calleth the things that are not as though they were" [Rom.4:17], the things that are not yet as though they were now subsisting. Thus he calls Abraham the "father of many nations" before even Isaac was born. And thus Christ is called "the Lamb slain from the foundation of the world" [Rev. 13:8]; though he was not slain, in fact, till some thousand years after. In like manner, God calleth true believers "elect from the foundation of the world," although they were not actually elect, or believers, till many ages after, in their several generations. Then only it was that they were actually elected, when they were made the "sons of God by faith" (cf. Gal. 3:26]. Then were they, in fact, "chosen and taken out of the world, elect" (saith St. Paul) "through belief of the truth" [cf. 2 Thess. 2:13]; or (as St. Peter expresses it) "elect according to the foreknowledge of God, through sanctification of the Spirit" [I Pet. 1:2].

This election I as firmly believe as I believe the Scripture to be of God. But unconditional election I cannot believe; not only because I cannot find it in Scripture, but also (to waive all other considerations) because it necessarily implies unconditional reprobation. Find out any election which does not imply reprobation and I will gladly agree to it. But reprobation I can never agree to while I believe the Scripture to be of God; as being utterly irreconcilable to the whole scope and tenor both of the Old and New Testament...

How will you reconcile reprobation with the following Scriptures, which declare God's willingness that all should be saved? ... [Mt. 22:9; Mk. 16:15; Lk. 19:41; Jn. 5:34; Acts 17:24ff.; Rom. 5:18; 10:12; I Tim. 2:3,4; 4:10; Jas.1:5; 2 Pet. 3:9; I Jn. 4:14].

How will you reconcile reprobation with the following Scriptures which declare that Christ came to save all men, that he died for all, that he atoned for all, even for those that finally perish?... [Mt. 18:11; Jn. 1:29; 3:17; 12:47; Rom. 14:15; I Cor. 8:11; 2 Cor. 5:14f.; I Tim. 2:6; Heb. 2:9; 2 Pet. 2:1; I Jn. 2: 1,2].

You are sensible, these are but a very small part of the Scriptures which might be brought on each of these heads. But they are enough; and they require no comment. Taken in their plain, easy and obvious sense, they abundantly prove that there is not, cannot be, any such thing as unconditional reprobation.

But to be a little more particular. How can you possibly reconcile reprobation with those Scriptures that declare the justice of God? To cite one for all ... [Ezek. 18:2-31 is quoted *in extenso*]...

Do you say, "Nay, but it is just for God to pass by whom he will, because of his sovereignty; for he saith himself, 'May not I do what I will with my own?' and, 'Hath not the potter power over his own clay' " [cf. Rom. 9:21]? I answer: the former of these sentences stands in the conclusion of that parable wherein our Lord reproves the Jews for murmuring at God's giving the same reward to the Gentiles as to them. To one of these murmurers it is that God says, "Friend, I do thee no wrong. Take what thine is and go thy way. I will give unto this last even as unto thee" [cf. Mt. 20:13-15]. Then follows: "Is it not lawful for me to do what I will with mine own? Is thine eye evil, because I am good?" As if he had said, "May I not give my own kingdom to whom I please? Art thou angry because I am merciful?" It is then undeniably clear that God does not here assert a right of reprobating any man. Here is nothing spoken of reprobation, bad or good.

But you add, "Hath not the potter power over his own clay" [Rom. 9:21]? Let us consider the context of these words also. They are found in the ninth chapter of the Epistle to the Romans, an epistle, the general scope and intent of which is to publish the eternal, unchangeable purpose or decree of God. "He that believeth shall be saved; he that believeth not shall be damned" [Mk. 16:16]... Those words - "Hath not the potter power over his own clay" - are part of St. Paul's answer to that objection that it was unjust for God to show that mercy to the Gentiles which he withheld from his own people. This he first simply denies - saying, "God forbid!" - and then observes that, according to his own words to Moses, God has a right to fix the terms on which he will show mercy, which neither the will nor the power of man can alter (v.15,16), and to withdraw his mercy from them who, like Pharaoh, will not comply with those terms (v.17). And that accordingly, "he hath mercy on whom he will have mercy" (namely those that truly believe), "and whom he will" (namely, obstinate unbelievers), he suffers to be "hardened".

But "why then," say the objectors, "doth he find fault" with those that are hardened, "for who hath resisted his will" (v.19)? To this insolent misconstruction of what he had said, the apostle first gives a severe rebuke and then adds, "Shall the thing formed say unto him that formed it, Why hast thou made me thus?" Why hast thou made me capable of salvation only on those terms? None indeed "hath resisted this will" of God. "He that believeth not shall be damned." But is this any ground for arraigning his justice? "Hath not," the great "potter power over his own clay to make" (or appoint) one sort of "vessels" (namely, believers) "to honour" and the others to "dishonour"? Hath he not a right to distribute eternal honour and dishonour, on whatever terms he pleases - especially considering the goodness and patience he shows, even towards them that believe not - considering that when they have provoked him "to show his wrath, and to make the power" of his vengeance "known, yet" he "endures, with much longsuffering," even those "vessels of wrath" who had before "fitted" themselves "to destruction"?

I have spoken more largely than I designed in order to show that neither our Lord in the above-mentioned parable nor St. Paul in these words had any view to God's sovereign power as the ground of unconditional reprobation. And beware that you go no further therein than you are authorized by them. Take care, when you speak of these high things, to "speak as the oracles of God" [I Pet. 4:11]. And if so, you will never speak of the sovereignty of God but in conjunction with his other attributes. For the Scripture nowhere speaks of this single attribute as separate from the rest. Much less does it anywhere speak of the sovereignty of God as singly disposing the eternal states of men. No, no: in this awful work, God proceeds according to the known rules of his justice and mercy, but never assigns his sovereignty as the cause why any man is punished with everlasting destruction.

Now then, are you not quite out of your way? You are not in the way which God hath revealed. You are putting eternal happiness and misery on an unscriptural and a very dreadful footing. Make the case your own. Here are you, a sinner, convinced that you deserve the damnation of hell. Sorrow, therefore, and fear have filled your heart. And how shall you be comforted? By the promises of God? But perhaps you have no part therein, for they belong only to the elect. By the consideration of his love and tender mercy? But what are they to you, if you are a reprobate? God does not love you at all: you, like Esau, he hath hated even from eternity. What ground then can you have for the least shadow of hope? Why, it is *possible* (that is all) that God's sovereign will may be on your side. Possibly, God may save you, because he will! O poor encouragement to despairing sinners! I fear "faith" rarely "cometh by hearing" *this!*

The sovereignty of God is then never to be brought to supersede his justice. And this is the present objection against unconditional reprobation (the plain consequence of unconditional election). It flatly contradicts, indeed utterly overthrows, the Scripture account of the justice of God...

How shall God in justice judge the world, if there be any decree of reprobation? On this supposition, what should those on the left hand be condemned for? For their having done evil? They could not help it. There never was a time when they could have helped it. God, you say, "of old ordained them to this condemnation" [Jude 4]. And "who hath resisted his will?" He "sold" them, you say, "to work wickedness," even from their mother's womb. He "gave them up to a reprobate mind" [cf. Rom. 1:28] or ever they "hung upon their mother's breast." Shall he then condemn them for what they could not help? Shall the Just, the Holy One of Israel, adjudge millions of men to everlasting pain because their blood moved in their veins? Nay, this they might have helped, by putting an end to their own lives. But could they even thus have escaped from sin? Not without that grace which you suppose God had absolutely determined never to give them. And yet you suppose him to send them into eternal fire, for not escaping from sin! That is, in plain terms, for not having that grace which God had decreed they should never have! O strange justice! What a picture do you draw of the Judge of all the earth?

Are they not rather condemned for not doing good, according to those solemn words of the great Judge, "Depart, ye cursed; for I was an hungered, and ye gave me no meat; I was thirsty, and ye gave me no drink ...

Upon *your* supposition might they not say (O consider it well, in meekness and fear!): "Lord, we might have done the outward works; but thou knowest it would have but increased our damnation. We might have fed the hungry, given drink to the thirsty, and covered the naked with a garment. But all these works, without thy special grace, which we never had, nor possibly could have (seeing thou hast eternally decreed to withhold it from us) would only have been 'splendid sins.' They would only have heated the furnace of hell seven times hotter than before." Upon *your* supposition, might they not say, "Righteous art thou, O Lord; yet let us plead with thee. O why dost thou condemn us for not doing good? Was it possible for us to do anything well? Did we ever abuse the power of doing good? We never received it, and that thou knowest. Wilt thou, the Holy One, the Just, condemn us for not doing what we never had the power to do? Wilt thou condemn us for not casting down the stars from heaven [cf. Dan. 8:10], for not holding the winds in our fist [cf. Prov. 30:4]? Why, it was as possible for us to do this as to do any work acceptable in thy sight! O Lord, correct us, but with judgment! And, before thou plungest us into everlasting fire let us know how it was ever possible for us to escape the damnation of hell."

Or how could they have escaped - suppose you assign that as the cause of their condemnation - from inward sin, from evil desires, from unholy tempers and vile affections? Were they ever able to deliver their own souls, to rescue themselves from this inward hell? If so, their not doing it might justly be laid to their charge, and would leave them without excuse. But it was so. They never were able to deliver their own souls; they never had power to rescue themselves from the hands of those bosom enemies...

Should you not rather say that unbelief is the damning sin and that those who are condemned in that day will be, therefore, condemned "because they believed not on the name of the only-begotten Son of God" [cf. Jn. 3: 18]? But *could* they believe? Was not this faith both the gift and the work of God in the soul? And was it not a gift which he had eternally decreed never to give them? Was it not a work which he was of old unchangeably determined never to work in their souls? Shall these men then be condemned because God would not work, because they did not receive what God would not give? Could they "ungrasp the hold of his right hand, or force omnipotence?"

There is, over and above, a peculiar difficulty here. You say, "Christ did not die for those men." But if so, there was an impossibility, in the very nature of the thing, that they should ever savingly believe. For what is saving faith but "a confidence in God through Christ that loved *me,* and gave himself for me?" Loved *thee,* thou reprobate? Gave himself for *thee?* Away! thou hast neither part nor lot herein. Thou believe in Christ, thou accursed spirit, damned or ever thou wert born? There never was any object for thy faith; there never was any thing for thee to believe. God himself (thus must you speak, to be consistent with yourself), with all His omnipotence, could not make thee believe Christ atoned for thy sins, unless he had made thee believe a lie.

If, then, God be just, there cannot, on your scheme, be any judgment to come. We may add, nor any future state, either of reward or punishment. If there be such a state, God will therein "render to every man according to his works" [cf. Rom. 2:6]. "To them who, by patient continuance in well-doing, seek for glory and honour and immortality: eternal life; but to them that do not obey the truth but obey unrighteousness, indignation and wrath: tribulation and anguish upon every soul of man that doeth evil."

But how is this reconcilable with *your* scheme? You say, "The reprobates cannot but do evil, and the elect, from the day of God's power, cannot but continue in well-doing." You suppose all this is unchangeably decreed; in consequence whereof, God acts irresistibly on the one and Satan on the other. Then, it is impossible for either one or the other to help acting as they do; or rather, to help being acted upon, in the manner wherein they are. For if we speak properly, neither the one nor the other can be said to act at all. Can a stone be said to act when it is thrown out of a sling, or a ball when it is projected from a cannon? No more can a man be said to act, if he be only moved by a force he cannot resist. But if the case be thus, you leave no room either for reward or punishment. Shall the stone be rewarded for rising from the sling, or punished for falling down? Shall the cannon ball be rewarded for flying towards the sun, or punished for receding from it? As incapable of either punishment or reward is the man who is supposed to be impelled by a force he cannot resist. Justice can have no place in rewarding or punishing mere machines, driven to and fro by an external force. So that your supposition of God's ordaining from eternity whatsoever should be done to the end of the world, as well as that of God's acting irresistibly in the elect and Satan's acting irresistibly in the reprobates, utterly overthrows the Scripture doctrine of rewards and punishments, as well as of a judgment to come.

Thus ill does that election which implies reprobation agree with the Scripture account of God's justice. And does it agree any better with his truth? How will you reconcile it with those plain assertions? ... [Here again Wesley quotes Ezek. 18:23-32; 33:11 in extenso.]

But perhaps you will say, "These ought to be limited and explained by other passages of Scripture wherein this doctrine is as clearly affirmed as it is denied in these." I must answer very plain: if this were true, we must give up all the Scriptures together; nor would the infidels allow the Bible so honorable a title as that of a "cunningly devised fable" [2 Pet. 1:16]. But it is not true. It has no colour of truth. It is absolutely, notoriously false. To tear up the very roots of reprobation, and of all doctrines that have a necessary connexion therewith, God declares in his Word these three things, and that explicitly, in so many terms:

1. "Christ died for all," namely, all that "were dead" in sin, as the words immediately following fix the sense. Here is the fact affirmed.
2. "He is the propitiation for the sins of the whole world," even of all those for whom he died. Here is the consequence of his dying for all. And,
3. "He died for all, that they should not live unto themselves, but unto him which died for them," that they might be saved from their sins. Here is the design, the end, of his dying for them. Now, show me the Scriptures wherein God declares in equally express terms (1) Christ did not die *for all,* but for some only; (2) Christ is not "the propitiation for the sins of the whole world." And (3) he did not die for all, at least, not with that intent "that they should live unto him who died for them." Show me, I say the Scriptures that affirm these three things in equally express terms. You know there are none. Nor is it possible to evade the force of those above recited but by supplying in number what is wanting in weight by heaping abundance of texts together whereby (though none of them speak home to the point) the patrons of that opinion dazzle the eyes of the unwary and quite overlay the understanding both of themselves and those that hear them.

To proceed: what an account does this doctrine give of the sincerity of God in a thousand declarations, such as those ... [Deut. 5:29; Ps. 81: 11-14]...

Our blessed Lord does indisputably command and invite "all men everywhere to repent" [Acts 17:30]. He calleth all. He sends his ambassadors, in his name, "to preach the gospel to every creature" [Mk. 16:15]. He himself "preached deliverance to the captives" [Lk. 4:18], without any hint of restriction or limitation. But now, in what manner do you represent him while he is employed in this work? You suppose him to be standing at the prison doors, having the keys thereof in his hands, and to be continually inviting the prisoners to come forth, commanding them to accept of that invitation, urging every motive which can possibly induce them to comply with that command; adding the most precious promises, if they obey; the most dreadful threatenings, if they obey not. And all this time you suppose him to be unalterably determined in himself never to open the doors for them, even while he is crying, "Come ye, come ye, from that evil place. For why will ye die, O house of Israel" [cf. Ezek. 18:31]? "Why" (might one of them reply), "because we cannot help it. We *cannot* help ourselves, and thou *wilt* not help us. It is not in our power to break the gates of brass [cf. Ps. 10:16), and it is not thy pleasure to open them. Why will we die? We must die, because it is not thy will to save us." Alas, my brethren, what kind of sincerity is this which you ascribe to God our Saviour?

So ill do election and reprobation agree with the truth and sincerity of God! But do they not agree least of all with the scriptural account of his love and goodness: that attribute which God peculiarly claims wherein he glories above all the rest? It is not written, "God is justice," or "God is truth" (although he is just and true in all his ways). But it is written, "God is love" [I Jn. 4:8) (love in the abstract, without bounds), and "there is no end of his goodness" [cf. Ps. 52:1]. His love extends even to those who neither love nor fear him. He is good, even to the evil and the unthankful; yea, without any exception or limitation, to all the children of men. For "the Lord is loving" (or good) "unto every man, and his mercy is over all his works" (Ps. 145:9, B.C.P.).

But how is God good or loving to a "reprobate," or one that is not "elected"? You may choose either term, for if none but the unconditionally elect are saved, it comes precisely to the same thing. You cannot say, he is an object of the love or goodness of God, with regard to his external state, whom he created (says Mr. Calvin plainly and fairly) "to live a reproach and die everlastingly." Surely, no one can dream that the goodness of God is at all concerned with this man's eternal state. "However, God is good to him in this world." What? When by reason of God's unchangeable decree, it had been good for this man never to have been born, when his very birth was a curse, not a blessing? "Well, but he now enjoys many of the gifts of God, both gifts of nature and of providence. He has food and raiment, and comforts of various kinds. And are not all these great blessings?" No, not to him. At the price he is to pay for them, every one of these also is a curse. every one of these comforts is, by an eternal decree, to cost him a thousand pangs in hell. For every moment's pleasure which he now enjoys, he is to suffer the torment of more than a thousand years; for the smoke of that pit which is preparing for him ascendeth up for ever and ever. God knew this would be the fruit of whatever he should enjoy, before the vapour of life fled away. He designed it should. It was his very purpose, in giving him those enjoyments. So that, by all these (according to your account) he is, in truth and reality, only fatting the ox for the slaughter. "Nay, but God gives him grace, too." Yes, but what kind of grace? "Saving grace," you own, he has none; none of a saving nature. And the "common grace" he has was not given with any design to save his soul, nor with any design to do him any good at all; but only to restrain him from hurting the elect. So far from doing him good, this grace also necessarily increases his damnation. "And God knows this," you say, "and designed it should; it was one great end for which he gave it!" Then I desire to know, how is God good or loving to this man, either with regard to time or eternity? ...

"Natural free-will," in the present state of mankind, I do not understand. I only assert that there is a measure of free-will *supernaturally* restored to every man, together with that *supernatural* light which "enlightens every man that cometh into the world" [cf. Jn. 1:9]. But indeed, whether this be natural or no, as to your objection, it matters not. For that equally lies against both, against any free-will of any kind -your assertion being thus: "If man has any free-will, God cannot have the whole glory of his salvation," or, "It is not so much for the glory of God to save man as a free agent

- put into a capacity of concurring with his grace on the one hand and of resisting it on the other - as to save him in the way of a necessary agent, by a power which he cannot possibly resist."

With regard to the former of these assertions, "If man has any free-will, then God cannot have the whole glory of his salvation," is your meaning this: "If man has any power to 'work out his own salvation,' then God cannot have the whole glory"? If it be, I must ask again, what do you mean by God's "having the whole glory"? Do you mean, "his doing the whole work, without any concurrence on man's part"? If so, your assertion is, "If man do at all 'work together with' God in 'working out his own salvation,' then God does not do the whole work without man's 'working together with him.'" Most true, most sure. But cannot you see how God nevertheless may have all the glory? Why, the very power to "work together with him" was from God. Therefore to him is all the glory. Has not even experience taught you this? Have you not often felt, in a particular temptation, power either to resist or yield to the grace of God? And when you have yielded to work together with him, did you not find it very possible, notwithstanding, to give him all the glory? So that both experience and Scripture are against you here and make it clear to every impartial inquirer that though man has "freedom" to work or not "work together with God," yet may God have the whole glory of his salvation.

If then you say, "We ascribe to God alone the whole glory of our salvation," I answer, "So do we, too." If you add, "Nay, but we affirm that God alone does the whole work without man's working at all," in one sense, we allow this also. We allow it is the work of God alone to justify, to sanctify, and to glorify, which three comprehend the whole of salvation. Yet we cannot allow that man can only resist and not in any wise "work together with God," or that God is so the whole worker of our salvation as to exclude man's working at all. This I dare not say, for I cannot prove it by Scripture. Nay, it is flatly contrary thereto; for the Scripture is express that (having received power from God) we are to "work out our own salvation" [Phil. 2:12], and that (after the work of God is begun in our souls) we are "workers together with him" [2 Cor. 6: 1]...

This is my grand objection to the doctrine of reprobation or (which is the same) unconditional election. That it is an error, I know, because if this were true, the whole Scripture must be false. But it is not only for this (because it is an error) that I so earnestly oppose it, but because it is an error of so pernicious consequence to the souls of men; because it directly and naturally tends to hinder the inward work of God in every stage of it.

For instance. Is a man careless and unconcerned, utterly dead in trespasses and sins? Exhort him, then (suppose he is of your own opinion), to take some care of his immortal soul. "I take care!" says he.

"What signifies my care? Why, what must be, must be. If I am elect, I must be saved; and if I am not, I must he damned." And the reasoning is as just and strong as it is obvious and natural. It avails not to say, "Men may *abuse* any doctrine." So they may. But this is not abusing yours. It is the plain, natural use of it. The premises cannot be denied (on your scheme), and the consequence is equally clear and undeniable. Is he a little serious and thoughtful now and then, though generally cold and lukewarm? Press him then to stir up the gift that is in him, to work out his own salvation with fear and trembling [cf. Phil. 2:12]. "Alas," says he, "what can I do? You know, man can do nothing." If you reply, "But you do not desire salvation, you are not willing to be saved." "It may be so," says he, "but God shall make me willing in the day of his power." So, waiting for irresistible grace, he falls faster asleep than ever. See him again, when he thoroughly awakes out of sleep; when, in spite of his principles, fearfulness and trembling are come upon him and an horrible dread hath overwhelmed him. How then wilt you comfort him that is well nigh swallowed up of overmuch sorrow? If at all, by applying the promises of God. But against these he is fenced on every side. "These, indeed," says he, "are great and precious promises. But they belong to the elect only. Therefore, they are nothing to me. I am not of that number. And I never can be, for his decree is unchangeable." Has he already tasted of the good word, and the powers of the world to come [cf. Heb. 6:5]? Being justified by faith, hath he peace with God? Then sin hath no dominion over him [cf. Rom. 6: 14]. But by and by, considering he may fall *foully* indeed, but cannot fall finally, he is not so jealous over himself as he was at first. He grows a little and a little slacker, till ere long he falls again into the sin from which he was clean escaped. As soon as you perceive he is entangled again and overcome, you apply the Scriptures relating to that state. You conjure him not to harden his heart any more, lest his last state be worse than the first [cf. Mt. 12:45]. "How can that be?" says he.

"Once in grace, always in grace; and I am sure I was in grace once. You shall never tear away my shield." So he sins on, and sleeps on till he awakes in hell.

The observing these melancholy examples day by day, this dreadful havoc which the devil makes of souls (especially of those who had begun to run well) by means of this antiscriptural doctrine, constrains me to oppose it from the same principle whereon I labour to save souls from destruction. Nor is it sufficient to ask, "Are there not also many who wrest the opposite doctrine to their own destruction?" If there are, that is nothing to the point in question; for that is not the case here. Here is no *wresting* at all. The doctrine of absolute predestination naturally leads to the chambers of death.[46]

Addressing a prominent Calvinist, Wesley said, "You represent God as worse than the devil; as more false, more cruel, and more unjust ... You say you will prove it with the Scripture? Hold! What will you prove by Scripture? That God is worse than the devil? It cannot be."[47]

Calvinists have tried to portray the differences on these issues as a battle between the orthodox view of God's sovereignty (Calvinism) and a semi-Pelagian theory (Arminianism). This portrayal is little better than a trick. What we have here, rather, is a battle between fatalism [Calvinism] and historic Christianity. Arminians had many valid criticisms of Calvinism but their theology does have its own flaws as well. It was Jacob Arminius, however, who correctly pointed out that Calvinism's unconditional predestination makes God "the author of sin." In addition, he shows that Calvinism "is void of good news; repugnant to God's wise, just, and good nature, and to man's free nature; 'highly dishonorable to Jesus

---

46 John Wesley, "Predestination Calmly Considered", op. cit., 432-9, 449, 470-1

47 Erwin W. Lutzer, *All One Body - Why Don't We Agree?*, op. cit., 202-3.

Christ'; 'hurtful to the salvation of men'; and that it 'inverts the order of the gospel of Jesus Christ' (which is that we are justified after we believe, not prior to our believing.'[48]

Two modern critiques of the theories of Luther and Calvin should now be considered. Luther's exegesis and method of interpretation has been stringently scrutinized by a well-known Anglican theologian, John MacQuarrie of England:

> Luther himself believed that the doctrine of *sola gratia* can be clearly derived from the New Testament, especially from the writings of Paul which had become for him a kind of canon within the canon. He was especially impressed by Paul's account in Romans of his unavailing struggles to fulfill the law, and likewise with Paul's strong opposition, expressed in Galatians, to those Judaizing elements who wished to impose some residual elements of the law of Moses on Gentile converts to Christianity. Luther saw these oppositions in extreme terms: on the one side, a harshly legalistic Judaism in which salvation was to be gained through good works performed in obedience to the law, and on the other side, Christianity as a religion of grace in which redemption has been gained for us by the cross and salvation is offered to us as a free gift, without regard to our merit or lack of merit. The recent work of such New Testament scholars as W.D. Davies and E.P. Sanders has called into question this simplistic but highly influential exegesis inherited from Luther. Davies puts the point quite mildly when he warns us that 'it is possible to make too much of the contrast between Pauline Christianity as a religion of liberty and Judaism as a religion of obedience,' and he expresses the opinion that 'justification by faith is not the main factor in Paul's thought.' These remarks have been greatly strengthened by the important studies of Sanders, who shows that in the Palestinian Judaism of Paul's time there was a stress on grace as well as works, and that Paul's own position was not so very different from that of his Jewish teachers. Sanders claims that 'the Rabbis kept the indicative and the imperative (i.e., grace and works) well balanced and in the right order.'

---

[48]   Walter A. Elwell, ed., *Evangelical Dictionary of Theology* (Grand Rapids, Michigan: Baker Book House, 1984), 80.

Luther's exegesis of Romans was developed by him into a polemic against the Roman Catholic church, which he equated with legalistic Judaism and contrasted with the Reformation religion of grace. But now that the New Testament basis of his contrast between first-century Judaism and early Christianity has been placed in doubt, his application of this model to the relation between Roman Catholic and Protestant versions of Christianity must also be doubtful. It is interesting to note that Barth, in spite of his championship of grace versus good works, is careful to distance himself from Luther's misuse of Galatians, *still uncritically accepted by many Protestant writers* [emphasis added] ...

While the champions of sola gratia have concentrated their attention on some passages of scripture and have probably interpreted even these in a onesided way, *there are other passages, even in the writings of Paul, where the element of cooperation in the work of salvation seems to be clearly recognized* [emphasis added]. It is Paul who, after the magnificent hymn in praise of Christ's redeeming work, in his letter to the Philippians, goes on immediately to say to the Christian believers: 'Work out your own salvation with fear and trembling; for God is at work in you' (Philippians 2:12). The thought here seems clearly to be that God's work and man's work go side by side in the realization of salvation. In another epistle he writes: 'Working together with him, then, we entreat you not to accept the grace of God in vain' (2 Cor 6:1). *A straightforward interpretation of these words seems quite incompatible with any rigorous doctrine of sola gratia* [emphasis added]. For what does it mean 'to accept the grace of God in vain' but to fail to make any response to this grace, to refrain from any answering work? The expression 'working together with him,' which has also been translated 'as co-workers with him,' is in Greek *synergountes*, from which we derive the English word 'synergism,' cited at an earlier stage in the discussion. This word 'synergism' is the usual theological term for the point of view I have been commending, namely, that human salvation is accomplished neither by man's own unaided efforts nor by an act of God entirely outside of man, but by a synergism or co-working, in which, of course, the human contribution is also necessary and cannot be left out of account. Before we leave the New Testament on these questions, let us call to mind in addition to the Pauline material the letter of James. Luther was so unhappy with this letter that he questioned whether it should ever have been included in the canon of the New Testament. It seems inconsistent with Paul's insistence that we are justified by faith, not by works, *or perhaps we should say, with Paul's view of these matters as interpreted by Luther* [emphasis added]... One should say that faith, as decision, is itself the beginning of the work. [49]

MacQuarrie draws our attention to the implications of the view of "grace alone" for human freedom:

The principle 'by grace alone' has remained a shibboleth of orthodox Protestant theology. It is prominent, for instance, in the work of Karl Barth. On this view, fallen man is so disabled by sin that he is totally unable to help himself. Grace alone can redeem him, and he can contribute nothing ... Redemption is not, in his view, to be considered as an ongoing process in which we have some part, but as the once for all act of God long before we were born - though it is hard to know whether this act in the past is the death of Christ on Calvary or the eternal predestinating decree of God in the very beginning. But it is all complete already without us.

Now, if one conceded Barth's point, then I think one would have to say that he is indeed treating human beings like sheep or cattle or even marionettes, not as the unique beings that they are, spiritual beings made in the image of God and entrusted with a measure of freedom and responsibility. This fundamental human constitution remains, even though ravaged by sin. Human beings are still human, not mere things or animals. If Barth were correct in what he says on these matters, it would make nonsense of the struggles of history, of the training and preparation of Israel, of the very incarnation of the Word, of the redemptive mission of the Church, of the preaching of the gospel and the ministration of the sacraments. These events in time could have no real significance, for everything has been settled in advance. Human beings, on such a view, have no freedom and no responsibility. They are not beings made in the image of God with some small share in the divine cre-

---

[49] *Mary for all Christians*, London: Collins, 1990, 106-110.

ativity and rationality, they are things to be passively manipulated and pushed around. Fortunately for us - or so we are assured - we are manipulated by grace rather than by a malignant fate or blind chance, nevertheless, we are manipulated. This seems to me a degradation of the concept of humanity implicit in the biblical accounts of creation. Feuerbach's words about Luther remain, alas, true of much of the theology that stems from him and from other leading Reformers: 'The doctrine is divine but inhuman, a hymn to God but a lampoon of man.' It is understandable that Feuerbach, Marx, Nietzsche and a whole galaxy of modern thinkers came to believe that Christianity alienates them from a genuine humanity."[50]

We must note that Calvin's god is unspeakably cruel since he deliberately predestines the majority of the human race for Hell. A former Calvinist, Clark Pinnock, explains that their view of divine sovereignity forces Calvinists to make God the author of evil since they have no place for freedom and everything is determined by God:

> The first and the best discovery I made [in Scripture] was that there was no "horrible decree" at all. Calvin had used this expression in connection with his belief that God in his sovereign good pleasure had predestined some people to be eternally lost for no fault of theirs (*Institutes* 3.23)...
>
> Of course I had always known how morally loathsome the doctrine of double predestination is and how contradictory it is to the universal biblical texts but I had not known previously how to avoid it. But now with the insight of reciprocity in hand, which had just surfaced for me in rethinking the doctrine of perseverance, it became possible for me to accept the scriptural teaching of the universal salvific will of God and not feel duty-bound to deny it as before. I was now in a position to rejoice in the truth that God's will is for all to be saved (I Tim. 2:4), and that God's grace has appeared for the salvation of all people (Titus 2:11).
>
> The dark shadow was lifting; the logic of Calvinism could no longer blind me to these lines of biblical teaching. All mankind has been included in the saving plan of God

---

50   Ibid.

and in the redemption of Jesus Christ. By the obedience of the Son, there is acquittal and life for all people (Rom. 5:18). Thus the invitation can go out to all sinners sincerely urging them to repent and believe the good news that offers salvation to everyone without hedging. The banquet of salvation has been set for all people: God has provided plenteous redemption in the work of Christ, sufficient for the salvation of the entire race of sinners. All that remains for any individual to benefit from what was accomplished for him is to respond to the good news and enter into the new relationship with God that has been opened up for all persons...

Predestination proved to be less of a problem, surprisingly enough. Familiarity with the dynamic character of God's dealing with human beings according to the biblical narrative had prepared me to see predestination in terms of God's setting goals for people rather than forcing them to enact the preprogramed decrees. God predestines us to be conformed to the image of his Son (Rom. 8:29). That is his plan for us, whether or not we choose to go down that path. God's plan for the world and for ourselves does not suppress but rather sustains and includes the spontaneity of significant human decisions. We are co-workers with God, participating with him in what shall be hereafter. The future is not stored up on heavenly video tape, but is the realm of possibilities, many of which have yet to be decided and actualized. Peter gives us a nice illustration of this when he explains the delay of Christ's return as being due to God's desire to see more sinners saved - God actually postponing the near return of Christ for their sakes (2 Peter 3:9).

Previously I had had to swallow hard and accept the Calvinian antinomy that required me to believe both that God determines all things and that creaturely freedom is real. I made a valiant effort to believe this seeming contradiction on the strength of biblical infallibility, being assured that the Bible actually taught it. So I was relieved to discover that the Bible does not actually teach such an incoherence, and this particular paradox was a result of Calvinian logic, not scriptural dictates. Having created human beings with relative autonomy alongside himself, God voluntarily limits his power to enable them to exist and to share in the divine creativity. God invites humans to share in deciding what the future will be. God does not take it all onto his own shoulders. Does this compromise God's power? No, surely not, for to create such a world in fact requires a divine power of a kind higher than merely coercive. When predestination is viewed in this light, there is immense relief also in the area of theodicy. The logic of consistent Calvinism makes God the author of evil and casts serious doubt on his goodness. One is compelled to think of God's planning such horrors as Auschwitz even though none but the most rigorous Calvinians can bring themselves to admit it. But if predestination is thought of as an all-inclusive set of goals and not an all-determining plan, then the difficulty for theodicy is greatly eased.[51]

In another book, Pinnock examines the arguments of the Calvinist John Feinberg and shows again how terrible a view of God it presents:

[Feinberg] even shrinks from saying that God only "permits" some atrocity like the Holocaust, as some less stout Calvinists inconsistently do, because this would suggest it originated outside God's sovereign will. Far be it from Calvinists to deny God the glory of causing everything! It should be clear to the reader why the number of strict Calvinists is relatively small. It involves one in agonizing difficulties of the first order. It makes God some kind of terrorist who goes around handing out torture and disaster and even willing people to do things the Bible says God hates. Some time ago a madman murdered twenty people in a McDonald's near San Diego. According to Feinberg, although God does not like this sort of thing, he decreed it anyway... One need not wonder why people become atheists when faced with such a theology. A God like that has a great deal for which to answer. In my view the Bible does not teach this.[52]

Another Evangelical, Bruce Reichenbach, shows that the denial of man's freedom again makes God the author of evil:

---

51 Clark H. Pinnock, "From Augustine to Arminius: A Pilgrimage in Theology," in Clark H. Pinnock, ed., *The Grace of God, The Will of Man* (Grand Rapids, Michigan: Academie Books, 1989), 21.

52 Clark H. Pinnock in *Predestination and Freewill*, David Basinger and Randall Basinger, eds. (Downer's Grove, Illinois: Inter Varsity Press, 1986), 58.

Many people do evil and not all will be saved. What of those who do evil? It follows from Feinberg's position that it is possible that God has to persuade someone to do evil. This sounds absurd, but consider what follows from his view of authority. According to Feinberg, God has at one time decreed all that comes about. This means that God has decreed the evil as well as the good. Further, this is done prior to and independent of any human action. Now suppose that someone desires to do good rather than the evil which God has decreed he do, or to accept God rather than reject him as God has decreed. Since all must occur as God has decreed, God is put in the indelicate situation of persuading the individual that it is rational and in his best interests to do evil rather than good or to reject God rather than accept him. God's sovereignty has been preserved, but at the cost of his wisdom and goodness...

Feinberg argues that the doctrine of eternal security entails that the indeterminist view is false. If the believer is able to do what he wills, he could apostasize following his reception of God's grace. But is the doctrine of eternal security either biblical or true? ... Many passages in Scripture teach that apostasy is possible and must be guarded against (Heb 6:4-6; 10:26-29; Lk 8:6-7,13; Jn 15; Rom 11:22; Rev 3; Acts 5:1-11). For an extended, careful treatment of the topic, see Robert Shank, **Life in the Son.**[53]

In a welcome retreat from the grip of Calvinism, a group of prominent Evangelical theologians recently produced a book refuting this theology titled **The Grace of God and the Will of Man.**

E. THE FALSE ISSUE OF FAITH VS. WORKS: IN CALVINISM IT IS NOT FAITH ALONE THAT SAVES BUT PREDESTINATION ALONE

The discussions here show that the theological issues at stake only superficially concern the question of faith and works. Just as the slogan of *Sola Scriptura* masks the question of private interpretation the slogans of *Sola Fidei* and *Sola Gratia* mask the ques-

---

53 Bruce Reichenbach in *Predestination and Freewill,* op. cit., 50-1,54.

tions of man's freedom and God's salvific will. The doctrines of "salvation by faith alone" and "faith without works" are simply a cover for an underlying view of God's plan of salvation that is simply horrifying. It is not "faith alone" and "grace alone" that is being affirmed but God's predestination of a few men to salvation and His predestination of the rest of humanity to damnation. Those who are saved, on this view, are saved not "by faith alone" but "by predestination alone." Also the "righteousness by imputation" theory maintains that no substantial change takes place in our nature when we make the act of faith and commit ourselves to the obedience of faith. This becomes a self-fulfilling prophecy because we cannot grow in holiness if we do not believe that it is possible to grow in holiness.

In short the issue is not whether salvation comes from faith alone but whether we have freedom and whether God desires the salvation of all. Are we puppets or free beings? Does God love only a tiny minority of men while deliberately creating most of humanity solely in order to damn them - or does He love every person infinitely? The Christian answer is that each one of us is a free being who is loved infinitely by the God Who does not want to lose even one of His sheep. If we are saved it is because we freely respond to His free offer of salvation. We cannot earn salvation but we can turn it down.

When we talk of faith and works or salvation by faith alone or saving faith we also have to be clear as to what we mean by "faith." Simple intellectual assent to the revelation of Christ is not what is meant by faith in the New Testament. Faith that is simply intellectual assent is not "saving faith." Paul uses "faith" in three senses. For Paul "saving faith" requires belief, hope and love. The idea of "the obedience of faith" is very important here as we shall see.

It has been shown that the "faith alone" view of salvation is actually a Calvinist claim that those who are saved are saved because God preprogrammed them with "saving faith." There is no merit in their act of faith, they make no contribution to their salvation because the whole process was irresistibly directed by God. They are robots programmed for salvation while the lost are robots programmed for damnation.

A minority of Fundamentalists have found the Calvinist view to be repulsive and agree that the act of faith has to be free and available to all if we wish to be consistent with Scripture. While affirming this they still hold to the position that believers are saved only because of their act of faith and this act has no merit in itself. We have shown that this claim is self-evidently false. If salvation depends on a free act of faith and if some people are not saved because they deliberately and consciously refuse to make this act then it is senseless to say that those who *do* make such an act are not doing something infinitely important and commendable [which is the same as saying that they are doing something meritorious]. If there is an incalculable demerit attached to a conscious rejection of the act of faith - because it leads to damnation - then there has to be an incalculable merit attached to a conscious performance of the act of faith. Now we are able to make the act of faith only because of the grace of God but the merit lies in our acceptance of this grace and cooperation with it. If we say it is totally grace with no role for man's response or cooperation then we return to Calvinism with its claim that some are irresistibly saved while others are irresistibly damned.

If we reject Calvinism then we have to acknowledge that the act of faith is a free act which is a meritorious act of human cooperation with divine grace. Calvin himself rightly saw that any claim of "faith alone" and "grace alone" that rejects human cooperation is consistent only with his rejection of freewill ["We shall never be clearly convinced as we ought to be, that our salvation flows from the fountain of God's free mercy, till we are acquainted with his eternal election, which illustrates the grace of God by this comparison, that he adopts not all promiscuously to the hope of salvation, but gives to some what he refuses to others."[54]].

The question of merit in the act of faith can be better understood by reference to the works of Fundamentalists who deny this possibility. In his **Protestants and Catholics: Do They Now Agree?**, an attack on the recent joint statement of Evangelicals and Catholics, John Ankerberg tries in vain to reconcile his view on the central significance of faith with an affirmation of the total insignificance of making the act of faith:

---

[54] John Calvin, *Institutes of the Christian Religion*, op. cit., 170-1.

Faith is only the instrument by which we are saved and is
not deserving of merit on our part. Picture that burning building and the frightened man trapped on the third floor. He is
urged to jump - in other words, to have faith in the firemen
below that they will catch him in their net. But if the man
jumps, his faith will only be that belief which caused him to
jump. It will not be that which actually saves his life. Rather,
it will be the firemen holding the net who actually save him.

In a similar manner, concerning salvation, it is not ultimately the instrument of faith which actually saves us; rather,
it is Christ in whom our faith is placed that saves us.[55]

This example is amusing in that it proves exactly what
Ankerberg is desperate to deny. If the man jumps he is thereby saving his life because he is making a free choice that he does not need
to make. He is saved by the net below but he could not be saved if
he did not choose to jump. It is the decision to jump that we are
talking about. If his decision was to stay where he is he would die.
But he decides to jump and thus saves his life. So his decision makes
all the difference in his survival. Of course, it is not the jumping
alone that saves him. The net had to be there and the firemen had to
call him. But ultimately his choice saves him. *The Calvinist position is that the tenants of the building are not capable of making the
decision to jump and that those who fall into the net fall in because
God pushes them into it while leaving the vast majority to burn.*
The Christian position is that the man who jumps is offered the net
by God and called by God to jump. But it is his response and cooperation that are of paramount importance.

In trying to save his picture of faith-with-a-free-response-but-
without-merit, Ankerberg appeals to a text by Norman Geisler:

Catholic insistence that a right standing can be obtained
without works misses the point. Namely, that this standing
for Catholics does not entail the gift of eternal life. Further,
the Catholic argument that this is a gift that is merited by
work (though not deservedly earned) is insufficient. For even
if one is given, say, a million dollars from someone for getting a loaf of bread for him (which he obviously did not

---

55 John Ankerberg and John Weldon, *Protestants and Catholics: Do They Now
Agree?* (Eugene, Oregon: Harvest House Publishers, 1995), 118.

earn), nonetheless, he did do some work and, hence, it was not by grace alone. Likewise, if someone spends a lifetime of works (however long) as a condition for receiving eternal life, then it was clearly not by grace alone.[56]

We see again that the main issue is not addressed. If the man of faith is given the million dollars for nothing (not even for "getting a loaf of bread") though he does not earn the million dollars he still has to accept it as a gift. And whether you call it a work or not, it is a free response, a free act of cooperation, which is meritorious because it could easily have been a "No." And Scripture unmistakably shows us [as we have seen] that believers have to "persevere to the end" to be saved - a fact which wishful thinking Fundamentalists do not want to face.

Elsewhere Geisler writes: "Salvation is an unconditional act of God's election. Our faith is not a condition for God's giving salvation, but it is for our receiving it. Nonetheless, the act of faith (free choice) by which we receive salvation is not meritorious. It is the giver who gets credit for the gift, not the receiver."[57]

This again misses the point. Of course, the giver gets the credit for the gift: both for the gift of salvation and for the gift of faith. But the receiver is a receiver because he decides to accept a gift which he could just as easily have turned down. If it is wrong to turn down the gift then it is right to accept it. If it is bad to turn it down it is good to accept it. If it is reprehensible to turn it down it is commendable and praiseworthy to accept it. To do something commendable and praiseworthy is to do something meritorious.

In the same work [**Predestination and Freewill**] we see clearly that Geisler wants to have his cake and eat it too. He wants to be a Calvinist while holding that our actions are free. He makes the incredible statement that

"God *determined* that Judas would *freely* betray Christ."[58]

---

[56] Quoted in *Protestants and Catholics: Do They Now Agree?*, op. cit., 86.
[57] Norman Geisler in *Predestination and Freewill*, op. cit., 80.
[58] Ibid., 72.

Another of the contributors to the volume has no trouble in showing the contradiction in this statement:

> We will begin with Geisler's contention that free acts are self determined. He claims that Judas's act of betrayal was both determined by God (in that all that occurs is determined by God) and a free act determined by Judas and not by another (self determined). But this is contradictory. If the act of betrayal is determined by Judas and not by another, it cannot be determined by God, and vice versa.
>
> Furthermore, if a person is free he is able to do otherwise than he does in those cases where he is free. If Judas's treachery was a free act, then Judas could have done otherwise than he did. He could have chosen not to have betrayed Jesus. But since all events are determined by God according to his eternal plan, the act of treachery was necessary and Judas could not have done otherwise than he did, for, as Geisler tells us, God effects his plans with certainty. This too is a contradiction. If the act was necessary, it could not have been performed otherwise than it was, and vice versa...
>
> If God determines, controls and directs every action, then the action itself cannot be contrary to what God determines, and as such, it is not the result of a *free* act of the agent.[59]

Both Scripture and historic Christianity tell us that the act of faith is free and meritorious. Contemporary Fundamentalists are blinded to this historic affirmation simply because they blindly accept the interpretations of Luther and Calvin. Ankerberg, for instance, constantly cites the authority of the interpretation of Luther and his followers in defending his position:

> After meditating on Romans P:16,17, this works-tormented Catholic monk [Luther] *realized* the true nature of biblical justification ...
>
> Rome's decrees were obviously contrary to *Luther's beliefs* - beliefs which were *clearly based* in Scripture and not Church tradition.

---

[59] Bruce Reichenbach in *Predestination and Freewill*, 90-1.

Luther taught the opposite *based on* Galatians, chapters 2 and 3, Romans 5:1-10, and Ephesians 2:8,9.

But in Romans 4:3-5 *Luther discovered* the imputation of God's righteousness apart from works, a legal declaration provided (imputed) by God.

Luther found justification by faith alone in Romans 3:24, but Trent decreed ...

Luther could not help but believe that Acts 13:38,39 stated exactly what was condemned by Rome.

Luther found in John 3:16; 5:24; 6:29,47 and Galatians chapters 2 and 3 that the believer did not have to keep the commandments of God and the Church in order to acquire salvation.

No more authoritative analysis of the Council of Trent has been penned than by Lutheran theologian Martin Chemnitz.

But what is wrong with Rome's claim? In *his definitive critique* of the Council of Trent, Lutheran theologian Martin Chemnitz (1522-86) *correctly noted* ...[60]

This appeal to Luther is no different from a Catholic's appeal to the authority of the Pope's interpretation. In trying to reconcile James and Paul, Ankerberg cites the authority of the Calvinist R.C. Sproul:

> James' concept is not contrary to Paul's. But once you asssume the Roman Catholic interpretation, there is no conceivable manner under the sun that James can be harmonized with Paul. Unfortunately, the manner in which the Roman Catholic Church has dealt with this is to avoid Paul like the plague. They have made serious attempts at harmonization, but I believe it has been a miserable failure every time it is tried.[61]

Sproul's own words call his bluff. Catholics do not see any contradiction between Paul and James. They see a contradiction

---

[60] John Ankerberg and John Weldon, *Protestants and Catholics: Do They Now Agree?*, op. cit., 46-9, 85-86.

[61] R.C. Sproul quoted in John Ankerberg and John Weldon, *Protestants and Catholics: Do They Now Agree?*, op. cit., 38.

between James's teaching and Luther's interpretation of Paul. Sproul does not see this contradiction because he "buys" the interpretations of Luther and Calvin. Ironically, and fatally for Sproul, Luther himself saw a contradiction between his interpretation of Paul and the teaching of James. That is why Luther called James "an epistle of straw" that should be excised from the Bible! It is tragic that a proponent of sola scriptura would refer thus to the holy Word of God when parts of it do not agree with his (novel) interpretation.

Fundamentalists must realize that they are ignoring the witness of Scripture as a whole while clinging to Luther's interpretation of *Galatians*, an interpretation that even many Protestant exegetes admit is flawed. They must also understand that there is something basically wrong with the idea that there is no merit in doing good or in doing something right. Such an idea is an attack on the whole moral order, on the infinite Good Who is God. The equal and opposite error is that there is no demerit in doing evil because, it is claimed, we are totally evil any way. Christianity, on the contrary, says that God is all-holy and infinitely pure and that all good and holy acts by men glorify God and are therefore praiseworthy and to be encouraged. In addition, all men have the obligation to resist evil and all evil is to be condemned and avoided.

Fundamentalists have some idea of the law of cause and effect in the spiritual and moral worlds because they believe that Original Sin had terrible consequences for the human race and that Jesus died in order to reverse these consequences by His Atonement. But it is wrong to suppose that the death of our Lord allows those who accept Him to flout the moral law without consequences. A Christian who sins will suffer the consequences of the sin. Jesus Himself tells us this: "Sin no more, lest a worse thing come unto thee." [*John* 5:14]. A Christian is not a robot who is incapable of resisting evil or doing good. The grace of God enables him to do good and to resist evil. But a Christian can easily resist grace and do evil. When he does evil he suffers the consequences - and sometimes he can turn so totally against God as to damn himself. "Behold therefore the goodness and severity of God: on them which fell, severity; but toward thee, goodness, if thou continue in his goodness: otherwise thou also shalt be cut off." [*Romans* 11:22]. This is written to believers.

And it is precisely here that the Calvinist error is so dangerous. IF YOU SEE YOURSELF AS A PUPPET, YOU THINK AND ACT AS A PUPPET. IT IS IMPOSSIBLE FOR A PUPPET TO DO GOOD OR TO AVOID EVIL. HE IS INCAPABLE OF DOING GOOD AND SO THERE IS NO POINT IN TRYING TO BE HOLY OR DOING GOOD. WHY SHOULD HE AVOID EVIL SINCE THERE IS NO MERIT IN AVOIDING EVIL AND NO CONSEQUENCES IF HE FALLS INTO SIN? Wesley has shown this implication better than anybody else. The danger of the doctrine of "faith alone" is that it removes all moral constraints, degrades the majesty of the divine moral law, harms our view of the integrity of Divine holiness and blinds us to the inevitable consequences of our sins until it is too late.

The tragedy of this doctrine is illustrated most clearly by Martin Luther himself in a letter he wrote to Melanchthon, August 1, 1521: "Be a sinner, and sin boldly, but believe and rejoice in Christ even more boldly ... No sin will separate us from the Lamb even though we commit fornication and murder a thousand times daily."[62]

This view is nothing less than monstrous. Could anyone imagine such unholy counsel coming from the Son of God Who throughout His teaching exhorts us to greater holiness while warning us of the consequences of evil. While we are able to do good and avoid evil only because of God's grace working in us, it is possible for us to reject His grace and thereby suffer the consequences of our rejection. Luther's letter should remind us of *Hebrews* 10:26-9: "For if we sin wilfully after that we have received the knowledge of the truth, there remaineth no more sacrifice for sins, But a certain fearful looking for of judgment and fiery indignation which shall devour the adversaries. He that despised Moses' law died without mercy under two or three witnesses. *Of how much sorer punishment, suppose ye shall he be thought worthy, who hath trodden under foot the Son of God, and hath counted the blood of the covenant, wherewith he was sanctified an unholy thing*, and hath done despite unto the Spirit of grace?"

---

[62] *Luther's Works*, American Edition, 48, 281-82.

F. JUSTIFICATION AND SALVATION: BRINGING FREEDOM BACK

The previous discussions have been concerned with the questions of what we must do to be saved. Almost all Christians, Catholics, Orthodox and most Protestants, agree that we must be justified with God to be saved. It is also generally agreed that justification can come only through the grace of God and through faith. Differences arise when we consider the relationship of justification to sanctification and sanctification to salvation.

We are not saved by our works. Neither does our salvation depend on whether we have done more good deeds than evil ones. But experience, Scripture and the historic Faith tell us that we have the freedom to accept or reject God's grace, that we can continue to cooperate with God's grace and grow in holiness and that our ultimate salvation depends on our perseverance to the end. Some Catholic apologists have spoken of salvation as a process but this terminology could be misleading. Salvation by definition is the state of being saved from the consequences of sin. At each moment in life we are either saved or not saved. We could cut ourselves off from God and not be in a saved state at any time. But it is a state rather than a process. The state of our soul at the end of our earthly life - is it "saved" or "damned" - will determine where we spend eternity.

There is also the question of whether justification makes any difference to our souls. Luther and the Fundamentalists say that when we accept Christ, God "declares us righteous." Justification, for them, was a legal transaction. Historically, however, Christians have believed and taught (on the basis of Scripture and the apostolic testimony) that God does not simply declare it so but makes it so. In I *Corinthians* 6 we see that justification also begins our sanctification. Almost all of Paul's epistles warn believers to turn from evil, lest they fall away, and to pursue holiness. 2 *Peter* 1:4 tells us that believers become "partakers of the divine nature." To clinch it all, *Hebrews* 12:14 warns: "Follow ... holiness, without which no man shall see the Lord." Although Luther wrote that men can do good works after they have made the act of faith, he ascribes these good works totally to Christ acting in them: these good works, according to Luther, are works done *by Christ through us* in opposition to our evil nature rather than works done *by us through Christ* as we cooperate with the grace He gives us in transforming our sinful nature.

The mistake made by Luther and Calvin was to rule out any role for the human response. According to them our salvation or damnation is predetermined by God and we have no role in choosing Heaven or Hell. It is not our faith that saves us but God's predetermination. Hence they could see no need for growing in holiness and no possibility of rejecting God - since those who were predestined for salvation would be saved no matter what they did and those who were predestined for damnation would be damned no matter what they desired.

This interpretation of Luther and Calvin is entirely at odds with Scripture itself and the constant teaching of the Christian Faith. Here we will cite several major presentations of the historic teaching on faith and works, justification and salvation, predestination and freedom:

William Marshner:
Justification by Faith

For Luther, good works were merely *symptoms* of confident faith; for Calvin they were symptoms of irresistible grace. Few Protestants today are familiar with the details of Luther's or Calvin's personal thought; what they have inherited from these great forebearers is rather a general orientation, whose core is the conviction that according to St. Paul, we are justified *sola fide* (by faith alone) or *sola gratia* (by grace alone), either formula being understood to exclude any essential role of good works...

Catholic and Protestant views on the respective roles of grace, faith and works cannot be compared meaningfully, unless one specifies what stage of the justifcational process one is talking about. In the preparatory stage, for instance, in which prevenient graces first stir a person towards an interest in religious truth, towards repentance, and towards faith, Catholics, Lutherans and Calvinists are at one in saying *"sola gratia."* A second stage is the very transition from death to life, which is the first stage of justification proper. Here the parties are at one in saying "sola fide " though they seem to mean different things by it. Protestants tend to mean that, at this stage, by the grace of God, man's act of faith is the sole act required of him; Catholics mean that faith is the beginning, foundation and root of all justification, since only faith makes possible the acts of hope and charity (i.e. love-for-God) which are also required. However, since most Protestants have a broad notion of the act of faith, whereby it includes elements of hope and love, it is often hard to tell how far the difference on this point is real and how far it is a matter of words. Finally, however, there comes a third stage, that of actual Christian life, with its problems of growth and perseverance. The man justified by faith is called to "walk" with God, to progress in holiness. It is at this stage that the parties sharply diverge. Catholics affirm, and Protestants strenuously deny, that the born-again Christian's good works *merit* for him the increase of grace and of the Christian virtues. As a result, Protestant piety has no obvious place for the self-sacrifices, fasts, and states of perfection which are prominent features of Catholic piety.

Now this divergence over works in the third stage is partially due to a Protestant allergy to the word 'merit,' but only partially. The real reasons are much deeper, which brings me to my second point.

At each stage, neither the apparent agreements nor the apparent disagreements can be understood without looking at certain metaphysical quarrels, the chief of which is over the very existence of what Catholics call "grace."

In the natural order, a doctor ministers to a moribund patient and restores him to life; he does so by really changing the condition of the patient's body; he restores to it a quality called health. Can something analogous happen in the supernatural order? If so, what Catholics call "grace" exists. It is the quality thanks to which the soul is made alive and enabled to function as God intended it to function, just as health is such a quality to the body.

Of course, as is the case with all analogies, there are points at which this one breaks down. The human doctor is a finite physician; he can heal the sick but not the dead; God, on the other hand, restores spiritual health to those dead in trespasses and sins (Ephesians 2:5), so that God's act is not so much a cure of the sick as it is a downpayment on the Resurrection (Ephesians 2:6). So the analogy limps.

It fails to reflect the fact that grace is not only like health but also like brand-new life. Still, between life and health there is a deep connection, so that this limp is not fatal to the analogy. However, there is another problem with it.

Thanks to his instruments, chemical and surgical, the doctor is the principal cause of the patient's restored health; but it would seem odd to say that the man's health is wholly the doctor's gift, even if the doctor collected no fee. After all, it is the patient's own natural powers, his own natural capacity for health, which allows the doctor's work to be successful. So there *is a cooperation* here between the doctor's art and the patient's nature, thanks to which the restored health is not wholly the doctor's gift but partially also the patient's own achievement. Such things cannot be said of the initial, justifying grace. As Catholics understand it, this grace is a quality for which man has no natural capacity, to which he has no natural right, and towards which he has no natural inclination. It is a pure surprise, a pure gift, *an elevation* of our nature rather than a part of it; and this was true even before the Fall. Now, to be sure, Catholics believe that once *we have* been elevated to grace, we become capable of cooperating with God's further graces, since He has now given us the capacity and the inclination for such things. But this does not cancel the original picture; it only means that our very capacity to cooperate is a gift to us, something not natively ours; as a result, every God-pleasing act of ours remains so rooted in God's initial gift that it is simply an actuation of that gift. So the analogy between health and grace limps in this second way: it fails to reflect the fact that grace is so totally a gift that it exceeds our natural capacities and hence never becomes simply "our property," even after it has been given.

Thanks to these difficulties, what Catholics call "sanctifying grace" or "habitual grace" turns out to be a deeply mysterious entity: a quality of man which is a property of God. In order to cope with such an entity one needs a sophisticated metaphysics of participation. The Church Fathers and their successors, the Scholastic Doctors, took the trouble to work out such a metaphysics because the existence of grace as a real entity in man - ontic grace - was and is the foundation, without which the whole Catholic understanding of justification makes no sense.

The Protestant Reformers, however, impatient with metaphysics, preferred not to cope with such an entity and denied its existence. To them it seemed simpler to say that grace is something *wholly* in God, namely, His favor towards us. But then, if grace is not something real in man, our "justification" can no longer be received as a real change in us; it will have to become a sheer declaration on God's part, e.g. a declaration that, thanks to the work of Christ, He will henceforth *consider us* as just, even though we remain inwardly the sinners we always were. Hence, the Protestant doctrine of "forensic" or "extrinsic" justification. Now watch what happens to our own act of faith: it ceases to be the foundational act of an interior renewal and becomes a mere requirement devoid of any salvific power in its own right, which God arbitrarily sets as the condition on which He will declare as just. Whereupon watch what happens to our good works: they cease to be the vital acts wherein an ontologically real "new life" consists and manifests itself; they become mere human responses to divine mercy - nice, but totally irrelevant to our justification - or else they become zombie-like motions produced in us by irresistable divine impulses, whereby God exhibits His glory in His elect.

Now, again, few Protestants have thought these matters through. Most do not realize that the theology they have inherited derives historically from nominalistic assumptions, which led Luther and Calvin to deny the existence of sanctifying grace. Rather, they feel that they are simply reading St. Paul. "By grace are ye saved, through faith; and that not of yourselves: it is the gift of God, not of works, lest any man should boast" (Ephesians 2:5f). They feel that an extrinsic, purely declaratory justification is the obvious meaning of such passages... We must show that St. Paul's real position is far closer to that of Trent than to that of Luther...

The place to begin is with the fact that St. Paul expounds and contrasts two economies of justification or two orders of righteousness. Thus, Philippians 3:9 says: "(I counted all things loss) that I might be found in Him, not having my own justice which is from the Law, but the justice which is from the faith of Jesus Christ, the justice that comes from God through faith." Here the main contrast is between justice *from the* Law and justice *from* faith, whereupon a second contrast emerges betwees my own justice and justice from God.

This second contrast reappears in Romans 10:3, "(The Jews) not knowing the justice of God and seeking to establish their own justice, did not submit to God's justice."

We learn the result of this Jewish conduct in Romans 9:30-32, "What shall we say then? The gentiles, who were not pursuing justice, laid hold of justice, but the justice which is from faith. Israel, however, pursuing the law of justice, did not attain the law" (i.e. did not accomplish or fulfill it). The exact interpretation of this text has been debated, but for our purposes it suffices to see that Paul was speaking of a justice pursued by way of works and that such justice was the great ambition of the Jews in connection with the Law of Moses...

How does he [Paul] explain the failure of anyone to be justifed before God by the works of the Law? Here are the steps of his answer.

1. "For through the law comes knowledge of sin" (Romans 3:20). The law makes sin better known. What else?

2. "The law works (God's) wrath. For where there is no law, there is no transgression" (Romans 4:15), meaning, of course, no transgression of positive law.

3. Such transgression is deadly. "For while we were in the flesh, the passions of sins, which were through the law, worked in our members so as to bring forth death" (Romans 7:5). The passions or causes of sins were stirred up by the law. "While we were in the flesh" describes the situation of Christians before their baptism. So the law is clearly being given some part of the responsibility for the existence or activity of the passions which lead to various sins. What is this responsibility?

4. The answer is given in Romans 7:7-25, a text which falls into two parts, verses 7-12 and 13-25. Here is the first part. "What shall we say? Is the law sin? Far from it. But I would not have known sin except through the law. For indeed I would not have known covetousness, if the law had not said, 'Thou shalt not covet.' But sin, taking occasion of the commandment, produced in me all covetousness; for without law sin is dead. So long

as there is no law, I was alive; but when the commandment came, sin revived, and I died, and the commmandment which was for the sake of life turned out to be for death. For sin, taking occasion of the commandment, seduced me and, through it, killed me. So then the law is holy, and the commandment is holy, just and good."

There is a human story here, but whose story is it? St. Paul's "me" is certainly not meant to refer *exclusively* to himself. Some interpreters have thought he meant the young Jew in general and then, perhaps, by analogy, any young person. For just as the young Jew gains awareness of sin through learning the revealed Law, so also the young Gentile learns sin through the emergence of his conscience at the age of reason. On this interpretation, the time when I was alive without the law was the time of my non-responsible childhood. Thus Origen and St. Jerome.(8) Other interpreters have thought that Paul's "me" is the subject of human history. Man knew sin before Moses but not with the same killing exactitude. It is one thing to have nature or conscience as one's accuser and quite another to have God Himself. Hence the time when I was alive without the Law was the time before Moses. Thus Chrysostom and Aquinas. Still others have thought that Paul was speaking of universal human experience as prototyped in Adam. Our first parent "lived" until God gave him a commandment, of which sin was able to take advantage. Thus Theodore of Mopsuestis. It may be the case that St. Paul had something of each of these possibilities in mind...

We are now ready for the second part of this text (Romans 7:13-25), which clearly depicts the state of life under the law of Moses. "Did what is good then become death for me? Far from it. But sin, in order to appear as sin, gave me death by means of a good thing, so that sin might be held the more guilty through the fact of the commandment... For we know that the law is spiritual; but I am corporeal ... For what I should like to do, I do not do; but what I hate, I do... Thus it is one and the same me who serve the Law of God through my reason but the law of sin through my flesh."

Here the "me" is no longer considered in its state of relative innocence. Sin has emerged, and an inner conflict is unfolding under the most unfavorable conditions. Sin is no longer an agent external to man, as in the case of innocent Adam, nor an interior but latent principle, as in the case of a small child. Sin has become a "law" of the flesh. Given this new power of sin, there emerges a new "me," whom Paul says has fallen into the power of sin.

Nearly every ancient commentator, plus a virtual unanimity of modern exegetes Catholic and Protestant alike has understood this new "me" to be *the Jew* existing under the *Mosaic Law.* What makes this exegesis inevitable is the fact that Paul in the verses which follow immediately, makes this sorry state of inner defeat, this impotency of one's better self, a foil for the totally different experience now available in Christ. Through him we are able to behave "not as our corporeal nature dictates but as the spirit dictates" (Romans 8:4).

Such was also St. Augustine's exegesis, until at the end of his life and in further reaction to Pelagianism he changed his mind and extended the "me" of Romans 7 to the Christian. (St. Augustine's example on this point was followed by St. Gregory the Great, Peter Lombard and Thomas Aquinas.) Needless to say Luther, Melanchthon, and the Calvinists were delighted to adopt such an idea. To this day, the sad doctrine that our justification must be something merely declaratory has one of its most powerful roots in this fateful mistake: what St. Paul considered the paradigm experience of the Jew under the Law is confused with the paradigm experience of the Christian under the power of grace. And it is interesting to note that the revivalist wing of Protestantism tends to escape this mistake. Encountering Christ in deep experiences of conversion, they taste the power of His victory over sin in their own lives; having tasted it, they have not a doubt in the world that they have been changed inwardly, that God has given them new hearts, and that the nightmare experience of Romans 7 is over for them. Of course, the Christian can fall back into that nightmare. This is the grain of truth in St. Augustine's later exegesis. The Christian can cease to live in the power of Christ; he can neglect prayer, grow cold, and find himself thrown back on his own resources; when he does so, inevitably, he will repeat within himself the experience of the Jew under the Law.

Though it may seem odd to summarize our discussion in that way, introducing suddenly the mention of grace, there is a reason for doing so. Romans 7, with its abstract dialectic of Law and sin, better self and concupiscence, has to be understood consistently with what St. Paul has already said in Romans 2. There he seems to treat the keeping of the commandments as *a real* possibility: "for when the gentiles, who do not have the Law, naturally do the things of the Law..."(Romans 2:14). In fact, he says, "God will render to each man according to his works: eternal life to those who, dedicating themselves with perseverance to good works, seek glory, honor and immortality ... glory honor and peace to all who do good, to the Jew first and to the Greek" (Romans 2:7) and this in a contest in which the revelation of Christ is not even under discussion yet.

These words certainly show that St. Paul did not regard good works as impossible, misguided, or pernicious, as some Protestant exegetes have tried to hold. Quite the contrary. But if St. Paul seems to admit justifying works in Romans 2 and to exclude them in Romans 7, the most plausible explanation is that he is speaking of the *total* human condition in chapter 2, where grace is at work among Jew and gentile alike, whereas in chapter 7 he is showing what happens when the Law is isolated from grace. Such isolation is exactly what is sought, when man seeks his own righteousness on the basis of law.

Moreover, what we have been saying squares with St. Paul's remarks on the function of the Law in God's overall plan of salvation. "The Law intervened so that sin might abound" (Romans 5:20) ...

St. Paul's conviction that God intended the Law to be provisional has its roots in the earliest preaching of the Church. Stunned by the death and resurrection of Jesus whom they had thought to be the Messiah, the first disciples were compelled to search the Scriptures for a clue to the meaning of these events... If the Messiah was supposed to suffer and die, mankind's religious problem had to be quite different from what the Jewish picture contemplated. What was needed was a clue to a whole new picture. This clue was found in the Servant Songs of Isaiah (especially Isaiah 52:13-53:12), where the suffering and death of the Servant are presented as a vicarious atonement for sin. "By his suffering shall my servant justify many, taking their faults upon himself" (Isaiah 53:11)...

At the very origin of Israel, Paul found in Abraham's faith the thread resumed in Christ; whereupon the entire Mosaic sub-plot could be read as a parenthesis ordained to Christ.

The Jewish project to seek one's own justice from the Law, then, was not only psychologically impossible (Romans 7) but also contrary to the plan of the ages, in which the Law had no function but this: in leading us to Christ, to render *itself* obsolete. Now we can understand why Paul cried out in frustration at the obtuse Galatians: "If the Law can justify us, there is no point in the death of Christ" (Galatians 2:21).

And the time has come to examine that other kind of justice mentioned by Paul: the justice which comes *from God through faith.*

"For in it (the Gospel) the justice of God is revealed from faith to faith, as it is written, 'The just shall live from faith'" (Romans 1:17). What is this justice "of God" (dikaiosune theou)? ...

Now, if what Paul means by *dikaiosune theou* is not something to remain in God but something meant to be conferred on us, then we must reckon with that mysterious possibility: a quality of man which is the property of God! Does St. Paul say anything to indicate a knowledge of this possibility? Indeed he does: "God has made him who knew no sin to be sin for us, so that we in him might become justice of God" (II Cor. 5:21). This verse is the pattern on which Athanasius would learn to say, "God became man, so that man might become divine." It is not a question of replacement but of participation, and the participation is real in both directions. First in Jesus: just as really as the Word took our humanity, just that really his humanity became God. And then in us: just as really as Christ-God took our sins (so really that even the Father forsook Him - Mark 15:34), just that really we receive God's justice. For if we dare to believe that in the Incarnation our nature, without ceasing to be a human nature, received *God's* subsistence, then we may easily believe that we, in Christ, receive *God's* justice as our quality. In fact, St. Paul even has a name for this quality, In the very next verse (II Cor. 6:1) he says: "As

God's co-workers, we beg you once again not to have received God's grace in vain." What we should not "receive in vain" is exactly what Paul has just said we have "become" in Christ. God's justice is His grace, a gift *given* to men. That is why the justice *of God is* identically "the justice which *comes from* God through faith" (Philippians 3:9).

What emerges from these texts, then, is the *existence* in man of a justice conferred by God. But this justice is tied into faith, whether before Christ's coming, as in the case of Abraham, or afterwards, as is our case. What we must explore next is the nature of this tie-in between justice and faith.

St. Paul's most important test on faith is Romans 10:13-17: "Whoever shall call upon the name of the Lord shall be saved. But how shall they call upon one in whom they have not believed? And how shall they believe in one of whom they have never heard? And how shall they hear if no one preaches? And how shall anyone preach unless he has been sent ... But not everyone has obeyed (*hupekousan*) the Gospel. As Isaiah said, 'Lord, who has believed our report?' So faith depends upon preaching and preaching upon the word of Christ." We have here an order of necessary conditions, which inverts to yield the following order of precedence: (1) The word or teaching of Christ, i.e. the Gospel; (2) the mission to preach given to the Apostles; (3) their preaching; (4) our hearing, and finally (5) an act which may be described equally well *as faith (pistis)* and as obedience (*hypakoe*)...

Paul twice speaks of "the obedience of faith" (Romans 1:5 and 16:26, the genitive being appositional) and also why II Cor. 10:5 says that every thought (or every intellect) is to be brought into a captivity which is "obedience of Christ."

These texts indicate that what St. Paul called "faith" certainly *included* the scholastic sense of the term (assent or submission of the intellect to the truths taught by Christ to His Apostles, and by them to us, on the authority of God) but also included more. The reader should remember that the scholastic definition of 'faith' was designed to do a technical job, namely, to designate the common *content* of 'living faith' *(fides caritate formata)* and 'dead faith' *(fides informis)*. It does this job very well; the common content is intellectual assent to the revealed message. But St. Paul's term 'faith' was used by him to designate man's *rightful* response to Christ's message. Now, *where* this message consists of truths of faith (e.g. "Before Abraham was, I am"; "I and the Father are one," etc.) intellectual assent is all there is to the rightful response; but where the message contains imperatives ("Repent and be baptized"), consolations ("Fear not, I have overcome the world"), promises ("But I will see you again, and your heart shall rejoice"), examples ("When you pray, pray like this: Our Father...") etc. there the rightful response is to do as one is commanded, *take* the consolation, *trust* the promise, *heed* the example and so forth. Indeed, to believe in a command intellectually and then not do it, to accept a consolation intellectually and then not feel it, to acknowledge a promise and then not trust it - these are even unnatural responses. "Dead faith" is an ugly thing - not just "unformed" but deformed by sin and shot-through with the self-contradiction which lies at the heart of every sin.

So a rightful response to Christ's total message must not only include faith in the narrow sense but must be what St. Paul calls "obedience of faith," which is just what Catholic theology calls the acts of faith, hope and love.

We are now in a position to see the tie-in between faith and justice. Observe first of all how St. Paul expresses the connection in prepositions. He speaks of God's "justice which *is from (ek)* faith" (Romans 9:30;10:6); he says we are "justified from faith" (Gal. 2:16; 3:24). So justice is distinct from faith; it proceeds from it. Justice has its source and point of departure in faith. However, lest we should get the idea that justice is a direct "output" of faith, or a natural derivative, it is vital to see that a divine action intervenes between faith and justice: "God *justifies* the Gentiles from faith" (Gal. 3:8,30; cf. Romans 3:24). This divine action is highlighted by Paul's other favorite preposition, the instrumental *dia*, through. "God's justice is through faith" (Romans 3:22; Phil. 3:9) "he justifies the gentiles through faith" (Romans 3:30). So man gets justified, but God does the justifying, and He does it by means of faith, using faith as an instrument. Elsewhere we have it (Phil. 3:10) that "the justice from God is on the basis of faith (*epi*)" and (Hebrews 11:7 "according to faith (*kata*)."

These prepositions instruct us on how to take Paul's meaning when he dispenses with prepositions in favor of a simple instrumental dative: "For we think that man is justifed by faith" (Romans 3:28); "through Him (Christ) we have access by faith" (Romans 5:1). The meaning is the same as before. Faith remains God's instrument in justifying, and not (as Luther supposed) man's instrument in getting justified.

But how does God use this instrument? We have an indication from Romans 4:3f. "Abraham believed God, and it was reckoned to him *(elogisthe)* for justice." In the Hebrew of Genesis 15:6, the verb is active: "God counted it as justice." So the mystery is being described as an accounting procedure. God credits *pistis to* Abraham's account as having the value of dikaiosune. Now the question is what kind of accounting this is. Luther supposed that God took a thing of no real value (our faith) and made it stand for something oú value. God doctored the Book of Life! Such an idea has no foundation in the text. The key verb here *(logizomm)* is used throughout the Septuagint (Psalm 106:31; Isa. 40:17), and even in Koine Greek, and in the New Testament (Acts 19:17, and even in St. Paul's epistle to the Romans (2:26; 9:8), to mean an honest reckoning, based on a real equivalence of value between the two things. Nowhere does the crediting presuppose a disproportion between the thing furnished (e.g. faith) and the value put on it (e.g. justice). No, indeed; what Abraham's faith is said to count for in Gen.15:6 is the very thing which the keeping of the Law is said to count for in Deuteronomy 6:25 and 24:13. Living faith is worth righteousness. Yes, but not in *the way* that works are worth it. Hear how Paul continues the passage which he started about Abraham (Romans 4:4f): "To the one who works, his wages are not credited to him according to grace but according to what is owed. But to the one who does not work but believes in Him who justifies the wicked, his faith is credited to him for righteousness." So, if faith is eeally worth righteousness, it is not worth it in the way that works are. The latter have their value in the order of strict justice, whereas faith has its value in the order of grace (*kata charin*).

Does it follow, then, that the order of grace is arbitrary, unreal, an order in which the worthless is accorded fictitious worth? Not at all! We have seen what living faith really is. It is that *rightful* response to the Gospel, whereby man assents to the truths, heeds the commands, feels the consolations, trusts the promises - in short, it is that total attitude toward God from which (as from a source) or through which (as by a means) God can draw for every good work with the further help of His actual graces. Between such faith as a basis and the "measure of the stature of the fullness of Christ" an an apex, there is a real continuity and proportion. That is why God can use faith to justify us, and why He can, without dishonesty, credit that faith to our account as the root and foundation of all justlce.

For as St. Paul himself says ... "We are God's handiwork, having been created in Christ Jesus to do good works, which God prepared beforehand that we should walk in them" (Ephesians 2:10). Our new creaturehood in Christ Jesus is our reception, through grace, of the "obedience of faith." Through that faith, as through an instrument, God has refashioned us, making us now prompt to obey. Our new estate is thus ordered to good works as to its intrinsic and God-intended finality. With what joy, therefore, do we walk in them, we who believe. And woe to us if we do not walk in them, for then we betray our faith and frustrate God's handiwork.

So we have, and are intended to have, works. Does it follow that we may boast? Not at at all! For our works, unlike the works attempted by the Jew under the Law, are not from us but from God. Rooted in God's gift, brought forth by living faith, God's instrument in us, these works are grace-works. They are our justice through faith, and therefore they are justice in the order of grace (*kata charin*), not in the order of self-achievement where boasting arises.

Living faith: our quality but God's instrument; good works: our deeds but God's handiwork; our deeds as men living in Christ, not tbe motions of "graced" zombies still dead in sin.[63]

Tim Staples:
The Bible Made Me Do It

Many Protestants accuse the Catholic Church of teaching a system of salvation based on human works independent of God's grace. This is not true.

63 William Marshner, "Justification by Faith," in *Reasons for Hope*, Jeffrey A. Mirus, ed. (Front Royal, Virginia: Christendom College Press, 1982), 219-237.

The Church does teach the necessity of works, but so does Scripture. The Church condemns the notion that salvation can be achieved through "works alone." Nothing, whether faith or works, apart from the grace of God, can save us. It is works of grace that we do as a result of the grace of God moving us to act and helping us to bring the meritorious acts to their completion.

Father [Mitch] Pacwa summed it up nicely when he explained that we are saved by grace through faith which works by love (cf, Gal. 5:6). But we must choose to allow God's grace to work through us. He does not force us to "continue in grace" (cf. Acts 13:43). This made sense to me, but I was still confused by Paul's emphasis on salvation being a past-tense event: "For by grace you *have been* saved" (Eph. 2:8). And then there was 1 John 5:13: "These things have I written unto you that believe on the name of the Son of God; that ye may know that you *have* eternal life."

Father cleared up both of these problems. He agreed that salvation is in a sense a completed action in the life of all who have been baptized (Matt 16:16, Rom. 6:3, Gal. 3:27). But salvation is also spoken about in the present tense for example Paul says, "The message of the cross is foolishness to those who are perishing, but to us who *are being saved* it is the power of God" (1 Cor 1:18). Salvation is also described as a future event: "He who endures to the end *will be saved*' (Matt.10:22).

I did an exhaustive word study on the Greek terms related to the English word "justification," and I found that not only is it inextricably linked to the issue of sanctification (the two concepts are actually one and the same thing) the Bible also speaks of justification in the past, present, and future tenses, implying that it is an ongoing process of sanctification in the life of each believer: "Therefore since *we have been justified by* faith, we have peace with God through our Lord Jesus Christ" (Rom. 5:1); [we are] "being justified freely by his grace through the redemption that is in Christ" (Rom. 3:24); and "But if, in *seeking to be justified in* Christ, we ourselves are found to be sinners, is Christ then a minister of sin? Of course not!" (Gal. 2:17).

What can separate us from the love of Christ? Fundamentalists claim to have an absolute certainty of their salvation. But ... the Bible explicitly says that Christians do not have *an absolute* assurance of salvation.

Paul said "It does not concern me in the least that I be judged by you or any human tribunal; I do not even pass judgment on myself; I am not conscious of anything against me, *but I do not thereby stand acquitted;* the one who judges me is the Lord. Therefore do not make any judgment before the appointed time, until the Lord comes, for he will bring to light what is hidden in darkness and will manifest the motives of our hearts, and then everyone will receive praise from God" (1 Cor. 4:4-5). Other verses which show this are Romans 11:22; Hebrews 10:26-29; and 2 Peter 2:20-21.

In Matthew 5:19-30, Jesus first tells us that there are "least commandments" that a person can break and still go to heaven though he will be "least in the kingdom of heaven." And then he tells us of sins that leave a man "in danger of hell fire." St. Paul gives us a number of lists of deadly sins about which he says, "They which do such things shall not inherit the kingdom of God" (Galatians 5:21, see also Eph. 5:5-7 and 1 Cor. 6:9-10).[64]

William Most:
Faith Alone: Luther's Discovery?

Is it true that there is salvation by faith alone? Definitely, yes. St. Paul teaches it over and over and it is the chief theme of Galatians and Romans. But James wrote in his Epistle (2:24) "See that a man is justified by works, and not by faith alone."

Because it was contrary to his personal philosophy, Luther rejected that Epistle. But if we look closely, we will see that the critical point lies in the meaning of the word *faith.* Not everyone uses every word in precisely the same sense. St. James and St. Paul, both working under inspiration, could not contradict each other. But they did use the word *faith in* different senses. St. James clearly uses *faith* to mean, narrowly, just intellectual acceptance of a revealed truth. So we can see why St. James feels the need to add works. Even St. Paul talks similarly at times; for instance *in Romans 2:6-13:* "He will repay to every man according to

---

64   Tim Staples, "The Bible Made Me Do It," in Patrick Madrid, ed., *Surprised by Truth* (San Diego: Basilica Press, 1994), 233-5.

his works. For not the hearers of the law are just before God, but the doers of the law shall be justified." As we will explore later St. Paul does not mean that works earn salvation - but violations of the law can earn eternal ruin. Thus, St. Paul does not disagree with St. James, but his use of the word *faith* is much broader. *By faith,* Paul means *total adherence of a person to God in mind and will.* This, in turn, implies several things: If God speaks a truth, we believe with our minds. This is the sense St. James had in mind (see I Thes. 2:13; 2 Cor 5:7). If God makes a promise we are confident He will keep it (see Gal. 5:5; Rom. 5:1; 1 Thes. 5:8), If God gives a command, we obey (see Rom, 1;5). And all should be done in love (Gal. 5:6).

In contrast, the Lutheran Augsburg Confession taught (20:23), "Faith does not mean knowledge of an event. . . it means a faith which believes ... also in the effect of an event, namely ... the remission of sins, i.e, that we have, through Christ, grace, righteousness, and remission of sins." Modern Protestants often express this as meaning that one takes Christ as his *personal Savior, or, has confidence that the merits of Christ are credited to his account.* It is as if there were a ledger with a credit and a debit page for each man. If he "takes Christ as his personal Savior," he can write on the credit page the infinite merits of Christ. On the debit page go his sins: past, present and future. Of course the balance is always more than favorable.

Hence, they see no need for confession, no need even to make an act of contrition even out of love. Protestants believe that Jesus paid in advance for one's sins and nothing more needs to be done...

Even many Protestant scholars today modify the old notion of faith substantially. A standard Protestant reference work on Scripture, the *Interpreter's Dictionary of the Bible,* Supplement Volume, tells us, "Paul uses *pistis/pisteuein* [Greek words for *faith* and *believe] to* mean, above all, belief in the Christ *kerygma* [proclamation or preaching], knowledge, obedience, trust in the Lord Jesus." Note the word *obedience.* The *Interpreter's Dictionary* admits St. Paul includes it in an important place in his idea of faith.

In fact, Paul sometimes identifies *faith* and *obedience* when he speaks of the "obedience of faith." Here, the *of* has the same sense as it does when we say the "city of Chicago." We mean: the City that is Chicago (see Rom. 1:5; 16:26, and in a similar sense, Rom. 10:16; 6:16; 15:18; 2 Thes. 1:8)...

The Protestant view tells people they can be infallibly *saved once for all* by just one act, taking Christ as their personal Savior. St. Paul had no such notion. If anyone should have been saved that way, it ought to have been St. Paul. Yet Paul told the Corinthians, "But I chastise my body, and bring it into subjection: lest perhaps, when I have preached to others, I myself should become a castaway." (I *Cor.* 9:27). So Paul knew he had to tame his flesh by mortification, much as athletes at the Isthmian games went into training. Hence, in 2 *Cor.* 11:23-27, he added fasting to all the great hardships that came with his apostolic work. He did not want to fall and risk being rejected at the Judgment. If he were "infallibly saved," there would be no need of acts of mortification, because no matter how much he might fall, he would still be saved.

Again, in I Cor. 10:1-12, he is trying to induce the Corinthians to be willing to give up meat at times to avoid scandal, and he tells them in effect, "Do not just say, we are the People of God - look at the first People of God. God did not approve of many of them, so He often had to strike them, even to strike them dead." So Paul concluded in 1 Cor. 10:12, "Wherefore he who thinks that he stands, let him take heed lest he fall." If they were all infallibly saved there would be no need for such a warning.

Again in Romans 5:3-5, Paul wrote, "But we glory also in tribulations, knowing that tribulation produces patience; and patience trial; and trial hope; and hope does not disappoint us." These verses make "character" needed for salvation, character coming from endurance in suffering. This is hardly the same as an easy once-for-all declaration of "taking Christ as my personal Savior."[65]

William Most:
On Predestination

Even though Scripture does not speak explicitly of predestination, it does so implicitly... 1) He [God] wants all

---

[65] William G. Most, *Catholic Apologetics Today* (Rockford, Illinois: TAN Books, 1986), 106 ff.

His children to be saved; 2) He looks ahead to see who will resist His grace so much that he cannot be saved. (This is just our way of speaking because there is no "future" for Him as we perceive it.) Remember, grace is a divine power to save us and if one throws it away too often, he cannot be saved. So then, sadly, God determines *to reprobate or reject those who have earned it fully.* (3) He then turns to all the rest, to those who are not forcing their own loss, and He decrees to predestine or save them. Why? Not because of their merits or good lives. He has not even looked at such things yet. He has been looking only at resistance to His grace. Further, it is not even because of their lack of such serious resistance. No, the bottom-line reason He will save them is simply this: He always wanted to do that - He wants to save all - and those He saves are not stopping Him by throwing away the means that could save them or His grace.

To sum it up, *predestination is determined without* consideration *of merits* or good living; *reprobation is decided with or because of consideration of demerits,* resistance to grace...

How much resistance to grace will bring reprobation? We can hazard a guess. It is the amount which will bring spiritual blindness that makes us incapable of even perceiving that God is calling us by His grace, at a particular moment to do His will. If we cannot even perceive His call, the rest of the process cannot happen either. Such blindness comes from repeated sinning, especially from sinning *in presumption,* in the attitude that says, "I will get my fill of evil, and then later tell God that I wish I had not done it." ...

In spite of his words about salvation by faith and not by law, St. Paul says many times that if one violates the law he will be eternally lost. For example, in 1 Cor. 6:9-10, "Do you not know that the unjust shall not possess the kingdom of God? Do not err: neither fornicators, nor idolators, nor adulterers, nor the effeminate, nor those who lie with men, nor thieves, nor covetors nor drunkards, nor slanderers nor extortioners, shall inherit the kingdom of God." So if one breaks the law on a major point, he will not be saved. (St. Paul has similar statements in Eph. 5:5 and Gal. 5:19-21.)...

We can easily make sense of all these statements with the help of Romans 6:23, as we said, "For the wages of sin is death. But the gift of God, life everlasting." That is, eternal death can be earned by breaking the law but eternal life is a free gift of God. Our keeping the law does not earn it; not even faith earns it. It is our "inheritance" as sons. Note the word "inherit" in I Cor. 6:10 - they who break the law will not "inherit the kingdom."

Consequently, a Christian must follow the Spirit of Christ, who teaches him to live as Christ did. Then he need not even look at the law. 1 *Timothy* 1:9 says, "Knowing this that the law is not made for the just man, but for the unjust and disobedient." If the just man breaks the law, he loses his inheritance.[66]

Hyacinthe-M. Dion:
Predestination in St. Paul

In Paul's writings on predestination nothing can be found which smacks of an exclusive choice of a small number of privileged ones, as Augustine's exegesis would lead us to believe. There is rather a pure message of hope to his Christian brethren, persecuted and despised in this world - plus a great admiration at the Father's plan to gather all men, Jews and Greeks alike, around his Son.

This attitude corresponds perfectly to the Pauline universalism crystallized in I Tm: "God our Savior. . . desires all men to be saved and to come to the knowledge of the truth. For there is one God, and there is one mediator between God and men, the man Christ Jesus, who gave himself as a ransom for all, the testimony to which was borne at the proper time. For this I was appointed a preacher and apostle" (I Tm 2:3-7).

Finally in Paul's eyes, can the divine will be blocked by the revolt of man? How can he maintain that the divine will always accomplishes its purposes, if not all of humanity is truly saved and particularly if some Christians, some of the predestined, do not succeed in reproducing perfectly the image of the Son?

We know that Paul envisioned the eventual loss of a considerable number of sinners, Jews as well as Gentiles. The following passage is particularly significant in this regard: "The coming of the lawless one by the activity of Sa-

---

[66] Ibid., 114.

tan will be with all power and with pretended signs and wonders, and with all wicked deception for those who are to perish because they refused to love the truth and so be saved. Therefore God sends upon them a strong delusion, to make them believe what is false, so that all may be condemned who did not believe the truth but had pleasure in unrighteousness" (2 Thes 2:9-12).

We easily forget that for Paul the same danger continued to threaten Christians, the predestined. In 2 Tm 2:10 he even says that his own sufferings are still needed to help somehow toward the salvation of those who are already "elect." This implies that even predestination is not quite identical with an absolute *guarantee of* salvation. This thought underlies a large number of exhortations to prayer and imitation of Christ and Paul himself.[67]

Once we return to the historic Christian Faith we return also to the constant striving for holiness and sanctity that should mark all followers of Him Who said "Be ye perfect as your Father in heaven is perfect."

G. FROM THE THEOLOGY OF "ONCE SAVED ALWAYS SAVED, ONCE DAMNED ALWAYS DAMNED" TO THE GOD WHO ASKS US TO PARTICIPATE IN HIS SCHEME OF SALVATION

The Christian God is the God revealed in Scripture and the historic Faith Who desires the salvation of all men but has given every man the freewill to choose or reject Him. This is the doctrine of faith, works and salvation given not just in scriptural texts but in the testimony and authoritative interpretation of the Christian community dating back to the age of the Apostles. A sampling of reflections from the Fathers of the Church revered even by the Reformers shows that salvation is a gift of God which nonetheless must be accepted through faith and through our choices and actions:

---

[67]   Hyacinthe-M Dion, "Predestination in St. Paul," *Theology Digest*, 1967, 148-9.

Justin Martyr [154 A.D.]:

"We have learned from the prophets and we hold it as true that punishments and chastisements and good rewards are distributed according to the merit of each man's actions. Were this not the case, and were all things to happen according to the decree of fate, there would be nothing at all in our power. If fate decrees that this man is to be good and that one wicked, then neither is the former to be praised nor the latter to be blamed." [*First Apology*, 43]

Theophilus of Antioch [181 A.D.]:

"He who gave the mouth for speech and formed the ears for hearing and made eyes for seeing will examine everything and judge justly, granting recompense to each according to merit. To those who seek immortality by the patient exercise of good works [Romans 2:7], he will give everlasting life, joy, peace, rest, and all good things, which neither eye has seen nor ear has heard, nor has it entered into the heart of man [1 Cor. 2:9]. For the unbelievers and the contemptuous and for those who do not submit to the truth but assent to iniquity ... there will be wrath and indignation (Rom 2:8)." [*To Autolycus* 1:14].

Hippolytus [215 A.D.]:

"Standing before [Christ's] judgment, all of them, men, angels, and demons, crying out in one voice, shall say: 'Just is your judgment,' and the justice of that cry will be apparent in the recompense made to each. To those who have done well, everlasting enjoyment shall be given; while to lovers of evil shall be given eternal punishment." [*Against the Greeks*].

Cyprian [253 A.D.]:

"You who are a matron rich and wealthy, anoint not your eyes with the antimony of the devil, but with the collyrium of Christ, so that you may at last come to see God, when you have merited before God both by your works and by your manner of living." [*Works and Almsgiving* 14].

Cyril of Jerusalem [350 A.D.]:

"The root of every good work is the hope of the resurrection, for the expectation of a reward nerves the soul to good work.

Every laborer is prepared to endure the toils if he looks forward to the reward of these toils." [*Catechetical Lectures*, 18:1].

Augustine [396 A.D.]:
"We are commanded to live righteously, and the reward is set before us of our meriting to live happily in eternity. But who is able to live righteously and do good works unless he has been justified by faith?" [*Various Questions to Simplician* 1:2:21].[68]

Once we recognize the reality of human freedom, as the historic Christian Faith has done, the vital role of Mary in salvation history becomes evident: "Accept the possibility, asserts Barth, of man co-operating in the divine economy of salvation and of his elevation to the glory of God then the Mariology of Catholic tradition must follow as a natural conclusion."[69]

We have seen already that Scripture calls us to participate in Christ's work of redemption: "I Paul ... rejoice in my sufferings for you, and fill up that which is behind of the afflictions of Christ in my flesh for his body's sake, which is the church." [*Colossians* 1:24].

If it is possible to cooperate in God's plan of salvation, it is possible also to mediate God's grace to others. Both the New Testament and all of salvation history shows that mediation through various human beings and sometimes angels is the process by which God brings the message and grace of salvation to humanity. Even the most rigorous Fundamentalist has to admit that God's salvation is mediated to the human race through written documents [the New Testament], individuals [the Apostles, family, friends, missionaries], and so on.

Some Fundamentalists have interpreted 1 Timothy 2:5, "There is one God, and there is one mediator between God and men, the man Christ Jesus," in such a way as to rule out any possibility of intercession or mediation involving Mary or other holy individuals in salvation history. This interpretation contradicts other passages in Scripture as well as the experience of every Christian both Fundamentalist and non-Fundamentalist. All our knowledge of God comes through multiple mediators. The New Testament itself is a

---

68   Citations in *This Rock*, March 1994, 35ff.
69   A. Lancashire, *Born of the Virgin Mary* (London: The Faith Press, 1962), p.140.

written document mediating the Word of God just as the Apostles mediated the true Faith. Prophets, patriarchs and angels have all been mediators. In fact 1 *Timothy* 2:1-7 is a call for all Christians to be mediators and intercessors for humanity with Paul concluding that he himself is a mediator. We should read 1 *Timothy* 2:5 in the same light in which we read Our Lord's command "Do not call anyone your father on earth." (*Matthew* 23:9). Clearly this command does not mean that a son should not call his father "father." It simply states that no one is "father" in the unique sense in which God the Father is the "father" of all that exists. Similarly 1 *Timothy* 2:5 simply states that no one is a mediator between God and man in the unique sense in which Jesus, God-man and Redeemer of humanity, is a Mediator.

The most comprehensive study of 1 *Timothy* 2:5 that remains true to the historic interpretation is given to us by the exegete Manuel Miguens. Below is an excerpt from his analysis:

> All theological, grammatical and linguistic considerations seem to suggest for 1 Tim 2:5 the following translation: "There is one and the same God [for all], there is also one and the same mediator [for all]." The loving and saving care of God is for all (not only for a few, for Christians), and the redeeming mediation of Christ is "for all" too.
>
> The linguistic analysis of 1 Tim 2:5 proves the nonexclusive meaning of the text... In fact at least three kinds of mediation emerge in the bible.[70]

This analysis of 1 *Timothy* 2:5 is further developed in *This Rock*:

> The principal point of Paul's teaching in 2:1-5 is that we must pray for everybody because God is everybody's God. There is no other. Christ alone is for *everyone* the only way to the Father. Gentiles, even harsh rulers, are men and women. Christ the God-Man is their Christ too. He is the go-between for them and not just for us. Paul hammers this teaching home in 2:6-7 by noting that Christ gave himself

---

[70] Manuel Miguens, *Mary "The Servant of the Lord": An Ecumenical Proposal* (Boston: Daughters of St. Paul, 1978), 176-7.

as a ransom for *all*, not just for those already Christian. Paul reminds Timothy and his group that he (Paul) was appointed preacher and apostle to the Gentiles (*Gentiles* yet!).

The fact is that in 1 Timothy 2:1-7 (the whole context, mind you), Paul commands *all* Christians to be mediators and intercessors for all men because God is God of all and Christ is Christ for all. He concludes by saying that he himself is a mediator too, as preacher and apostle.

The high point of the passage is verse 5, where he enthrones Christ, the mediator par excellence, who by uniting us to himself makes mediators of us all for all. The whole passage, verses 1-7, is a unit and must be read as a unit. Its message is broadly ecumenical; it is a missionary message, a message of outreach. (44).

A more detailed study of mediation is carried out in the other two volumes of this Trilogy. It is shown there that the denial of mediation by human beings in God's plan of salvation leads inevitably to pantheism.

Ironically both Liberals and Fundamentalists say on the one hand that we have no freedom (Liberals say that our choices and actions are governed by our social environment while Fundamentalists say that God predestines all our choices and actions) and on the other hand claim to be champions of freedom (Liberals claim to have the freedom to choose what they want to take as true from the Bible, Fundamentalists claim that every man can interpret the Bible as he pleases as long as he says it is the Word of God).

Neither Liberals nor Fundamentalists have understood either the fact or the real nature of freedom. Historic Christianity has affirmed consistently that we are free beings who must in this life make the choice between God and self, Heaven and Hell, salvation and damnation. This freedom is a great mystery and in some senses a terrifying mystery. The thought that we can refuse the grace of God brings us to our knees. Perhaps this is what drove Luther and Calvin and many others to the view that we are puppets programmed by God. But such a view of God is truly terrifying as well as horrifying. The God Who gives us freedom loves us infinitely and does

---

[71] Father Mateo, *Refuting the Attack on Mary: A Defense of Marian Doctrines* (San Diego, CA: Catholic Answers, 1993), 15.

1-189

everything possible to bring us to Him. We have no reason for terror because our loving Father wants to take all of His prodigal children Home and will come after even the one lost sheep. In exercising our freedom we look at Mary: she is the one human person who said "Yes" to God at all levels. She is not just a model but the one whom her Son has given to us as a Mother to bring us to Him. And it is to the theme of Mary we turn now.